ROBINSON FAMILY GOVERNESS: LETTERS FROM KAUA'I AND NI'IHAU, 1911-1913

BY JUDITH MARION BURTNER

FROM THE ORIGINAL LETTERS OF
HETTIE BELLE MATTHEW

PUBLICATION
CONSULTANTS
· We Believe In The Power Of Authors

PO Box 221974 Anchorage, Alaska 99522-1974
books@publicationconsultants.com—www.publicationconsultants.com

ISBN: 978-1-59433-827-4
eISBN: 978-1-59433-828-1
Library of Congress Catalog Card Number: 2018966772

Cover design by Christina Olsen Burtner

Manufactured in the United States of America.

Letters are among the most significant memorial a person
can leave behind them.

– Johann Wolfgang von Goethe

FOREWORD

A thousand years ago, the ancestors of both my mother and father crossed the English channel around the same time, in the last successful invasion of England. But after that they separated. My mother's people later went west into the American colonies and followed the American frontier until they arrived in California. Meanwhile, my father's ancestors eventually went east around the world, first into New Zealand and then finally onto the Hawaiian islands of Kauai and Niihau. There these two lines of my family would meet again, a thousand years later, exactly halfway around the world from England, on the opposite side of the planetary globe.

Now here is the story of how my father met my mother....

When my father Lester was some 7-9 years old, his father Aubrey Robinson decided he needed a tutor-governess to instruct the boy. On a trip to California (where he had earlier worked on a construction project in Menlo Park in 1900-1901), Aubrey met a man named Allan Matthew. Allan recommended his own adventurous young sister, Hettie Belle Matthew, for the job. She stayed in the job for two years from 1911-1913, right in the middle of the great 1911-1914 Hawaiian drought, when no rain at all fell on Niihau island for three years.

Many years passed. My father graduated from Harvard in 1924, worked in the pineapple industry on Oahu for a while, and then finally came home to Kauai to work in the family business.

In 1935, out of the blue, a letter arrived from Dad's old governess, now Hettie Belle Marcus – her young niece, the daughter of Allan Matthew, was about to go on a tour of Hawaii – so, for old times sake, would someone from the Robinson family be willing to show her the sights on Kauai when she eventually visited the island?

Hettie Belle's letter arrived at a most inconvenient time – the entire Robinson family was just about to leave for a relaxing, fun-filled, two-week vacation on the nearby island of Niihau. And in order to accommodate Hettie Bell's request, someone would have to give up his vacation and stay behind to "do the honors." Eventually, my father was "sacrificed" for the job, since Hettie Belle had been his old governess. And so, at the age of thirty-four, he got left behind and stood disgustedly fuming alone on the dock as the sampan containing all the rest of the family sailed off for Niihau. As he told me many years later, the last thing in the world that he wanted to do just then was to waste two weeks squiring around some silly little ten-year old girl with pigtails.

In reality, the "little ten-year old girl in pigtails" was approaching or just past her twenty-fifth birthday. Born and raised in California, Helen Marion Matthew loved animals, was fascinated by cowboys, and enjoyed horse and mule pack-train camping trips to the high Sierras. Just now, during the part of her stay on Oahu, she was exercising the polo ponies of a rich, rising-star army colonel named George Patton – then temporarily marooned in Hawaii without his tanks. Helen Marion loved Colonel Patton's polo ponies, but she didn't care too much for the good colonel – she thought he was a bit crude and had a roving eye for the ladies. But soon, on the Kauai part of her Hawaiian tour, she would meet the man of her dreams – a Harvard-educated cowboy, expert in horse training, and cattle roping, and all other aspects of livestock work. They would have two weeks together (only accompanied by her brother) before the rest of the Robinson family returned from its Niihau trip. And by that time, my father realized that he had discovered a woman who would make an ideal rancher's wife.

During 1911-1913, in her two years as my father's governess, Hettie Belle Matthew kept a diary of her experiences in letters to her family. It is published here in this book. I have read it and regard it as a good, representative chronicle of the social life of upper-class women and children in Hawaii in those last years of peace, before World War I changed the world. Unfortunately, in her line of work, Hettie Belle was necessarily confined to a somewhat cloistered existence, and she apparently never saw the hard, sweaty, action-packed working world of Hawaii's men. Therefore, since I come from that other world and am a hard working "loner," and as I am almost totally bored by parties and the "social whirl," I read her account with only mild interest.

Hettie Belle did very accurately describe Aubrey Robinson, her employer – although he was rich, he was also a generous man who helped other and employed more people that he actually needed.

This, then, is an account written by a young woman living and working among the upper classes of pre-World War I Hawaii. If it seems a bit frivolous and superficial, it must always be remembered that she was still single and at a time of life when girls focus on the "social whirl" in order to find future husbands. Eventually, my mother's "Aunt Hettie" would marry and settle down, and she would develop a far more serious attitude as she faced the trials and cares and responsibilities of full adulthood.

Keith Robinson
Descendant of the prominent land-owning Western-Kauai family

Contents

APPENDICES

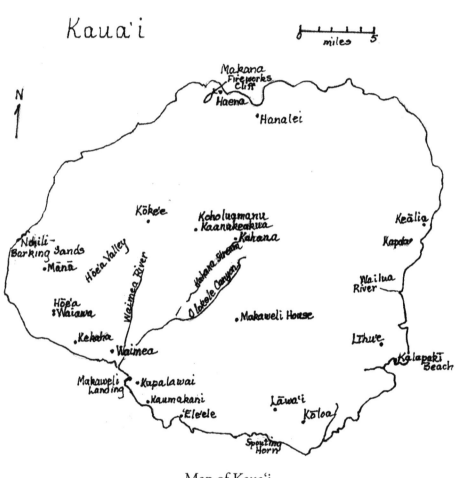

Map of Kaua'i

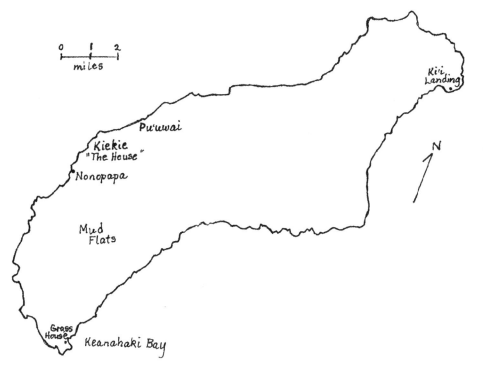

Island of
Niʻihau

0   1   2
miles

Puʻuwai

Kiekie
"The House"

Nonopapa

Mud
Flats

Grass
House

Keanahaki Bay

Kiʻi
Landing

N

Map of Niʻihau

PREFACE

My grandmother had definite expectations about proper behavior, especially when she served formal dinners in her San Francisco home with a maid in attendance. She taught me to set a table using forks, spoons, glasses, and even finger bowls in the correct layout. A stately woman, she wore large jeweled rings and hats with veils when going out for dinner and cards at the Palace Hotel with other widowed friends. Every Christmas I was thrilled to see gift books wrapped in shiny gold paper under the tree, books like Pearl Buck's *My Several Worlds,* which enticed me with stories of foreign lands. She told me fairy tales, taking the part of the troll or stepmother as we acted out the stories. Granny took me shopping at the high-end department store, I. Magnin, in San Francisco for a dream dress of soft, green wool with white angora trim. While my siblings and I carefully balanced pre-dinner juice and crackers on our laps, she sat at her grand piano to play, and she filled the room with heartfelt emotion. I would never have imagined my imposing, even formidable grandmother as an adventuresome young woman, playing piano in a sprawling compound in an exotic place called Kapalawai, or chasing two children dressed in Edwardian white suits through the Hawaiian hills.

Still fiercely independent even into her eighties, my grandmother traveled extensively to visit her far-flung family, and she ventured to India, China, France, and many times to the Hawaiian Islands. She had a love of tropical beauty that spilled into her garden set with mossy stones and a small fishpond with golden koi. A tangle of brightly colored flowering plants surrounded the patio, with bougainvillea growing along the wall.

A few years ago, my mother handed me a large shoebox, directing me, "Here, I think you might do something with these letters from Granny." Giving them a cursory glance, I saw that my grandmother had written them when she was a governess on the island of Kaua'i between the years 1911 and 1913. I had been to Kaua'i twice as a young woman and remembered being wrapped in the warm air and welcoming aloha spirit. I let the letters sit for a few years; then, enticed by memories of Granny, in addition to my own love of the Hawaiian Islands, I began to read.

Here was my grandmother as a young woman named Hettie Belle, off on a great adventure in a place far removed in time and place from my mountain home in Alaska. I was soon drawn into her life as governess to two lively children on a Kaua'i plantation/ranch one hundred years ago, not just any plantation, but one belonging to one of most important families on Kaua'i: the Robinson/Gay clan. Their land, shaped like a hefty slice of pie, stretches for over 21,000 acres from the ocean into the folded cliffs of the island's center, all the way along the shore from Waimea to Hanapepe. The Robinsons also own the entire "forbidden island" of Ni'ihau. A private family, they are known for rigorously protecting the largely undeveloped island's isolation and its rich aquatic life. I was intrigued to learn more about this family and their place in the community at the time my grandmother lived with them.

Over the next few years, as I transcribed the letters, I became curious about the time period that Hettie Belle had spent on Kaua'i, when Hawai'i was a newly acquired US territory. I started reading about Hawai'i's colorful yet often tragic history, going back to the early Polynesian settlers. I learned how their lineage and history were told in epic chants, poems, and songs called *mele*. I read Queen Liliuokalani's sorrowful account about the takeover of her government and her imprisonment. Studying Edward Joesting's book, *Kauai: The Separate Kingdom*, I learned how Kaua'i had a unique history with its own royalty and fight for autonomy. To help understand Kaua'i and Ni'ihau today, I followed the current local news, filled with stories of development versus protection of the land and the resurgence of native cultural activities. I learned that the Robinsons continue to struggle to protect Ni'ihau from over-fishing and tourism. I began to see Hawai'i as a complex mix of cultures, of varied landscapes, and of conflicting issues, not simply as a tropical paradise. My Granny's letters seemed to shed light on a missing piece of Kaua'i's published history.

I started spending long periods of time on Kaua'i, where I visited most of the sites mentioned in Hettie Belle's letters, including the church she attended, one of the homes she stayed at, and Ni'ihau, getting a tantalizing view of the seldom-visited island on a helicopter tour. I delved into the archives and photos at the Kaua'i Museum and the Kaua'i Historical Society. I scrolled through microfilm of the local newspaper, *The Garden Island,* at the Līhu'e Library, reading the issues published while Hettie was on the island.

In Honolulu, O'ahu, I went to the Bishop Museum, where I pored through photos and felt the power of the historical mele. At Iolani Palace, I saw the bedroom where Queen Lili'uokalani was imprisoned when she tried to restore the Hawaiian monarchy that was wrested from her by the Provisional Government. A deep sadness and shame fell on me, realizing that this Provisional Government had been acting with tacit approval from the United States. On O'ahu, I also searched the Honolulu Public Library and the Hawai'i State Archives for information.

Wanting a more direct contact with Hettie's past, I sought out Robinson family descendants, Keith Robinson and Lois Sommers, who graciously provided me with information on their family and places on the islands. Keith, who owns Ni'ihau with his brother Bruce, gave me the rare opportunity to visit that island with him. Chris Faye (first as curator at the Kaua'i Museum and later as director of Kōke'e Natural History Museum in Kōke'e State Park, which includes some of the original Robinson/Gay land) spent time helping me with early research. Historian Andy Bushnell read Hettie Belle's letters and made suggestions concerning the people she met who were of significance in Hawaiian history. Aletha Kaohi, manager of the West Kaua'i Visitor Center, twice pulled me, a stranger, into her office to "talk story" about Hettie Belle's letters.

To place Hettie Belle's letters in context both historically and geographically, I've incorporated the results of my research and my own personal knowledge of the island into a narrative thread that links the letters together.

Hettie Belle was hired in late summer of 1911 as governess for the youngest of the five Robinson children, Eleanor and Lester. Sinclair and Aylmer had recently graduated from Harvard and were learning the family business, and Selwyn was attending Harvard. Also in the household were two grandmothers, Mrs. Helen Robinson and Mrs. Jane Gay. They were sisters, daughters of the original pioneer to Hawaiʻi, Mrs. Eliza McHutcheson Sinclair. Another of their sisters, Mrs. Anne Knudsen, and her children are also prominent characters in this story, as is grandmother Gay's son, Mr. Francis Gay. These Gay/Robinson family members along with extended family are recorded in Appendix A.

Most of Hettie Belle's letters were addressed to her mother, but as the sixth of twelve children, she often wrote to her siblings, as well. She frequently mentions her eldest sister, Margie, who was, at the time, working as a secretary for the YWCA in Japan. The younger siblings back in Boise, Idaho, were referred to by their pet names: Marian, "Mutt"; Theodore, "Dordie"; John, "Fats" or "Johnny Boy"; and Gertrude, "Babe." Her nickname for her brother Raymond, who was musically involved like her, was "Boy Dear." Hettie Belle herself sometimes signed her letters as "Betty." A list of family members who appear in the letters, along with their nicknames, is included in Appendix B. The organization of both the Robinson and Matthew family trees follows the format that the Matthew family used for their large family gatherings and is explained in the Code Key in each of the appendices A and B.

Appendix C lists some facts about the important historical figures on Kauaʻi that Hettie Belle met during her stay. Brief comments on the Hawaiian royalty mentioned in the narrative are also included. These historical people are briefly noted in footnotes, and then more detailed information in Appendix C is listed in alphabetical order of last names. Bibliographic references, however, are placed as endnotes rather than footnotes.

In addition to leaving out letters that focused on Hettie Belle's longings for her family and the endless details of her travel arrangements, I have made minor editorial changes, such as adding paragraph divisions for clarity. Some letters were edited for length. In order to reflect Hettie

Belle's personality and spirit, I left her inconsistent spacing, spellings, and punctuation marks intact. For example, when meeting new people, she often misspelled their names initially, but later corrected her spelling. Her abundant dashes show her youthful thoughts were quickly flowing, so I have let those stand as they were. Hettie Belle was effusive with her use of underlines, sometimes making two or three strokes; these have been changed to italics for easier reading. A glimpse of her original penmanship style may be seen in Appendix D.

To flesh out Hettie Belle's story, I have also drawn upon a short memoir of her time in Hawai'i, which she penned in 1973 at the request of her daughters. Her recollections were colored by her many later visits to the islands over the years and sometimes differ from her earlier letters. I've included excerpts of the memoir in my narrative sections, sometimes paraphrased and sometimes quoted.

Hettie Belle's photos, which I later found in my mother's papers, were unlabeled. I have been able to identify some individuals by comparing them to people in other archived photos on Kaua'i and by questioning Robinson family descendants.

In her letters, Hettie Belle did not use the macrons (*kahakō*) and glottal stops (*'okina*) in Hawaiian words. These markings have not been important to Hawaiian speakers on Ni'ihau or to the Robinson family members who know the language. However, in my narrative passages, I have italicized words other than English and added the markings in order to assist English speakers with pronunciation. A short glossary of Hawaiian terms can be found in Appendix E.

Appendix F contains a page of Hettie Belle's unpublished memoir, and Appendix G holds the recipes mentioned in Hettie's letters. The maps of Kaua'i and Ni'ihau at the beginning of the book are ones I constructed from a variety of available maps. Places that Hettie Belle mentions are marked on the maps as accurately as I was able to determine, with help from Keith Robinson.

INTRODUCTION

Hettie Belle Matthew stood at the railing on the steamship *Korea* in the fall of 1911, watching fish with silvery wings fly over the water of the great Pacific Ocean. She had just finished breakfast in the dining room, served by Chinese wait staff with their long shining queues tucked into side pockets. She was proud to be the only woman present at the meal, the others all feeling ill.

Hettie Belle, a hardy, middle class girl of twenty-two years, was leaving her home and career in Berkeley, California to travel to Hawaiʻi, a trip that would change the direction of her life. Though she had not attended college, she was financially independent, an accomplished pianist and teacher with her own studio and pupils. When a friend telephoned her and asked if she would like to go to "the Islands" to teach for a year, she stated that she would not consider it because she was too musically involved in Berkeley. But she was later persuaded to meet Mr. Aubrey Robinson, a wealthy landowner, who had come from the remote island of Kauaʻi to find a teacher for his two youngest children. She fell under his charm. This daughter of a struggling Methodist minister, sixth of his twelve children, began to see the advantages of a year on Kauaʻi and decided to travel across the Pacific Ocean, over 2,500 miles, to a remote island in Hawaiʻi to become a governess in a wealthy home.

In the past, Europeans and Americans had referred to Hawaiʻi as "the Islands," short for the Sandwich Islands, a name given to that group of volcanic outcroppings by Captain James Cook to honor the Lord of

Admiralty, 4th Earl of Sandwich. Although many Europeans settled in Hawai'i and enjoyed economic prominence there, American influence strengthened when missionaries in the 1820s were sent from the Boston area to convert and educate native Hawaiians. For many years, Boston was America:[1] whalers, traders, missionaries all came from there into the Pacific. The Robinsons sent all their sons to Harvard, and Hettie Belle helped prepare their younger children for private high school on the east coast. The Robinson/Gay clan was comfortable traveling to and living in Boston. David Igler speaks of the American Pacific as a suburb of Boston, demonstrating the strong ties.

In 1893, a powerful group of mostly American businessmen (including many missionary descendants) staged a coup. President McKinley refused Hawai'i its rightful independence. Queen Lili'uokalani* was placed under house arrest in 1895 by a business clique asserting power, and the United States annexed Hawai'i in 1898. The 100-year-old Hawaiian kingdom came to an end. Christian capitalism/colonialism replaced the old, stratified Hawaiian society that had been weakened by disease and culture shock.[2] Hawai'i became a territory of the United States in 1900.

The island of Kaua'i was an unknown to Americans. Many pictured remote sandy isles of exile or wild jungles with naked inhabitants. Hettie Belle was soon to learn that proper Scottish Edwardians, like the Robinson/Gay clan, lived there along with a mix of ethnicities, including native Hawaiians. Life on the Islands was cosmopolitan, part of a vibrant Pacific trading community. Hettie Belle would find herself transported into the life of an elite Euro-Hawaiian family.

During the Edwardian Age, sail and steam connected the Pacific Rim.[3] Trade and travel between San Francisco, Hawai'i, and the Orient were common. Prosperous plantation owners like the Robinsons obtained furniture from overseas, animal hides and guano (bird fertilizer) from South America, and rugs from the Orient. Goods flowed from San Francisco back and forth between Canton and other Chinese cities, tying Sitka, Alaska and Vancouver, Canada to California and to South America, to the Hawaiian Islands, and to Japan. Mrs. Aubrey Robinson's

---

* Queen Lili'uokalani was the last ruler of the Kingdom of Hawai'i.

father, Captain Thomas Gay,[*] had been a whaler roaming the Pacific Rim, traveling from New Zealand to Alaska.

Mr. Robinson was a wealthy rancher and sugarcane planter. He and his wife Alice Gay had five children: Sinclair, Aylmer, Selwyn, Eleanor, and Lester. The three older sons were educated at Harvard, and Selwyn was a student there during Hettie Belle's stay on Kaua'i. Higher education linked the Robinsons to Boston. The family was also connected to California where a sister of Mrs. Robinson (Mrs. Welcker[†]) lived, and it was through her that Hettie Belle met Mr. Robinson.

The Robinson/Gay clan (descendants of the Sinclair family) had a history of adventure and travel. In the previous generation, the Sinclairs had emigrated from Scotland to New Zealand with their many children, then later sailed to the northwest American coast, and finally to Hawai'i in search of a place to settle. While stopping over in Honolulu, Eliza Sinclair,[‡] widow of the wealthy Captain Francis Sinclair, arranged to purchase the island of Ni'ihau from King Kamehameha IV[§] for $10,000 in gold. Finding that Ni'ihau did not have sufficient water to support the local Hawaiians and the business plans of the extended Sinclair family, Eliza later purchased 21,400 acres of Makaweli land on Kaua'i from Princess Victoria Kamāmalu.[¶]

By 1910 after Eliza Sinclair's death, Aubrey and Alice Robinson owned two homes on Kaua'i. Makaweli House was in the hills of the Makaweli *ahupua'a* (a land division usually extending from the uplands to the sea) comprised of several canyons descending from the Alaka'i Swamp to the coast. Makaweli means glaring, threatening eyes, perhaps

---

[*] Captain Thomas Gay, Scottish-born, married Jane Sinclair in New Zealand and was skipper of the bark that brought the Sinclair/Robinson/Gay family to Hawai'i.

[†] Elizabeth ("Eliza" or "Lila") Gay was Mrs. Robinson's sister.

[‡] Elizabeth "Eliza" McHutcheson (Mrs. Sinclair) was the matriarch of a line of strong women.

[§] King Kamehameha IV, Alexander Liholiho, ruled the Kingdom of Hawai'i from 1855 until his death in 1863.

[¶] Victoria Kamāmalu was the granddaughter of the first Kamehameha and the highest-ranking woman of Hawaiian royalty. King Kamehameha IV appointed her to the office of Kuhina Nui, to preside over the king's Privy Council.

from idols with fearsome, terrifying eyes from *heiau*, pre-Christian places of worship.[4] This upland house was used mostly in the hotter months. The Kapalawai house was within sight of the ocean and was built, under the direction of Aubrey Robinson, not long before Hettie Belle's arrival. The family also had a home on Ni'ihau called Ki'eki'e, known as "The House," and several small shelters around that island.

First School Year

CHAPTER ONE
LETTERS HOME

Hettie Belle Matthew was the sixth of twelve children in the family of Reverend Dr. Winfield Scott Matthew and Marion Lillian Pomeroy. Both of her parents were educated in Chicago. Her mother was one of few early female graduates of Northwestern University; there she met her future husband, Scott, who would later work for the Methodist church in various capacities: pastor, educator, writer, and editor. In his line of work, the family moved quite often. At the time of Hettie Belle's job interview with Mr. Aubrey Robinson, the Matthews and their four youngest children had been stationed away from California at a church in Boise, Idaho. The strong religious interests were probably important for both the Robinson and Matthew families in agreeing to Hettie Belle's travel to Kaua'i.

Because her parents were far from Berkley at that time, Hettie Belle went to her eldest brother, Allan, for advice. He immediately frowned on the offer, reminding her how very fortunate she was to be so musically connected in Berkeley with an excellent teacher, a lovely studio, and all the pupils she had time to teach. However, Allan agreed to go with Hettie Belle and meet Mr. Aubrey Robinson.

After assessing Mr. Robinson's intentions, Allan was convinced, and he helped Hettie Belle decide that a year on Kaua'i with the Robinson family could be a delightful and financially rewarding experience. Matters were settled as to salary, dates, and travel. All expenses were to be paid by the Robinsons.

Mr. Robinson told Allan that he would like Hettie Belle to take the same ship to Honolulu as he, so that she would be safely chaperoned. Also, he said, "Miss Matthew will have to have a completely different wardrobe, because of climatic differences. I wish permission to give her a check for the purchase of some appropriate clothing, so as to be comfortable. When we reach Honolulu, a friend of our family will help her find riding clothes and bathing suit."

Much activity ensued. Hettie Belle went to the local board of education and found all the books the children would require for a year. She located appropriate music. A friend, Luther Marchant of Mills College, took over her studio and all her students who wished to study with him.

The days flew by, and soon the sailing date for the *Korea* arrived in early September, 1911. Hettie Belle traveled first class with Mr. Robinson. At that time, a first class ticket from Honolulu to San Francisco cost $65.[5] The *Korea* was part of the Pacific Mail Steamship Company, built in 1909 at Newport News, Virginia. This steamer ship traveled between San Francisco and Japan and China. On board were accommodations for 220 first class passengers, 54 white passengers in steerage, and enough space for 1,144 Chinese. Advertisements stated, "Should the latter not be carried, the unoccupied space will be used for additional cargo."[6]

On the crossing, there was only one stormy day, and Hettie Belle proudly recalled in her 1973 memoir that she was the only woman in the dining room for breakfast. The sunrises and flying fish filled her with wonder. Time passed quickly, and soon they entered the Honolulu harbor, arriving on September 25, 1911.

In Honolulu, the Robinsons stayed at the Alexander Young Hotel in the middle of the commercial district. Hettie Belle spent several days in the city with Mr. Robinson as they waited for the inter-island steamer. Also, Mr. Robinson wished to have time with his two eldest sons, Sinclair and Aylmer, who were employed on a plantation not far from Honolulu, learning about the raising of sugarcane. They met the young men at dinner.

After several delightful days seeing Honolulu and meeting some of the Robinson family friends, Mr. Robinson and Hettie Belle took an inter-island steamer for Kaua'i. These ships sailed to the various islands, attending to all needs of the sugar and pineapple plantations, carrying the mail, supplies, and passengers. This young woman, aged twenty-two, had ventured miles from her family to what she jokingly referred to as a "desert isle," and her adventures on Kaua'i and Ni'ihau were about to begin.

Makaweli House

Sept. 29 - 1911

Dearest Mother –

I believe that my last to you said that I was about to embark on the good ship "Kinau" for Kauai, and that I looked forward to a very rough trip – the Kinau being slightly smaller than the Korea – and the waters between Honolulu and Kauai being noted for their roughness. Well, many of the Honolulu friends came to the boat to see us off – and Mr. Wichman* – a man we met on the Korea – brought a huge box of candy to the boat to me (this was in payment of a bet I had won while aboard). After the farewells we embarked and you cannot imagine how rough it was! It was *frightful!* And I feared that I would lose my reputation as a good sailor. But I still had my "sea legs" on – and enjoyed the trip hugely. We left Honolulu at five o'clock Tuesday evening – and arrived at Makaweli at seven o'clock the next morning Wednesday. If it had not been for two distractions on board, I would surely have been deathly sick. One distraction was a Mr. Fairchild,† friend of Mr. Robinson's – a man with a tremendous sense of humor –and a great store of good stories. The other distraction was a tiny baby, not yet three weeks old – you know how I love them. But think of a mother taking such a trip with such a tiny baby.

The most exciting part of the trip was the landing. There is no pier or wharf – you simply cling on to a rope ladder that is lowered over the side of the boat – below you the waves are dashing high and a row boat filled with natives is bobbing around fiercely. The captain of the "Kinau" does a deal of swearing – the natives are all talking in high pitched voices – and suddenly when things are calmest – you are grabbed bodily and set down in the row boat, quite out of breath – you have been too scared to breathe. Then when a few more passengers and baggage are placed in

---

* Henry F. Wichman was in the jewelry business in Honolulu.

† Mr. George Hendrick Fairchild was the manager of the Makee Sugar Company at Keālia and Territorial Senator from Kaua'i in 1911.

the rowboat in the same manner, you are rowed to shore. It was certainly one of the strangest experiences that has as yet come to your daughter.

When we were safely on shore – we found servants waiting with a carriage, and we drove immediately to "Kapalawai," which is the name of the Robinsons' home. The drive to the home was perfectly beautiful – the soil here is very red – so the roads are this lovely red with red stonewalls on either side. And all the trees are so green – the grass and ferns are *so* green. One does not know what *green* is until one comes here. Mrs. Robinson and the children were awaiting us on the porch – such a dear, sweet quiet woman she is – and the children are *dears!* They had come down from the mountain home to meet us – and said that they were going back up in the afternoon. So I was taken to my room – it is a dear pink and white room – (you know my failing for pink) with a door opening upon the court and one opening out on to the garden; a bathroom attached, of course. The dear little Japanese maid helped me unpack my trunks and repack my steamer trunk to take to the mountain home. Then she prepared my bath – and after a good bath and clean clothes – I felt quite at home. We had company for lunch – a Mr. Kanutzan [Knudsen]*– and after lunch prepared immediately for our trip up the mountain.

It is about an eight mile trip – the children went on horseback – while Mr. & Mrs. Robinson and I went in a buggy. You know when every tree, and plant, and flower is *absolutely* different from anything that you have ever seen before – you begin to think that you *must* be in a dream. This is the way that I feel. I have tasted so many new fruits and vegetables during the past week that I am quite bewildered. We wound higher and higher up the mountain until we reached this beautiful mountain home – "Makaweli House."

Mrs. Robinson,† Mr. Robinson's mother, and Mrs. Gay,‡ Mrs. Robinson's mother, are here. They are *sisters* – and two dearer old ladies never lived. They dress in lovely trailing black dresses and wear white caps. There are only ten servants

---

* Eric Alfred Knudsen was a younger cousin of both Mr. and Mrs. Robinson, a frequent visitor in their home.

† Helen McHutcheson Sinclair (Grandmother Robinson) was the daughter of Francis Sinclair and Eliza McHutcheson. She voyaged with her family from Scotland to New Zealand, where she married Charles Barrington Robinson. Her son was Aubrey.

‡ Jane "Jean" Sinclair Gay was the oldest of the three Sinclair daughters and Mrs. Aubrey Robinson's mother.

up here – five house servants and five yard servants. They have native yard servants, but Japanese house servants. This is an *immense* house, about half a block long – only two rooms thick. My room is a pink and white room, here, also – all apple-blossomy – I'm at the extreme right end of the house. In both front and back are great wide covered porches, called "lanai," running the full length. The school house is behind the house.

After arriving, I got thoroughly settled in my room, then took a look at the place, guided by little Lester. He took me to the top of the hill – showed me where to find the delicious strawberry guavas – then insisted that he could beat me to the bottom of the hill. Of course I had to let him prove it.

After dinner and worship I was more than ready to fall into bed – never to move until the sweet voice of the little maid said – "Goodee morning, Missee Matu – bath already"!

Thursday morning at nine school began – I found the children unusually bright – all has started well. In the afternoon I gave them their music lessons – in music also they will do *very* well. So after two days of school – I feel that I have taught school *always!* We have school from 9 - 12:30 with half-hour recess from 10:30 - 11:00. During recess we refresh ourselves with cocoanut milk. You shall have the descriptions of the two homes in my next letter – they will fill a letter by themselves. If I tell you the truth – it is that I have not had *one* unhappy moment since leaving Berkeley. I love you all so!

Hettie

Captain James Gregory of the inter-island steamer *Kinau* was a small stout man with a loud voice and rough vocabulary. For many years prior to his death, he efficiently captained this craft through rough island waters. During subsequent trips on the *Kinau*, Hettie Belle was allowed to sit in the pilothouse and listen to his stories.

The *Kinau*, owned by the Wilder Steamship Company, was elegantly appointed for its time. It even had electric lights. During Hettie Belle's stay, the *Kinau* or another inter-island steamer came to Kaua'i twice a week. She sent letters home each time it arrived.

Hettie Belle recounted that there were few staterooms on the *Kinau*. However, the Hawaiians were allowed to sleep on deck and could ride for free. Mr. Robinson told delightful stories about these trips. One night the seas were especially stormy. A Hawaiian alerted the Captain that a native woman had been washed overboard. As soon as possible, the Captain reversed his ship, and with a bright searchlight swept the waters. Sure enough, through the stormy sea came the woman, swimming vigorously and singing. She had removed her shoes, tied them together, and hung them around her neck.

Strawberry guavas (http://images.search.yahoo.com/images/view) Psidium cattleianum is an invasive tree. According to botanists at Limahuli Garden, this plant creates "monotypic stands which dry out the land, negatively affecting the forest's ability to retain water." People who introduced these exotic plants were not aware of the changes they would cause.

Makaweli Landing – men rowing passengers to or from an Inter Island steamship vessel. Hettie Belle thought the most exciting part of the trip was when she was "grabbed bodily and set down in the row boat, quite out of breath." (courtesy of the Kaua'i Museum)

Envelope from a Hettie Belle letter home written in the fall after her arrival on Kaua'i.

The Matthew children had been born about every two years. Hettie Belle said that she noticed only that her mother went up the stairs more slowly when she was about to birth another child. After the first six children, Hettie's mother, Marion Lillian, began assigning one of the older children to each successive baby, so that the elder six each had a special "baby" to help care for, to share secrets with, and to love especially. Hettie's was Gertrude, the last child. Hettie Belle was deeply concerned about all her siblings as she wrote to her mother, wanting to be involved in the family from afar. Sister Sally lost two babies, and her unsettled brother, Hurd, was a concern. Her special brother Raymond was also involved in music, and she longed for news of him.

Hettie Belle's mother, Marion Lillian Pomeroy Matthew (circa 1878) and father, Winfield Scott Matthew (circa 1906)

Matthew brothers by age, youngest at left to right: Theodore, John Britton, Raymond, Samuel Hurd, Winfield Scott, Melville Richard, and eldest Alan [Allan] Pomeroy. (Christmas 1913)

Matthew sisters by age, youngest left to right: Gertrude Willard, Marian Hilliard, Hettie Belle, Sarah Wheat (Sally), and eldest Margaret Lillian (Margie). (circa 1913)

Oct. 9 -1911 —

Darling Mutt —

Why don't you people write to me? I had barrels of steamer letters — and my! how I loved them, but since arriving on Kauai — I have only had two letters ⁊ one postal — and I am simply starving for news from you home people — I can hardly wait. Now I can appreciate just what it means to Margie to get letters from home.

Mutt darling — I shall never destroy your steamer letter to me. It was so sweet — so like you! You cannot know how it comforted me — won't you write me often — and such sweet comforting letters as that was, this year?

I told Mother that in my next letter you people should have a description of my new home. Well — there are two new homes to describe — the mountain home "Makaweli House" where we now are, ⁊ "Kapalawai" which means lowlands⁊ — and is the home down in the lowlands. When we arrived in Kauai, we went to Makaweli House almost immediately, only stopping at Kapalawai for lunch ⁊ to repack my trunk. But each Saturday we go down to Kapalawai, so as to be down in town where we can attend church on Sunday — then Sunday evening we come up here again to Makaweli House. This mountain home is about 8 miles above the lowland home — and you cannot imagine how cool and delightful it is here — and beautiful! There is a splendid road all the way, first passing thro' the lovely green sugar cane fields then thro' the woods. And Oh! Mutt darling — the trees are so interesting ⁊ beautiful — and everything is so green — and the ferns ⁊

flowers grow so thick and sweet. I couldn't have imagined such a beautiful spot as this island is. Makaweli House is a long house, as near as I can count it has thirty rooms – the schoolroom & servant quarters are behind it. It has great porches all around it – and great beautiful rolling lawns. There is a lovely garden behind the house, and in front of it, winding paths and bordered walks. A lovely tennis court is hidden among trees. But for the most part, it has been left wild – as a mountain home should be left – so when you take paths and go in different directions, it is all wild and wonderfully so. I love to go to the swimming pool – you have to pass thro' a great wilderness of bamboo – it is such lovely green lacy stuff. I think that I shall be married in that bamboo grove. That will probably be the only way that I shall ever get you people to come and see all this beauty that I am powerless to describe. There is a beautiful Steinway Grand piano here – and every evening they make me play by the hour. There is also a billiard table here – that is fun. But I started to tell you about the swimming pool – we take a lovely winding path (pass lots of peacocks on the way), and we wind in and out among beautiful trees, grass & ferns until we finally reach the lovely swimming pool set down among the rocks & simply surrounded by green – & by lovely begonias as tall as your head – growing wild – and you cannot imagine how beautiful the delicate pink of their blossoms is amongst the green fern. I cannot begin to tell you of the many new fruits that I have tasted – some so delicious – some so peculiar & tropical in taste. I have a dear room here – all pink & white. A bathroom attached of course – I take always two & usually three baths a day and change all my clothes – this is such a luxury. In the morning I take my cold shower – then a warm bath just before I dress for dinner & usually another before retiring.

I must tell you about our course of study. We have school from 9-12:30 & we study Arithmetic, Spelling, writing, History, Geography, English, (reading & Composition & grammar), German, Latin, (drawing & cooking twice a week), music (vocal & piano) and folk dancing. That seems like a lot doesn't it? But we get it all in. In the afternoon the children study from 2-3, and then we have our walk & romp with the dogs – go swimming or riding. Later in the P.M. the children finish their practising – they each get some in the A.M. before breakfast. I cannot tell you how I am enjoying my work here.

Makaweli House – "Makaweli House is a long house, as near as I can count it has thirty rooms – the schoolroom & servant quarters are behind it," wrote Hettie Belle. (circa 1912 by Hettie Belle)

One of the paths near Makaweli House where Hettie Belle said, "But for the most part, it has been left wild – as a mountain home should be left." (circa 1912 by Hettie Belle Matthew)

Now I must tell you about Kapalawai, the lowland home. It is built around a square court, a great porch all around the inside & around the outside. In the court are wonderful tropical flowers and a grass plot – and twining flowers on the porches. Surrounding the home are great stretches of lawn – acres & acres – and hundreds of palms & trees – you really cannot believe it without seeing it. And a tennis court and a fruit garden – and a lake, surrounded by cocoanut palms. There are about 40 rooms in this home – and many surrounding houses for servants etc. From the porches you have a wonderful view of the sea, and you can continually hear the roar & see the breakers – this is especially fascinating by moonlight. The view is not as wonderful as that from Makaweli House however – from here you have the beautiful green valley below you – then the blue sea stretching out with their beautiful island of Niihau in the distance. You cannot imagine how filled the two homes are with rare curios, beautiful furniture, rugs and silver! It's just like a book. But I must leave something to tell next time. I love you so dearly.

Please write your

Loving Muttress

Free-spirited Hettie Belle enjoyed all the activities in the mountains at Makaweli House: horse rides, long walks, and runs with the children. She was proud of herself as she learned new physical skills of swimming, rowing, tennis, and horseback riding.

The front of the Kapalawai house where Hettie Belle said "Surrounding the home are great stretches of lawn – acres and acres." (2013 by J. Burtner)

There was a great living room at Makaweli House. Off this room was a library with many enclosed bookcases. Hettie Belle remembered that at one time, Mrs. Robinson told the servants that she wished all the volumes to be "aired." To her great dismay, the airing revealed that bookworms had found their way into many of the treasured, rare first editions.

Kapalawai was one of the most perfect homes that Hettie Belle had ever seen, both for beauty and comfort. The form, a huge hollow square with wide verandas both outside and inside, had been planned by Mr. Robinson. In the inner court was a tropical garden with hibiscus, ginger, bleeding heart, and ferns. On the rear porch, besides the lounging chairs, there was a piano and a billiard table. From the front, one looked across a great expanse of lawn and garden, then open pasture cut through a grove of algaroba trees to a view of the sea.

At the lowland house, Hettie Belle's room was next to the grandmothers' suite. Mrs. Robinson would go each night to bid the grandmothers good night, and then she would come into Hettie Belle's room for a little visit, and she would tuck Hettie Belle into bed.

The Kapalawai house was built around an inner courtyard. (2013 by J. Burtner)

Some of the schoolbooks Hettie Belle used are still stored in the
Kapalawai house. (2013 by J. Burtner)

The billiard table is still on the Kapalawai lanai and was a source of great
entertainment for family and visitors. (photo 2013 by J. Burtner)

The piano at Kapalawai where Hettie Belle sat to play on many evenings.
(2013 by J. Burtner)

Judith Marion Burtner

Oct. 9 - 1911

Dordie, dear –

Did you ever see a spider? No, you never have seen a *real* spider – 'cause you have never been on Kauai. *I* have seen one. First you *hear* it – coming across the floor – it is so heavy that it makes a noise as it walks. When first you see it coming – you think it is a kitten coming across the floor – but when you go to pet it, you realize your mistake. You can't kill it by stepping on it – at least you wouldn't want to – so you throw your shoe at it – it winks an eye at you and ambles off out the door. Ugh! But they are horrid things – but there are *lots* of wonderfully beautiful things here. Love to you, Hettie

Dear John,

I want to tell you about my midnight visitor. You know it is so hot here that we leave all windows and doors open. In the middle of the night, I was awakened by a peculiar noise. The bright moonlight was streaming in at my door & at my windows. It seemed to be a crunching and a chewing noise – finally as I could stand it no longer, I couldn't get to sleep – I quietly, but *bravely* got out of my bed and crept to the door. Instead of a fierce bepee [*pipi* or steer], as I had imagined might be there – it was only a donkey. I tried to shh him away, but failed. He was having too good a time eating the grass that grows just off my porch. So I tried shoes – missed him with the 1st but hit him square with the 2nd & off he went down the bank – & off I went to sleep – but the next morning my shoes were full of water – it rained before morning. Love to you,

    Hettie

Dearest Gertrude –

We have just come in, Eleanor, Lester and I – from the hill, where we have been gathering and eating strawberry guavas. They are a little wild fruit – and *so* juicy & sweet, I love them. Every afternoon after school we go for a run on the hills. You cannot imagine how beautiful it is here – if only you children could be here – what fun we could all have together. Eleanor is 13 and Lester 10 – and they are such *dear* jolly children – it makes me almost feel as if I were with *you* children again. Sometimes on our walks, we go over to the swimming pool, it is so beautiful there ⁊ we meet many peacocks on the way – also we have to pass thro' a grove of bamboo – it is lovely ⁊ green and cool. You children *must* write me, ⁊ write me *often*, or I shall just die! Love to *you*. Hettie

Makaweli House – Oct. 18th 1911.

Babe, dearest –

The little violets which you sent were still very sweet when I smelled of them – and you were a dear, sweet child to send them to me. The woods here are just *full of* blue and yellow violets – carpets of them everywhere – I hate to step in some places, almost, because I crush so many at each step. And thank you for the birthday dates! I am so glad to have them – and have asked for them several times. But I realize that it was a great deal of trouble for you to get them for me – I can just see you poring over the huge family Bible and copying them for me.

Now Gertrude – you must find time to write me a *long* letter. I want you to tell me *in detail* about your *music* and about your *studies* – you know that I am especially interested in all these things these days. Lester is in the 6th grade, I think, and Eleanor in the 8th. You must tell me what they have in those grades in Boise, and we can compare notes. Lester is awfully interested in stamps just now – has some *dandy* "traders"– and wants to know whether or not John would care to trade with him. If so, tell John to send some of his best "traders," and write Lester a letter – or enclose a note in a letter to me.

Are you going to make the badger skin into a muff? Tell him to get a few more ⁊ then you can make a muff and fur for your neck. You know I left my lynx furs for Sally to wear, it doesn't ever get cold here – I haven't worn a coat or wrap of *any* kind, since the 3rd day out on the Korea. When we drive I have to wear a duster and tho' it is thin linen, I nearly suffocate. So you can picture me in thin, *thin* clothes – while you are shivering and shuddering in a thunderstorm.

You will write me *soon* again won't you, dearie? I love your letters. Tell me all the *little* things. Your loving big sister – Hettie Belle .

Chapter Two

Class Distinctions and Squeaky Shoes

Far from distant England and Scotland, the Edwardian Age flourished in the Hawaiian Islands. In this era, land was power, and tradition kept the classes in line.

On the Robinson plantation there were definite divisions in society, and crossing boundaries was not permitted nor even considered, particularly by women. Ladies had to be always proper and dignified. However, when the men were away, Mrs. Robinson, Hettie Belle, and the children relaxed and frolicked about the house and grounds. In addition, Hettie Belle's youth and enthusiasm sometimes caused her to step outside the bounds of propriety and custom. Being a middle-class California girl new to the Islands, she didn't know what was expected, as the following story indicates.

Each weekend the Robinson family journeyed to the lowlands to attend the Sunday church service in the district. Shortly after her arrival on Kaua'i, when time came for the family to go down on a Saturday, Hettie Belle announced that she would like to walk down and thus see the cane fields and the wonderful view.

Hettie Belle scarcely noticed the stunned silence. As she went along the veranda toward her room, she overheard one of the grandmothers say sternly, "Of course you will not allow it!" Her feeling was that they thought the seven or so miles too much for her. (At this time, seven miles was nothing to Hettie Belle. When her family had lived in Marin County, CA, she and her siblings had happily walked all day, as much as seventeen miles.)

And so, down the hillside went the procession: the great carriage, a smaller conveyance for the servants, the children and cowboys on horseback. Hettie Belle walked, hatless but supremely happy and arrived covered with red dust. She did not know until years later that this provided a favorite Robinson "story," about the new teacher walking down the mountain road, when no one walks in that heat.

Makaweli House
Oct. 18th 1911.

Mother dearest –

Have you ever tasted *real* Scotch "short bread"? If you have you couldn't forget it. We made some in cooking school this P.M. It turned out beautifully, and was *lickin'* good! If you want the recipe – say so.

I covered myself with glory in more ways than one today. If *not* with glory – with *gory* blood. I was rough-housing with Eleanor, was chasing her – she flew into my room *&* banged the door shut, and I promptly went thro' the glass! Cut my little finger twice, and the under part of my arm, once. They are really mere scratches – I guess I did it mainly to prove what a splendid surgeon Mrs. R. is – and how brave I am at the sight of blood. In about 5 seconds I was all plastered up – and in my right mind. I intend to stay in that mind, and not go thro' any more glass doors. But one *has* to start something once in a while – else life would grow too monotonous altogether. By the time this reaches you, the plasters will be off and not even a scar will be in sight – so *don't* say, "Wasn't that a shame," and, "I'm afraid she didn't tell me how badly she was hurt," 'cause I *did* tell you all – even exaggerated, as usual.

Sixteen letters today! Among them your dear one with Babe's enclosed. You wrote on Oct. 1, and had not then had a letter from me – but *surely* you had one soon after. You asked about the climate – I find it *most* delightful. At the lowland home it is rather moist and warm but *not* disagreeable – but up here at Makaweli House, where it is 1800 ft. it is perfectly delightful – very much like Berkeley climate, making you *feel* like doing things. And yet I cannot quite understand it, for we wear *thin* things all day *&* evening and never need even a scarf extra – I think it *perfectly* *ideal. You know before I came I was worried as to what I should do with a maid! But now I wonder what I should do without! Little Japanese Ito is a dear! Such sweet, cunning half-apologizing little ways. In the morning, I hear – "Goodee morning, Miss Matu – bath already – seven o'clock." And presently I hear "Goodee morning, Teacher, half past seven." And once "Oh! Teacher. 5 minutes to eight – bell ring." And she popped me into my clothes. She cares for my room and bathroom, mends my clothes & stockings, runs in ribbons, cleans or blacks shoes, dresses me for dinner, brushes my hair each night – and a hundred other things that only a maid can think to do. She has fixed my mosquito canopy for the night turned down the covers & now waits to tuck me in – so goodnight with love. Hettie*

The class divisions of the Edwardian Age are illustrated in the way Hettie Belle referred to her Japanese maid as "little." Ito experienced a tragedy later, and Hettie Belle seemed to feel sorry for her but did not dwell on it for long.

Japanese people began coming to the islands in the late 1800s when sugar planters contracted them for work. By mid-1901, seventy-one percent of Kaua'i's workers were Japanese.[8] The Japanese experienced difficulties far from home, yet many stayed to help build the state of Hawai'i. Asahina Umekichi, the first of Francis Sinclair's original Japanese workers on Ni'ihau, eventually became a dentist in Hawai'i.[9] Many Japanese Nisei became successful business owners and elected officials, helping their new home to thrive.

Japanese men who were plantation workers sometimes sent photos to marriage brokers back in Japan. "Picture brides" would arrive, be married in a mass ceremony and then try to learn to adjust to a new land with a strange man.

Hettie Belle later fondly remembered the "splendid Japanese couple" in the kitchen at Kapalawai. She recalled Ketzu, the butler. He had been with the Robinsons for many years and was becoming old and "heavy-footed," as Hettie Belle said. Though slow, he was still completely capable, anticipating every need and wish of the family.

Instead of an "upstairs and downstairs" division, the Robinson family was in the big house and the others had quarters behind. The Japanese servants did household work and some gardening; the groundskeepers were Hawaiian, as were the *paniolo* (cowboys). Of course these cowboys' knowledge of the flora, fauna, and the culture of the islands was invaluable to the plantation families. The Robinson sons learned to speak Hawaiian, worked with the men to absorb their skills and local knowledge, and respected their expertise. According to David Larson who visited Niʻihau in 1942, the family did not give direct orders to Hawaiian workers; instead, Aylmer Robinson asked if the men could do something, and then asked how it should be done.[10]

Japanese women working on the grounds of the Robinson home.
(photo by Hettie Belle, circa 1912)

Makaweli House –
Sunday - Oct. 22 - 1911.

My own dearest Mother –

This is the first Sunday that we haven't been to church in Waimea, but Mrs. R.'s mother has been ill all week, and she didn't like to leave her. So we had prayers after breakfast – then sang hymns for about an hour. Then we went for a short walk up behind the house, before dinner. This afternoon I read six chapters of Matthew to the children and some Bible stories – since, I have been resting.

Even if your birthday letter was late – I loved it – and I was not unhappy on my birthday because of no word from you – 'cause I knew that you were loving me – I could feel it. And what do you suppose these dear people did? They didn't find out about it until my birthday was passed – then they gave me a lovely peacock lei – (a band for my hat about three inches wide, made of beautiful peacock feathers) – and the loveliest gold hat pin that you *ever* saw – has four lovely pearls and a large lapus lazuli set in it. They do such things in such a dear sweet way that you can't possibly feel uncomfortable or indebted to them.

Yesterday we had a *picnic* – no school of course on Saturday – so right away after breakfast Mr. R. and the two children and I started for a walk. And these are the loveliest hills for walking! We walked and walked – finally came to the "ditch" – which is about 8 ft. wide & 4 ft. deep and miles and *miles* long – brings the water from away up in the mountains down to irrigate the cane fields. Well, we found an old boat tied to a landing – and in we jumped, untied the rope, and away we went, slowly gliding along with the current, under small trestles and bridges – we must have drifted along for an hour or so – *then* we came to some locks and could go no farther. We got out and went home by the road, but it was *stacks* of fun. Mr. R. is just like a big boy – enters right into his children's fun or play – he can beat any of them running, too.

I don't believe I told you what I did *on* my birthday – In the P.M. the children & I went for a long run on the hills here. We must have been out over two hours. You probably think that I mean "walk" when I say "run"– but I mean *run* – something about this air or these hills, makes one *really* run – so fast that ones hair promptly comes down and streams behind in the breeze – and little Lester gallantly carries your hairpins & combs in his pockets. I *can* run! The children go barefooted usually, and sometimes I am almost tempted. Would *you* approve? On a desert island you know. On our runs we simply *stuff* ourselves with delicious red strawberry guavas – sometimes we chase peacocks and pheasants, lovely golden pheasants, and sometimes the pipis (wild cattle), chase us. I have learned to climb trees – this is a necessary art in these hills, for pipis cannot climb trees.

Lester is continually killing me with his funny remarks. Last evening I was writing in my room just before dinner, and along he came. "Miss Matthew, I am *so* disappointed," he said. "What is the matter?" said I. "Why my new shoes don't squeak a *bit!*" said he. Poor youngster – I tried to console him with a straight face – and didn't tell him that we consider a "squeak" a *calamity!*

Then this afternoon the Japanese gardener brought out his little son to show him off for the first time. He is the cunningest little brown eyed *curly* haired fellow, just walking – one year & 3 months old – and *imagine* they had him in tiny little short black trousers! Mr. R. & Eleanor and I were playing with him & making a good deal over him – and along comes Lester – he couldn't make out quite what the excitement was about – and he looked up at me, and said in the most innocent, wondering way, "What's the matter – was he *just born*?" Naturally we exploded.

Love to you all, and thank you for the dear birthday wishes.

Your own Hettie Belle

Lester thought it splendid to have shoes that squeaked. It seems that among the the youngsters of Kaua'i at this time, it was disappointing if shoes did not call out to those around, "Look at me!" After all, shoes were only worn for special occasions, and if they squeaked, then others might notice the new shoes.

Hettie Belle later reminisced about church on Ni'ihau. She especially loved it when the Robinson family all went to the Hawaiian church. The people of Ni'ihau dressed up for church and even wore shoes: "So—down the aisle—squeak, squeak! The singing was lovely, all the old hymns I knew, but in Hawaiian, of course, and with a very lovely, special lilt. After church, the Ni'ihau people all waited outside to greet the Robinson family, and then they removed their shoes and went off on happy bare feet."

Makaweli House–

Oct. 30 – 1911.

You dearest Mother –

Eleanor and Lester have just ladened me down with five or six lovely leis which they have just finished making. The ginger flowers make such lovely leis – they are so delicate in color and so very sweet and fragrant. Leis are worn so commonly here – you seldom see a native that he hasn't a lei around his hat made either of fragrant leaves, seeds or flowers. I love the custom.

Company – company – company! Never have I seen such a family for entertaining. Company for lunch and company for dinner. People to spend a few days – and people for the week-end. I don't wonder – for Mrs. Robinson is such a charming hostess, and Mr. R. the jolliest kind of a host. Today a Mrs. Knudsen,* nurse and two children came – are to spend a few days. She is perfectly lovely – has a small daughter of five and the *dearest* baby boy – a year and a half old – so you can imagine how happy I am, and how I put in my afternoon. He is the jolliest, sturdiest, handsomest little fellow – I had the time of my life playing with him.

It is now quite late – after dinner tonight, Mrs. R. and I played billiards and pool with Mr. R. & Mrs. Knudsen, and we beat them shamefully each game. After that I played for them – about an hour, I guess. The people here are simply *crazy* and *hungry* for music – and night after night I play for them – not one piece – but really by the hour. It is splendid practise for me – I have absolutely lost all nervousness about playing, which I once felt, and now I will play before anyone and any number of people and never mind it – I really *love* to. Am learning some very lovely new pieces. Let me tell you a very strange thing – I can memorize a piece very much more easily here than I could in Berkeley. I cannot quite account for the difference – perhaps it is that it is quieter here – at any rate, I find that I can memorize a piece almost as I read it the *first* time. You can imagine how delighted such a discovery makes me.

One day last week, *four* men were here to lunch – all of them married men, I must add. I am the *only* unmarried person in these Islands. Then there were three ladies & a gentleman here to spend the weekend. No school tomorrow – Mr. R. having declared a holiday – we start early in the morning on a long horseback ride. Hurrah! I am soon to be a *dandy* rider. They say that I sit my horse *beautifully*! Aren't you proud of me? At least, I am proud to be *your* daughter Hettie Belle. The Robinsons send Aloha!

As a governess, Hettie Belle was in a class slot of her own: an employee but not a servant; not a member of the family, but living with the family. The Robinsons made sure that she was not isolated in this position. They graciously took her into their social circle, introducing her to family and friends as well as to several bachelors and widowers. Hettie Belle voiced both humor at these efforts and increasing concern over her unmarried state.

---

* Cecilie Alexandra L'Orange was married to Eric Knudsen at that time. The children were Alexandra Lilikoi Knudsen and Valdemar L'Orange Knudsen.

In Hettie Belle's world, it was of great importance to find a spouse, but on the Hawaiian Islands in the early days, there were few choices. During the Edwardian Age, it was rare to marry across ethnic boundaries, religious lines, or class distinctions. In the 1800s, this was especially difficult with fewer foreigners on the islands. Although there were a number of marriages between *haole* (Caucasians) and Hawaiians, there were also marriages between cousins, and even first cousins. These marriages suited another priority on the plantations: to keep the land and wealth intact. Aubrey Robinson and his wife Alice Gay were first cousins. In the generation before, Francis Sinclair married his first cousin Isabella McHutcheson.

In a letter to her sister Marian, Hettie talks about plans for a trousseau stating, "I still have faith and hope to be married *some day*!" At other times, she tried to shock her parents with sly remarks about men and even sent them a leap year newspaper ad, suggesting that she could propose to a man and receive land in Hawai'i. Her mother's return letters are gone, but the distance and teasing appear to have concerned the family back in the states.

Kapalawai –

Nov. 5, 1911.

Mother, dearest –

Sunday morning – and we are again at Kapalawai – came down yesterday afternoon as usual. I think that we come down from the mountains next Saturday to stay – and I can't tell you how very badly I feel to come away and leave that beautiful mountain home – it is such a *perfect* place. I am writing you before breakfast – am I not a smart lady? This is the most glorious morning – a perfect Sunday. After breakfast we will sing hymns, have prayers, and then get ready and go to church. Mr. Millican [Milliken]* is the minister – and he gives us very good sermons. The only thing that I find hard to endure in church is the music. The singing drags unmercifully – the organist plays so slowly – I am tempted each Sunday to tear up into the choir loft, knock her off the organ stool, and play myself. But the *sermons* are good.

---

* C.D. Milliken was pastor of the Foreign Church from 1905-1916.

Waimea Foreign Church, 2018, now Waimea United Church of Christ, a landmark in Waimea. (courtesy of Christina Burtner)

I don't believe that I told you about the company that we had last week. Mrs. Knudsen, her two youngsters and their nurse, spent a few days with us. She is perfectly lovely and the children are *darlings!* And I want to tell you what we did one day. It was last Tuesday – Mr. Robinson declared a holiday and after breakfast we all started off on horseback – quite a procession of us, I tell you – Mr. & Mrs. Robinson, Mrs. Knudsen, Eleanor, Lester and I, and a native boy in the lead, to remove any possible obstructions from our pathway. We took a lovely winding, much overgrown path and went away up thro' the mountains. It was glorious. We crossed many streams, and climbed many rocky places. The trees were so beautiful – and the lovely ferns and flowers made such wonderful dense undergrowth. And such views as we had – when we came out into high open places – views of valleys, mountains and the wonderful sea below. It was almost too wonderful. We saw lots of wild pipi (cattle), wild pig and wild chickens. Wouldn't Father and the boys smack their lips? But we were not hunting, so left them in peace. But the Robinsons have promised that I can go with them on some hunts some day. We got home shortly before lunch – in the afternoon we all went over to the lovely swimming pool, and had a swim. That was fun, I tell you. Then in the evening Mrs. R. and I beat Mr. R. & Mrs. Knudsen shamefully at billiards – so we all sought consolation afterwards in the moonlight – went thro' the "Kissing Gate" and on up the hill where we could have the view of valley and sea below us. The "Kissing Gate" sounds interesting, doesn't it? I regret to tell you that I failed to find it so. Love from Hettie

Palm Sunday inside the Waimea United Church of Christ (J. Burtner)

The Foreign Church Hettie Belle attended was a segregated congregation of European/American settlers. (At that time the Hawaiians had their own church.) The beautiful, solid structure was designed by Reverend George Rowell,[*] built in the mid-nineteenth century and constructed from fine limestone and from *ʻōhiʻa lehua* logs hauled on a drag by teams of oxen owned by Deborah Kapule.[†]

Over the following years the Foreign Church experienced conflict and neglect as well as weather-related damage. Repairs that had begun after a huge rainstorm in 1885 were continued when a board was formed that included Mr. Aubrey Robinson as the auditor of the group. There were no "members" of this church at that time, but "subscribers" who gave and worshipped there. The subscribers selected the seven persons on the board of trustees who attended to the business of the Foreign Church. In this manner, those who had contributed money held control of the church. No offering was taken and no creed was enforced.[11]

Makaweli House –

Nov. 10 – 1911.

My dearest Mother –

What wild thing do you suppose we did the other morning? Got up at four o'clock and went away out on the hill to view the comet. There was supposed to be a beauty visible just at that time. But narry a comet did we see – possibly the moonlight was too bright – it was full moon, and as bright as day, I swear – and the valleys and sea bathed in moonlight were something to dream over – and Oh! yes the morning star was wonderfully beautiful – so we felt repaid, tho' we didn't see the comet. We staid out there enjoying the wonderful quiet until a wee boy remarked, chattering between words, "Let's go home and get something to eat, and have a game of billiards." But by the time we had reached home, we were too sleepy to think of billiards – and even something to eat didn't tempt us.

---

* George Rowell was an early missionary to Kauaʻi.

† Deborah Kapule was the favorite wife of Kaumualiʻi, the chief of Waimea and ruling chief of Kauaʻi. She was a bright and active participant in the history of Kauaʻi during the first half of the nineteenth century.

Hurd would say "that it's a *shame* to take the money." (What I am being paid for, I do not know – I lie awake nights wondering if I can conscientiously draw my salary.) It seems to me that we play more than we work. Both Thursday and Friday this week have been holidays. We went down (makai) Thursday A.M. for we were invited to a tennis party out at the Knudsens in the P.M. So we donned our "gladrags" and went out, sat on the side lines under the beautiful trees, on the lawn – had tea ⁊ sandwiches, punch and cake poked in our faces by fascinating little Japanese maids – watched the playing and tried to suppress unladylike squeals when the games waxed exciting. Next time I hope to wear a short white skirt and a "middy" blouse and be one of the players – I think it's a great game and I mean to learn how to play it. Met a whole stack of new and most interesting people.

We stayed at Kapalawai all night, this morning before coming up we had some more excitement. First we unpacked some lovely new furniture and rugs – then we went down to the pen and perched up on the fence and watched Kauhi, one of the native boys, break in a new horse. It was a new and thrilling experience for me. The horse was scared to death of both bridle and saddle in turn – then he was blindfolded and Kauhi jumped on – and that horse nearly went mad – my! how he reared and bucked and pranced and bucked! It was fully half an hour before that horse quieted down, but all that time Kauhi didn't even rise in his saddle – he is most fearless. Never mind I'll be breaking in horses, next. Tomorrow we are going for an all day horse-back ride away up thro' the mountains – and the children whisper that we are to have either a "horse drive" or a "pig hunt." Won't that be exciting?

This afternoon the children ⁊ I made some orange ice in some little new glass freezers and also made a batch of Scotch short bread. The minister, Mr. Millican came to dinner tonight – we played billiards after dinner, then I played to them for about half an hour – his comment on my playing was that I was the first person that he had heard in a long time that had made him think – he said that my playing was thoughtful. Then we had prayers, and he has retired, as have most of the household. But I had to write my mother a wee note at least – so that she might know that I still love her.

A foreign mail tomorrow – and I am *sure* that there will be a letter from *you* – and I will now go to bed happy in that thought.

Your own Hettie Belle

51

Chapter Three
The Grandmothers' Adventures: Scotland to Kaua'i

Kapalawai –

Nov. 17 - 1911

My own Mother –

We've just been having a terrific fight – Mrs. Robinson and I – and even Mr. R. joined in on the chorus. And all because I asked her a most simple question – namely, what druggist I should write to in Honolulu for some things that I needed. She asked me what things I wanted, that they should go right in on her order. "And then I can pay you," I said. "What!" She said –"why the *idea*. Why what an *absurd* idea– pay for talcum powder, Honey & almond cream, or little trifles like that? Why, no indeed – I couldn't *think* of letting you do that." But I said that I intended to pay for them – insisted upon it. Told her that I was accustomed to paying for all those things myself. But, she insisted, "We have always done it for all our other teachers – why not *you*?" But I couldn't see it that way. Then Mr. R. spoke up – he said, "Now listen to me – our family running expenses run anywhere from $1,000 to $2,000 a month – what difference do you think $5.00 or $10.00 more a month for any little things for you makes?" Well, that kind of knocked the breath out of me, but still I insisted. Then we compromised – he said that I should order any things that I wanted, & that he would write checks for me. "And then you will deduct their total from my monthly salary," I said. "We'll attend to that later," he smiled. It remains to be seen who really won out. But did you *ever* see such a family? Paying for my stamps is not enough, but they insist on paying for all the little extras. They are certainly generous to a fault.

52

The most exciting thing that has happened this week has been the moving down from the mountain home. Yes, we are makai for good, now. All the silver was packed away, beds were covered, doors and windows locked—and the huge caravan came down the mountain. The children and I rode down on horseback — ooh! It was a glorious ride! I cannot tell you how I love it. I'm just *crazy* about it. We got down yesterday about noon, and by evening were about settled. I shall certainly miss the mountains — but I cannot say that I do not love it here — for it is just as beautiful in a different way.

Today Mrs. Knudsen' and Miss Fergueson, her companion, came to lunch. Miss F. is a *dear* & an Oakland girl — so we are kindred spirits. Mrs. Knudsen, altho' a woman way past middle age — is one of the cleverest, brightest women you could wish to meet. She and Mrs. Gay (Mrs. R.'s mother) and Mrs. Robinson (Mr. R.'s mother) are all three sisters. You see, Mr. & Mrs. R. are first cousins, and their beautiful big family of perfectly beautiful children has almost exploded the "cousin theory" for me. I'm almost tempted to tell you one or two of the naughty stories that Mrs. Knudsen told today. She heard a minister give them from the pulpit — so I guess they are repeatable.

A mother was trying to impress her small son as to the value of prayer. She said, "You must pray — pray often — ask forgiveness when it is necessary — and strength that you may yield not to temptation, when it is strong." Well, the neighbor's cat used frequently and unwisely to come into little Johnny's yard, and little Johnny would always chase it and sometimes nearly killed it. His mother had rebuked Johnny again and again. Finally she said that she *must* punish him as long as he persisted in his evil doing. So she took him up stairs to his room — told him he must stay there and pray until he felt *sure* that he had God's forgiveness for his naughtiness. She started down stairs, and Johnny came clattering down almost immediately after her. "Why Johnny," said his mother, "are you quite sure that God has already forgiven you? Have you told him all about it?"

"Yes," said Johnny, "I told him all about it, and he said 'That's all right, Johnny, I'd have done the same myself.'" The next day the mother went out into the back yard and saw with great consternation that her young son was in the act of sliding

---

* Anne "Annie" McHutcheson Sinclair was the youngest child of Francis and Eliza Sinclair. She married Valdemar Knudsen. She was sister to both grandmothers in the Robinson household.

down the long steep roof of the barn. He was calling loudly, "Oh, Lord save me – oh! Lord save me." She joined in the same refrain with him, but suddenly little Johnny piped out – "Never mind, Lord, my pants have caught on a nail!"

Yes – I agree with you – what *awful* stories for a minister to tell – and the idea of a minister's daughter repeating them! ('Twasn't the same minister in each case, of course you know).

Thank you for your dear fat letter – am so glad you liked the tiny birthday gift.

You pronounce "pipi"– peepee – it is either singular or plural, meaning cattle or a cow. You shall have the "short bread" recipe very soon. I want your brown bread recipe.

Eleven o'clock! This is rank dissipation for me. I'm always in bed by 9:30 or ten o'clock. And oh! I'm growing *so* beautiful – so beautifully *fat*, I mean of course. But the things to eat are so lickin' good – I can't resist them. Guess I'm fated anyway, to be a second "Aunt Jane." Anyhow fat people can love their mothers an *awful* lot – do you believe it? Hettie

Soon after her arrival, Hettie Belle began serving as Mr. Robinson's secretary. She was stunned by the enormous wealth of the Robinsons. The $1,000 to $2,000 monthly household expenditures mentioned would equate to between $24,000 and $48,000 today. Although her own family struggled to survive, making do on her father's limited salary, the Matthews were financially responsible and fiercely independent. In contrast, starting back in Scotland three generations of Robinson/Gays had benefited from the merchant marine, wartime spoils, and whaling. The widow Eliza Sinclair passed the wealth on to her children, including her daughters who were the two grandmothers in the Robinson home. The Robinsons then made wise investments that had been financially rewarding.

In 1839 Jane, Helen, and Anne, along with their parents, Francis and Eliza, and three brothers, traveled from their home in Sterling, Scotland to New Zealand. (See Appendix A.) It was a four-month journey around the Cape of Good Hope.[12] Their father, Captain Sinclair, was awarded generous landholdings in New Zealand because of his service as a naval officer. He had been a member of the British Royal Navy, a hero of the battles of Trafalgar and the Nile in the Napoleonic wars. In that capacity, he was able to procure a fortune for those times, and utilizing his great spirit of adventure, he crossed the oceans halfway around the world with his wife and six children. Little Anne was a baby on this voyage.

More adventures awaited the sisters in New Zealand. The Maori were fierce and belligerent because the English were giving away their land. After scouting the North in a sailing vessel that Captain Sinclair built, they finally settled near Akarora, Canterbury at Pigeon Bay. The pioneering family lived a year in a hut with another family and then built their home, Craigforth, hand milling their own lumber.[13]

Jane became engaged, but her fiancé, father, and brother George were all lost at sea during a storm as they sailed to Wellington for business and supplies. Of course, their mother Eliza was devastated at this time. Bishop Selwyn and the Aylmer family neighbors helped the grieving Sinclairs. Helen's son Aubrey later gave two of his sons these names.

Jane and Helen, the two older sisters, did marry later in New Zealand. Jane married Captain Thomas Gay, a widower with a five-year-old son. He was one of the whaling captains who stopped in at Craigforth. These were the later days of the dangerous, grueling, and brutal whaling era, and captains were able to turn a generous profit. Captain Gay was a man of some wealth and leadership capabilities with knowledge of the Pacific Ocean.

Helen married an older man, Charles Barrington Robinson, and Aubrey was born to them in 1853.[14] However, it was not a good marriage and there were even rumors of infidelity with a Maori woman.[15] Helen did not say why she left, walking the fifteen miles back to Craigforth with her one-year-old son.

The sisters' adventures did not stop in New Zealand. When young Aubrey was nine years old, the widow Eliza and her children decided to emigrate from New Zealand to another spot where they could acquire a large tract of land and become pioneers again. Helen wrote: "It all seems like a dream, mother being at her age the leader for such an undertaking. But she says it will be done and we trust her implicitly."[16]

Jane's husband, Captain Gay, procured a 300-ton English bark, the "Bessie" (a small sailing ship with three masts, the foremast rigged square). They loaded their household belongings of books, animals, food, and even the piano, setting out in 1863 with the gold from the sale of their properties. The passengers included the entire family from grandmother to a two year old. They sailed up the southern Pacific to Tahiti, having a frightful experience with a giant octopus that tried to climb aboard and nearly capsized the bark.[17] They didn't find a place to their liking in Tahiti and decided to bypass Hawaii and try the coast of British Columbia, Canada.

Finding nothing suitable in British Columbia and being discouraged about the lack of adequate winter anchorage for their ship in frontier California, the family decided to find a place to settle in Hawai'i. While living temporarily in Honolulu, Eliza arranged to purchase the island of Ni'ihau from King Kamehameha IV for $10,000 in gold. The family were seaching for a large tract of land for ranching. During the Great Mahele, land distribution in the mid-1800s, those Hawaiians who had never owned the land they had occupied and worked could apply for ownership of their *kuleana* (home property). It was complicated for people who were unaccustomed to Western culture as they had to file, survey, and pay taxes even though the land was free. Since only one or two people on Ni'ihau claimed their kuleana, the king sold the island to the Robinsons. After King Kamehameha IV died suddenly, the deal was completed with King Kamehameha V,* and the Robinsons took the bark *Bessie* to Ni'ihau. Normally dry, Ni'ihau was verdant that year due to unusually plentiful rains.

On the island of Ni'ihau, Jane Gay gave birth to Alice, who would later become Aubrey's wife, Hettie Belle's Mrs. Robinson. Alice was the first white person born there.

The Sinclair family's first European visitor to Ni'ihau was a Norwegian, Valdemar Knudsen,† who fell in love with Annie. They married in 1867. She was the first of Eliza Sinclair's children to leave Ni'ihau, moving to Kaua'i with her husband. Later Eliza purchased the Makaweli land on

---

* King Kamehameha V, Lot Kapuāiwa, ruled the Kingdom of Hawai'i from 1863 until 1872.

† Valdemar Knudsen "Kanuka" married the youngest Sinclair, Annie. He had established a plantation in Mona soon after he arrived on Kaua'i in 1856.

Kaua'i due to lack of sufficient water on Ni'ihau. Eliza still spent summers on Ni'ihau with many of her family and numerous extended family and guests. Eliza's son Francis Sinclair* wintered on Ni'ihau for many years, tending the ranch there while his wife Isabella† painted the delicate wild flowers. Eliza Sinclair's family had traveled widely, and her three daughters never lost their sense of adventure or their love for their home on Ni'ihau.

Sinclair family 1893
Mrs. Francis Sinclair (Eliza McHutchison Sinclair) and family, 1893. Seated left to right: Mr. Francis Gay, Mrs. George (Jane or Jean Sinclair) Gay, Mrs. Francis (Eliza McHutchison) Sinclair, Mrs. Charles (Helen Sinclair) Robinson, Mrs. Aubrey (Alice Gay) Robinson with baby son Aylmer, Mr. Aubrey Robinson and young son Sinclair Robinson. Standing left to right: Miss Eliza Gay, Mr. Francis Sinclair, Mrs. Francis (Isabella McHutchison) Sinclair, and Mr. Wodehouse (a visitor). (Courtesy of the Kaua'i Museum)

---

* Francis Sinclair (1834-1916) was the fifth child of Eliza and Francis Sinclair. His poetry reflects the many years he spent as family caretaker on Ni'ihau.

† Isabella McHutcheson was the niece of Eliza McHutcheson (m. Sinclair) and married her cousin Francis Sinclair. She is remembered for her paintings of the flowers of Ni'ihau and Kaua'i.

Chapter Four
Naming Trees

Mother, dearest –

There's time for a little note to you before church, I guess. We had such a lazy day, yesterday, just played all day long. After breakfast, we went right over to the lake, and launched the new rowboat that Mr. R. had had built for us. It's a *beauty*, let me tell you! We pushed away from the shore – Mr. R. had the oars – just as we got into the middle of the lake, out came an oar-lock and sank to the bottom. As we only had one pair of oar-locks, this of course crippled us terribly, and we decided that the lost must be recovered. Mr. R. whistled for a native to come, but in the mean time Mrs. R. told Eleanor to go over the side and try to feel it with her feet, by holding to the side of the boat and lowering herself into the water. So Eleanor took off all that she decently could and went over the side and felt and felt – but in vain. Just as the native reached the lake, and was about to dive for it, Eleanor gave a cry of victory, dove under, and came up with the lost oar-lock. This we soon replaced – the sun dried Eleanor in a short time, and we went on our way rejoicing – taking a turn about at the oars. After this we are to have two pair of oar-locks and two pairs of oars – this will be much more fun.

The lake is perfectly *lovely* – about as large as Strawberry Lake in Golden Gate Park, but more beautiful. The banks are lined by cocoanut trees – they are so picturesque and their reflection in the water is so lovely. There are two islands, Long Island, a long narrow island – and Round Island, a small round one. This last we explored yesterday and found many ducks' nests – some had more than 30 eggs in them. Oh! We had a jolly time, I assure you – I found a cocoanut in the water that had sprouted – we took it home and planted it in the garden, and have named it "Hettie." So many of their trees are named – Lester will come in and say, "Isn't this a beauty, I picked it from "Grace"!

After our row, we walked in the garden, sampling any number of fruits, and thus spoiling our appetites for dinner. The "garden" meaning the fruit & vegetable garden is a little more than eight acres in size – and so beautifully laid out – beautiful paths and all beautifully bordered. Every imaginable fruit, they have and all the vegetables too. And I might say, that there are many trees and vegetables that you cannot imagine. Did you know that a banana tree has but one bunch of bananas then dies? I have learned many, many new things about fruits and vegetables, let me tell you. Sometime, at closer range, I'll impart some of my rich wisdom to you. In the afternoon we played croquet and tennis – I want to be able to take part at the tennis parties.

We have two engagements ahead for next week – lunch at the Gays' tomorrow and lunch and tennis on Thursday at Mrs. Knudsen's. Popular people, aren't we? What do you think we did the other morning? All got up at four o'clock in the morning, when it was still dark – got partly dressed, and went up on top of the wind mill, to view a great cane fire. I cannot tell you what an extraordinarily marvelous sight it was. It looked like pictures which I have seen of huge prairie fires. And such sputtering and crackling as you never heard before in your life. You see when the cane is ready to cut, they set fire to it – all the leaves & debris burn, leaving the bare stalks standing – then it is easier to cut. We watched it for about half an hour, and it was well worth getting up for. I nearly said, "worth getting out of a nice warm bed!" When it is raining and snowing with you – you can think of your daughter sleeping with all her windows and doors open, and not more than a sheet over me, if that.

Mrs. R. and I are contemplating a trip to Honolulu – we may possibly go next Saturday & stay until the following Wednesday. You see, Ito – one of their little Japanese maids – is going back to Japan, and Mrs. R. wants to see her safely off – she has many things in Honolulu that she wishes to do, also. She says that she wouldn't think of going without taking me with her. It will be awfully nice for me, and besides I ought to get some glasses. My eyes bother me when I read or sew, and I am doing both incessantly, so there is a continuous strain on them. I really should have had glasses before leaving Berkeley as my eyes have given me some trouble for a long time past as you know. Then it will be nice to see the friends that I made on my way down.

This little maid Ito's case was the saddest ever. Ten years ago, she was sent to Calif. to be educated. She is an intensely bright girl – had a splendid education and traveled much, going east two years ago as maid to the R.'s. Last year she decided to go home, but the Robinsons prevailed upon her to stay with them just until this Christmas. Last month, her mother died suddenly, and the poor girl is broken-hearted. It is very sad – the poor girl had worked so hard and was looking forward so to being with her Mother, and longing for her mother's approval and commendation. I'm awfully sorry for her. Am going to give her a letter to Margie.

Speaking of Christmas – I am going to begin my Christmas sewing immediately. Christmas is coming down so suddenly upon me that my breath is actually taken away. Especially as I realize that I cannot work up to the night before, and twelve o'clock at that. I really have to be ready by the middle of December. But I don't intend to kill myself.

I wish that you would tell me what date Thanksgiving Day is – I have no idea, and would like to know. These dear people being Scotch, do not celebrate, of course. And goodness sakes! I have more than ever to be thankful for this year. I hardly know what to do – I am so overwhelmed when I think of my very numerous blessings. I feel that I am one of the most fortunate girls that ever lived – everything comes my way – I do not see why it should be so – I am so very unworthy of it all. But I shall strive to make the most of it all.

Your loving Hettie Belle

Ponds stocked with fish were a way to procure a family's own food to enjoy at meals. The lake Hettie Belle knew was a fishpond fringed with coconut trees not far from the Kapalawai home. Famous on Kaua'i is another fishpond, the Menehune Fishpond near Līhu'e. It is estimated to be as old as a thousand years. Legend has it that the small Menehune people, who worked at night, built it in one night for a prince and princess.

Hettie Belle compares the size of the Robinsons' pond to "Strawberry Lake" in Golden Gate Park in San Francisco. That lake is now called Stow Lake and has a little hill in the middle named Strawberry Hill, once covered with wild strawberries.

Fish pond at Kapalawai, circa 1909. The children are Eleanor and Lester. The lady may be the previous governess or their mother. (Courtesy of Susie Somers)

The Robinson garden overflowed with papayas, pineapples, coconuts, breadfruit, star fruit, mangos, citrus fruits, guavas, bananas, and more. During their recess time, Hettie and the children often played tag on the great lawns or walked in the orchard. Sometimes they picked a ripe avocado for a snack, and Hettie would go to the kitchen for a knife and spoons. Although Hettie Belle thought banana plants died after producing once, they actually grow offshoots that come up around the base called a corm. These offshoots can produce more bananas, so in this way, the plant is a perennial.

The wonderful fruits that Hettie Belle sampled came from all over the world. European/American plantation owners traveled frequently to obtain exotic plants, trees, fruits, and livestock.[18] Upon his graduation from Harvard, Aubrey Robinson's grandmother Eliza gave him a year's trip around the world. During these extensive travels, he procured seeds of exotic plants, trees, and improved varieties of fruits.

Scientists estimate that the volcanic Hawaiian Islands have only a small number of indigenous plants. These are plants that arrived at the uninhabited islands via wind or migrating sea birds and a few by ocean currents. Some of these plants and their progeny speciated, providing thousands of unique endemic plants found nowhere else in the world. Many of them are now endangered or have disappeared.[19] Later, taro, sugarcane, ti, wild ginger, bamboo, yams, and other plants came with seafarers from the Marquesas, the first Hawaiians. When other Polynesians ventured to Hawai'i from the Society Islands, they brought additional plants and animals necessary to their survival and way of life. Finally, the European residents, like Aubrey Robinson, imported exotics from all over the world.

The Robinson family's interest in plants goes back to New Zealand and then Ni'ihau. The veranda in the Sinclairs' New Zealand home was covered with Banksia roses,[20] and later on Kaua'i, Mrs. Robinson treasured her rose garden housed in a glass house in the yard at Kapalawai. It was her pride and joy to produce roses for the dinner table when they had guests. Hettie Belle could not understand this fascination with what seemed common roses when there were "masses of a variety of gorgeous tropical flowers."

Naming trees was a tradition well established in the Hawaiian culture, and having her own namesake tree tickled Hettie. On Ni'ihau, for instance, there were five 'ulu (breadfruit) trees named for supernatural women who had come to Ni'ihau from Tahiti. When they overstayed their visit, they were said to have turned into these trees. Since the trees grew in a kind of ditch so the roots could reach water, one could pick the fruit at eye-level just standing beside the ditch. These trees were named for the women: Hikinaakala, Kulimodu, Hakaleleaponi, Kalama, and Nauluhuaikahapapa.[21]

Many homes on Kaua'i had names as well. According to Eric Knudsen, the Hawaiians' houses all had names. Grass houses stretched on the bluff from Waimea to Mana. "Every house site had a name. To find a man you had to find his house name. The natives seemed to know every name and would keep sending you along until you finally came to the spot you were looking for."[22]

Sunday – Dec. 10 -

"Kapalawai"

My dearest Family –

When last I wrote a real letter, I believe we were contemplating a trip to Honolulu – well, we went – and *such* a trip! We left here early in the afternoon, in autos, two weeks ago yesterday and went clear over to the other side of the island. We could have taken the steamer from here in the morning, which would mean that we would be rocked about all day as they went from one small port to another, shipping all day. This trip in the auto gave me a splendid chance to see more of the island, and it is indeed marvelously beautiful. The canyons and the rivers and the rugged, rugged mountains! And *such* coloring! Then all the cane in the lowlands was in tassel – and for miles it was just a purplish, lavender haze, a beautiful sight.

Before going aboard the "Kinau" we made a couple of calls in Lihue, and then had tea at Mrs. Charles Rice's* home. She is a *dear*, and *so* like Ida [the wife of Hettie Belle's brother Melville]. I have never seen two people more alike – it was hard for me to keep from calling her "Ida." She has two sweet little daughters and a jolly teasing husband – and a lovely home, built right on the beach – with a glorious outlook, and always the beating, beating of the waves. You know how thoroughly I enjoyed the tea, but at least I enjoyed the cake and short bread.

Soon it was time to go aboard – so Mrs. R., Eleanor and I & Ito were lifted aboard, and Mr. R. and Lester waved us off. As it happened there was a young man

---

* Grace Ethel King (Mrs. Charles Rice) was a member of the *kama'āina* (born on the land) King family. She lived in Lihu'e next to the landing at Kalapaki Beach.

on board, whom I met on the Korea, also some other interesting people – so we had a jolly time during the evening. But early to bed I went, for I had a strange feeling, and sad to relate, I lost my short bread and cake. But I am not ashamed to relate it, 'cause *everyone* is sick going between these islands on these tiny tubs of steamers. They say that the waters get rougher than in almost any other part of the world.

We docked at Honolulu at three o'clock Sunday morning – a spooky hour, I can assure you. The two "Harvard" sons were there to meet us with an automobile and we went right up to the Alexander Young Hotel. Going in at that unearthly hour in the morning, I felt more like an eloping couple than anything else. We had lovely rooms and although my bed looked tempting, I wrote letters until breakfast time. Had I realized the strain that was before me, I would surely have snatched a few hours sleep.

Wailele, the Gay home in Kalihi Valley, Oahu. Hettie Belle thrilled to see the "beautiful waterfall right by the house, and forming a splendid swimming pool – they dive off from the second story right into the pool." (courtesy of the Bishop Museum)

In the afternoon we went in autos up to "Wailele" (means waterfall), the Francis Gays'* new Honolulu home. They have more than 400 acres of that lovely mountain country – a stream going thro' the place, falling in a beautiful waterfall right by the

---

* Francis Gay was a businessman who in 1880 founded Gay and Robinson, Inc., the family corporation, with his cousin Aubrey Robinson and grandmother Eliza Sinclair. Francis was the son of Grandmother Gay and was Mrs. Robinson's brother.

house, and forming a splendid swimming pool – they dive off from the second story right into the pool. Everything about the place is fascinating – from the drawbridge to the grass thatched huts which they use for servants quarters. We had tea there, and met some interesting people. Then we went away down to the opposite end of the Island – the "Peninsula" they call it – and called on some delightful people, the Waterhouse* family. I shall never forget the glorious sunset that we saw on the way home.

Monday morning we were at the dressmakers by 7:30! It seems that it wasn't enough for Mrs. R. to give me the trip to Honolulu, but she *insisted* that she wanted to give me some little remembrance of our trip – therefore two dresses are being made for me in Honolulu – a little cream marquisete, and a thin white embroidered dress – gifts from her. I really wasn't threadbare – she just wanted to do something nice. She wanted to get me some hats, but I insisted that I had *plenty*. Well, we were whizzing from store to store, all morning – shopping in an auto. You should see Mrs. R. shopping – she walks into a store says, "I'll take this, and this, and this, and this" just as fast as she can speak – and we stand back and laugh at her. But you have to do that way when you make such a flying shopping trip. Well, we shopped until nearly noon leaving just time to don our gowns and large hats, for we were invited to a big luncheon party at the Hotel. Mrs. Francis Gay[†] gave it. I am sending you my place card. We had luncheon on the roof garden at a huge round table, with places for thirty ladies. The center was a *mass* of violets. How sweet they smelled! And the hostess was in a violet gown and a huge violet hat. It was a very lovely affair. More shopping in the afternoon – then out to Waipahu (the sugar plantation where the "Harvard" sons have been working for about half a year). [Waipahu is the area on O'ahu, not the name of the sugar plantation.] We saw the plantation, then called on the manager's sister. Then back to the other end of the island to a dinner at the Von Holts'– cousins of the Robinsons. They have the most beautiful home, a jolly *large* family, and we had a splendid time. Mrs. Von Holt[‡] is much as I imagine Cousin Eda must be – so charming, so musical – plays beautifully. The big, jolly father pretended to be *terribly* annoyed because I had not remembered meeting

* William Waterhouse was a former schoolmate of Mr. Robinson at Dole's School in Kōloa.

† Lily Hart, (Mrs. Gay) wife of Francis Gay, was the mistress of a beautiful home Wailele in Kalihi Valley on O'ahu. She was a noted Hawaiian beauty and later a well-known floral artist.

‡ Ida Elizabeth Knudsen (Mrs. von Holt) was the sister of Eric Knudsen and daughter of Valdemar and Annie Knudsen.

him when first I arrived in Honolulu. "Why," said he, "I came home and raved about you – and you don't even remember meeting me!" He declared that he would send me his picture – then I could not forget him.

Tuesday morning – the dressmakers again – more shopping. Then to the wharf to see the fleet come in – also the "Wilemena" bearing Miss Gay[*] (a niece of Mrs. R.'s from Coronada [Coronado Island, CA]). Tuesday noon Mrs. R. had a luncheon party for Miss Gay – in the afternoon we saw Ito off for Japan, made some calls, more shopping, and at five o'clock boarded the "Kinau" for Kauai. Can you wonder that I was dizzy, and that I dropped exhausted into my bunk? It was one mad whirl – I haven't told you *half* – the calls on us, the meeting people, etc. By the way, I had my eyes examined and got my glasses – it seems that I have strained my eyes badly – he said that "I had been *using* them too much"– they have joshed me terribly about his remark. So I must wear them when I read, write and embroider. He said that they, my eyes, would be perfectly strong after awhile – then I could discard the glasses. And I haven't had a headache since I put them on. Formerly for the past month, I had suffered with some frightful ones.

We took the most glorious trip one day, a whole party of us, sixteen in all – went up Olokele Ditch, an all day trip on horseback. We saw that day the most glorious scenery that I have *ever* seen in my life, and the Cropps[23] who have been all around the world, and say that there is *nothing* that surpasses it. It is about 17 miles each way – when you leave the lowlands and enter the mountains, you have to go single file along a narrow trail dug out of the solid cliff – a thousand feet sheer cliff above you, and more than a thousand feet sheer drop below you. Some of the party got dizzy and sick and had to get off their horses – and though I felt rather strange going around some of the sharpest corners, I did not get dizzy. But the marvelous heights and depths – the massive, rugged cliffs opposite – the river below – the marvelous view up the canon [canyon] and down the canon were simply indescribable – I had not dreamed that anything in this world could be so *awful* or so marvelously wonderful. We stopped half way up for lunch, then went clear on up to the head, where the waters fall in a huge thundering waterfall. It was a long, hard day but I wouldn't have missed it for anything – the sunset as we came home was something

---

[*] Ethel Eliza Gay was a cousin of the Robinson children, the daughter of George Gay, Mrs. R.'s brother.

[†] Harry Martens von Holt was a Honolulu businessman.

to remember. Everyone was nervously as well as physically tired – it was a strain. That was Thanksgiving Day, and we had to hurry home & dress for our Thanksgiving dinner. Mrs. R. said that as long as she had an American girl in her home, she needs must celebrate that great day. So we had a lot of extra company and a huge dinner, but I was too tired to eat much. Later in the evening we went over to Dr. & Mrs. Sandow" home to a musical evening. I played, and also accompanied a Mrs. Truscott, and a Mr. Hughes (from Calif.) when they sang. We had a delightful evening.

It was full moon going home and so warm and balmy that we had to take the longest way home which was about five miles out of our way. Well, I was tired the next day, but not dead as I fully expected to be.

Now, I must tell you two exciting things – I'll put them in order of their importance. 1st when we came home from Honolulu we brought with us an automobile – big 6 cylinder, seven passenger, $6,000 Peerless. A beauty, I tell you! If I could only run it, I would be perfectly happy – in the meantime I am quite contented to sail around in it. 2nd the Two Harvard Sons have come home to remain! One is 23, the other 25. Which would you prefer? Of course I can have either. Anyhow it will be more interesting from now on – the boating, tennis, swimming etc. will be more fun. They are awfully nice fellows – tho' very immature and young and quiet. Possibly their names might have some weight – well 23 is named Aylmer, and 25 Sinclair. Again – which would you prefer?

The Robinson's Peerless with Lester climbing aboard. Hettie Belle was eager to learn to drive, and Francis Gay let her try. (photo by Hettie Belle)

---

* Dr. Bruno and Eula Elmira Sandow were active members of the Waimea society where he served as physician.

The other night we had had a small dinner party after which I was playing for the people – in the midst of one piece a ghost appeared at the door, waited until I had finished, then calmly walked in, followed by eight or nine other ghosts. They had the *awfullest* looking masks on and trailing white sheets and grimly shook hands all round. We were at a loss to know *who* or *what* they were, but they finally, becoming too warm, peeled off – and it was a crowd that had been at another dinner party – the minister was among them, too. I didn't dream that people did such frivolous things here. We played billiards and had a jolly time generally.

A Norwegian lady, Madame Brunchorst, has been visiting us this week – she is a fascinating woman. We have had company to lunch each day and a dinner party each evening – and several trips besides.

Friday a large party of us rode on horseback out to the "Barking Sands"– great sand banks that make a barking sound when you slide down or shake some in a bag. Scientists have come from all over the world and examined the sand but cannot explain its peculiar character – and *why* it should make this peculiar sound. We clambered to the top of a bank – then two or three of us would link together and one of the boys would pull us down. It was fun, and *such* a strange noise as the sand would make, like the muffled bark of many dogs.

We had a glorious swim in the surf before lunch, then lunched at the Knudsens' beach home – the Japanese servants had been there before us, and everything was in readiness. We had a delightful ride home in the afternoon – had to ford a stream that was so deep that the horses had to swim, and I got my new riding boots all wet, but that didn't matter. I was burned thro' my shirtwaist, to a *crisp!* When I can again wear evening dress, I know not. I'm becoming a Kanaka [native Hawaiian] in color – you won't know your once beautiful (?) daughter. Speaking of horses, I still prefer horses to autos – there is *nothing* like horse-back riding. I'm crazier about it every time I ride.

Yesterday afternoon I went to an afternoon tea with Mrs. R. & Madame B. at Mrs. Brandt's.* She has the finest view of anyone in Waimea – she is up on a cliff – has a glorious sea view, beside a wonderful valley & river view. I was the only "spinster" at the tea. They all, therefore, gave me advice as to *when* to marry, *whom* to marry, *why* to marry and *how* to marry. The rest of their conversation was also edifying – scandals

---

* Claire Edesse Borron (Mrs. Brandt) lived in a large mansion in Waimea and was prominent in the Norwegian community there.

in high and low life – the best way to sleep at night – and recipes for desserts. But the "eats" were lickin' good, so the day was saved.

Have been to church and heard a splendid sermon on "What is man." Father is just beginning on his evening sermon now – but I shall *not* begin on another sheet.

I love you all – *heaps!*

Your Hettie Belle

Makaweli, spectacular Olokele area, 2012 (J. Burtner)

Barking Sands, "Sounding Sands, Nohili" (courtesy of the Bishop Museum)

The Hawaiian Sugar Company constructed the Olokele Ditch. Opened in 1904,[24] it had been dug out, cut into rock, piped, and tunneled to carry water thirteen and a half miles down from the Hanapēpē River in the mountains to the sugarcane fields belonging to the Robinsons and other plantation owners. The water also supplied the sugar mills. For each pound of sugar produced, it took about two thousand pounds of water applied in the field. Much of that water was recaptured. Today the ditch is used to generate electricity and carries 55 to 60 million gallons a day.

In one of the earliest guidebooks to the Hawaiian Islands, William R. Castle, Jr. described the "barking sands" Hettie Belle visited. "The wind on the sands makes them rustle like silk; to slide down them produces a sound like thunder; to stamp on them makes them cry out in different cadences."[25] Young people would slide down the sands, ride their horses down, or simply rub the sand between two hands to hear the barking noise. This part of Polihale Beach has mineral calcite sand, made up of fragments of coralline algae and skeletons of marine animals such as coral and clams. The abrasion of this skeletal material made a dog-like bark when the sand was moved under pressure.[26] It wasn't until years after Hettie Belle's visit that researchers solved this mystery.

Olokele ditch 2012 (J. Burtner)   1624

CHAPTER FIVE
PANIOLO CHRISTMAS

"Kapalawai"

Dec. 18, 1911.

Mother, dearest –

Now *what* do you think of me? I have already sent off 35 packages, 3 dozen postal cards, and nearly 2 dozen Christmas letters. And I made nearly all the things myself, that I sent as gifts. Did you dream that you had such a brilliant daughter? But *never* again – I don't believe in putting one's eyes out, even for those we love, and I nearly did.

I do hope that the things to you dear people will all arrive safely. There was something for each one, of course, so if someone's package does not arrive, please notify me immediately. I have left to make, Mrs. R.'s gift and Eleanor's. But I have all this week so feel sure that I can accomplish that much.

Some Christmas company arrives tomorrow. We are going to celebrate on Monday evening although their custom has been to celebrate Christmas eve. We are making *grand* preparations. We are to have 20 extra grown-ups to dinner, and 10 children. A tree afterwards, of course. Then Mr. R. has a Luau (feast) for all the natives, on Christmas day.

But *what* am *I* doing here? Didn't I promise you and myself that I would spend this Christmas with my own dear family in Boise? And here am I – 10,000 miles away. What strange things do happen in this world. Who would have dreamed that I would be *here*. Yes, strange things happen, and to *me* so many strange things have happened.

Well, Mudder, Mudder, dear – I must hie me to my virgin couch, and seek some rest, and some beauty sleep. I always practise for at least an hour before breakfast with the children, and we breakfast at eight. Yes, you may not believe it – Father won't – I have had a bath, am dressed each morning by seven o'clock.

I sat on the lanai (open porch) and sewed until ten o'clock tonight in an organdy dress. What did *you* do? Surely you didn't sit outdoors with nothing on. I'm *sure* it is still summer and not time for Christmas. More later. Hettie

Makaweli, Kauai

Dec. 21, 1911.

Mother – what do you think of this? The Robinsons say that it is certainly an offer worthwhile. Do you think I could meet the stipulations? If you think it wise to go ahead, *wire at once!* HBM

[Newpaper clipping]

Our Best Wishes for 1912
Kaimuki Land Company, Ltd.
Main office Tel. 1659
HONOLULU
Branch office Tel. 3208

LEAP YEAR GREETINGS

As the Kaimuki Land Company, Ltd. is about to leap into another year of development and prosperity, with greater opportunities for the establishment of happy homes than ever before, we wish to express our appreciation of the consideration shown us, by an offer to give away one, good size, residence lot to the first young lady, (widows excepted), who is married in 1912 by her own proposal. This offer is made up on the following conditions: First—the young lady must be a resident of Honolulu for 3 years or more. Second—she must live happily with her husband for 6 months, during which time she may retain possession of the lot and deed will be deposited in trust for delivery. Third—the lot must be improved within 12 months and used for home purposes only. Fourth—the selection of the lot will be made by the company.

Leap Year news article

Jan. 1, 1912.

Happy New Year! My dearest Mr. Poppitee! [Father] And how do you suppose we spent our New Year's day? I know how you folks spent yours—you had a big dinner and then you went and made New Year's calls – am I right? Well, we went for a horseback ride, away up Waimea Valley – this forenoon – and a most beautiful and picturesque valley it is. I did enjoy it *so*. It's lots of fun to ford streams on horseback, isn't it? We had to ford the river about ten times today. Nothing exciting happened – it just grew more and more lovely, and more and more I thought of our Wonderful Creator. We came home to a late lunch – and this afternoon we dressed here – then ran down to the sea in our bathing suits, and had a glorious swim. As a result I have a blistered nose – but such trifles are to be expected.

I was awfully glad that you had to play "nurse girl" that evening, for then you had a chance to write to me – and I *did* enjoy your letter *so* much. If my letters are interesting to you people, just remember that the tiniest happenings of my dear "family" are far more interesting than you can possibly know or realize. Possibly that is why I do not receive all the details that I desire. When you write, please tell me exactly *how* Mother is – and *what* the matter is, won't you?

Very, very lovingly –

Your Hettie Belle

You dear Boys –

I want to tell you all about our Christmas day – then you can tell me how it compares with yours. First, I must tell you about getting the Christmas tree. We all went on horseback to the mountains the Saturday before Christmas. Away back up into the mountains we rode until we found a beautiful Norfolk pine – this we cut down and marched home in triumph!

Christmas evening at 5:30 the children and ten of their little friends had their dinner. Then the tree was lighted and Santa Claus appeared. We had the tree on the lanai (great open porch) and it was a *gorgeous* sight! We had spent nearly an entire day decorating it – and it was brilliantly beautiful. The lanai was decorated in cocoanut palm branches, ferns, ti leaves and 130 maili [*maile*] leis were festooned around the sides and ceiling. It was beautiful.

Beside the children and this family, they had about twenty outsiders in. There were beautiful gifts for all – the billiard table was simply stacked *high* with gifts. Then Santa began his work of distribution, and there were excited, happy crys, as people opened their gifts. After the many thank yous and kissings, we went to the dining room – the dining room and living rooms were beautifully decorated too – maili leis and great bunches of poinsettias and lovely ferns. There were about thirty at the table – and such a feast as we had! While we ate, the Hawaiian band from Waimea played in the front yard. After dinner we sat on the front veranda – (in low neck evening dresses and *no wraps*), and listened to the music and watched the beautiful fire works which they set off. Then I played for the multitude and they departed in peace. Such a Christmas! I can't imagine anyone making more elaborate preparations, can you? But it was hard to realize that it was Christmas – and we laughed as we piled the artificial snow on the tree.

Early Christmas morning we were awakened by the lovely Hawaiian band singing Christmas carols & playing beautiful music. I heard it in the distance first – and it was so wonderfully sweet and sad that I just lay still and wept. Mr. R. had a great luau (outdoor feast) for all his men. It was so interesting to see them sitting around eating roast pig, poi [mashed taro root], taro, squid (dried octopus) etc. etc. But I preferred *our* dinner. Christmas night we were again serenaded, and last night and this morning, also. It is such delightful music – I am *so* fond of it.

Wish you could go boating with us one of these days.

Love to you – Hettie

Hettie Belle admired the paniolo on the Robinson ranch, and she loved their music. She aspired to be a fine horseback rider herself. The expectation in the Robinson family was that members would be accomplished riders, able to climb into the mountains, canter down rough ground, and join in roundups. It is said that the Sinclair/Gay/Robinson young men could ride like Comanches, able to pick up an object off the ground from the side of their horse while at a full gallop. Mrs. Robinson was an amazing horsewoman and had two magnificent steeds for herself alone: a beautiful white Arabian stallion, "Ni'ihau," and a gorgeous chestnut mare. Hettie Belle admired Mrs. Robinson's riding skill as she rode sidesaddle and taught her horses to jump small streams or fallen trees.

Richard Cleveland brought the first horses to Hawai'i in 1803 as gifts to King Kamehameha I.[*27] Ranching began in Hawai'i thirty to forty years before it did in many of the western states and thus was influenced by the *vaquero* (Spanish cowboy) tradition rather than

---

* King Kamehameha I, "Kamehameha the Great," was the founder of the Hawaiian Kingdom, uniting all the islands.

Western cowboy ways.[28] The Hawaiian paniolo riding equipment differed from the American cowboy gear.

Ranching developed together with the maritime industry of interisland shipping. The Robinson clan moved sheep and cattle between Ni'ihau and Kaua'i, then on to other markets by boat. This involved having the animals swim out to the inter-island steamer and be hoisted aboard, or taking them in a smaller boat out to the steamer.

The transporting of Ni'ihau products to market was difficult as illustrated by Eric Knudsen. He told this story: A schooner loaded with a cargo of wool was anchored in Waimea Bay. The crew swam ashore, and the captain was alone on the ship when a storm came up and pushed it onto a reef. Since he was unable to swim, the captain tied himself to the mast. A girl on shore, Mele, asked the men why someone did not rescue the captain. They replied that they were tired. Mele stripped off her *holokū* (dress), swam out, and towed the horror-stricken captain back to the beach thru the storm. She refused his only coin, saying that what she did was only fun.[29] The captain was saved but the cargo of wool was lost.

Aubrey's father, Charles Robinson, purchased Durham short-horned cattle from England for his land in New Zealand. Later, the family probably brought some cattle on the bark *Bessie* along with Merino sheep. They imported more shorthorns for the Ni'ihau and Kaua'i ranches. On Aubrey's travels throughout Europe, India, and Asia, he studied and procured different kinds of stock, plants, and birds. In the 1880s, he imported fine Arabian horses for use on the ranches.[30]

Keith Robinson tells of his father, Lester, and his grandfather, Aubrey, rescuing a young lamb on Ni'ihau. It was bogged down in the half-dried mud of a disappearing lake. Aubrey told Lester to rope it and help it out. Lester was concerned about a muddy rope that would then dirty his saddle and pants. Disgusted, Aubrey said, "You can't even do that? What's the matter with you young people now days?" He then pulled out his own rope and lassoed the lamb with a 40-50 foot throw, pulling the animal from the mire. There was not a speck of mud on the rope! Aubrey Robinson was an accomplished paniolo.

Aubrey had traditional luaus for all the cowboys at Christmas. It was a British tradition to serve the household help a feast the day after Christmas, Boxing Day. Also each time they arrived on Ni'ihau, he and later his son Aylmer provided a luau, where poi and often lamb were served to all the paniolo.

It took a lot of manpower to get cattle to market. (Blackstad Family, courtesy of the Kaua'i Historical Society)

The life of a paniolo required endurance, working under difficult and dangerous conditions, mastering the harsh realities of breaking a horse, of branding, and of slaughtering animals. Despite this rugged life, Hawaiian cowboys often had a great sensitivity to beauty. Their hat lei were of Kaua'i maile or *kolohala* (pheasant) feathers. These lei were fragrant or decorative and the mass of feathers helped to weigh down their hats in the wind. Paniolo music touched the heart and still resounds in present day Hawaiian songs.

Chapter Six

Shells and Sugar

"Kapalawai"

Jan. 8, 1912.

Mother, dearest –

We stopped school at eleven today (recess time) and went for an auto ride. Mrs. Robinson (the grandmother) was going out for her daily airing and she invited us to accompany her. It was a *perfect* morning, just the kind for an auto ride – we took a lovely cliff ride with a splendid view of the sea all the way, and this morning the sea was very blue, indeed. I do so love to live near it, as we do – so close that we can constantly hear its roar.

In a letter from one of the girls, lately ▯▯she asked if the "masculines were beginning to flit, yet." Possibly I ought also to report to you on that question. Yes, some are – you know my capacity for attracting "freaks"– well, it apparently holds good in this country. A little man, to whom I have said, "How d'ye do," to, just *three* times at church has fallen prostrate at my feet. His name is Mr. Oser [Aaser]* (that may not be the way to spell it, but it pronounces "Oh! Sir!") He is a rather good-looking Swede or Dane, I know not which, a bookkeeper at one of the mills. He asked to call, and Mrs. R. said "certainly"– but she declares that I am the cause for he has lived in the "district" for ten years, and never before asked to call. Well, he came ▯▯but brought with him Mr. Hans L'Orange,† for moral support I suppose. We had a delightful evening – but did I tell you the funny thing that happened when we went

---

* Frederik Hjorth Aaser was a bookkeeper at Kekaha Sugar Company.
† Hans L'Orange was Erik Knudsen's brother-in-law, visiting from Norway.

to play billiards around on the lanai? Mrs. R. and I were going to play with Mr. Oser & Mr. L'Orange. Of course you play with partners – and the gentlemen did not speak up as to who they would take as their choice. So Mrs. R. put two balls behind her, a red and a white. "Now," she said, "I am the red ball, and Miss Matthew is the white." Then she turned to Mr. L'Orange and said, "which will you take?" (meaning of course, right or left hand). He thought a long time then said, "I'll take the *white!*" You can imagine how we *howled.* He really said it innocently – you see he has only been in this country a week or so, and does not understand all our ways.

Well, Mr. Oser asked to come again this week – and Mrs. R. took compassion on him & asked him to come to dinner. The minister, also, came that night to dinner & spent the evening.

Now Mr. Oser insists that I must start a collection of shells – says that he has some beauties that he wants to give me to start me in. I insisted that I didn't care much for collections of any kind – and further more didn't want to rob him – but he insists that I *must* start a collection. Now he wants me to go horseback riding – but I draw the line at that.

I'm going calling tomorrow – going to take my sewing and spend the afternoon with Mrs. Ewart, a lovely lady (the wife of Robinson's manager). I had the choice of going in auto, carriage or on horseback, and I chose horseback. I *love* it!

Love to *each* dear Matthew – and stacks of it. Your loving Hettie Belle

Oh! I forgot to describe Mr. Oser – he goes around on his tip toes, *never* touching his heels to the ground – sometimes I get so exasperated that I want to yell at him –"Why don't you *walk* like a real man." He *never* talks above a whisper, and I pretend that I am hard of hearing – and often beg him again and again to repeat himself – this he does until he is quite red in the face. You can't really admire a man that goes tip-towing around, bowing and scraping and apologizing for being alive – assuring you that it wasn't his fault – can you?

---

* Elizabeth Lindsay's husband was George Ewart, the manager of Gay & Robinson, Inc.'s Makaweli Sugar Plantation at that time. Her brother Alexander Lindsay was Attorney General of Hawai'i.

Years later, Hettie Belle remembered Mr. Aaser, a Norwegian bookkeeper:

> He was a quiet little gentleman, completely uninteresting to me — but he would telephone about once a week, asking to call. One thing that distressed us was that he came in a taxi, and had it remain. We could not help but hear the meter running!
>
> However — because of his visits — I came to possess a *very* valuable shell collection — his gifts to me from the beaches. This friend, Mr. Aaser, brought me tiny shells in medicine bottles — a splendid, exquisite collection. I sadly learned much later that he had only one eye! Imagine finding these tiny shells. He also brought me music — and always asked me to play.

Mr. Aaser, this popular young bachelor in the district, had many opportunities to meet young ladies. Although she later fondly remembered him, Hettie Belle could not "fall" for him.

Mr. Frederick Aaser on left, 1908. He is pictured with young women at Queen Emma's rock, Kōke'e. Mr. Aaser and other bachelors would be invited on Sundays to mingle with the young women as guests of the Fayés, Danfords, or Knudsens who spent the summers at Kōke'e. He courted Hettie Belle and gifted her with delicate shells. (Photo courtesy of Christine Fayé)

The tiny shells of Niʻihau were already well known in the late 1800s and have since become famous and highly valued. The Robinsons helped people on that remote island to market their handiwork,[31] selling some to the jewelers in Honolulu, one being Wichman & Company of which Hettie Belle spoke. Today the shell lei can be purchased on Kauaʻi at the Robinson's Niʻihau Helicopter office in Kaumakani, as well as at other locations. Hettie Belle had several Niʻihau shell necklaces that are now treasured by her great-grandchildren.

Shell lei (courtesy of Luc Nadeau, Hettie's great-grandson)

"Kapalawai"

Jan. 13, 1912.

My dearest Mother –

Well – I did call on Mrs. Ewart – and it was the first time that I had gone anywhere alone – yes, I went *quite* alone. I had the choice of going in auto, carriage or on horseback – and as you may imagine, I went on horseback. I could go in my riding clothes – for she said that it was to be an informal call – that I was to bring my sewing and spend the entire afternoon. So "Gopher" was saddled for me – and Mr.

R. showed me how to make a fancy knot, when I tied him up. It is only about a mile to Mrs. Ewart's – so Mr. R. suggested that instead of coming directly home – I should take a round-about way and have a little more of a ride. He carefully described my return route – and when he saw that I feared that I would lose my way – he laughed – and insisted that I try – so as to prove to myself the absurdity of such a thing. I spent a most delightful afternoon with Mrs. Ewart – she is a charming woman, a sister of Mrs. Faye.[*] At about 5 o'clock I turned my steps homeward – that is I went out to untie my horse – but Mr. Ewart[†] came riding up, and gallantly offered to untie my horse. I begged him not to – declared that it was unnecessary – for you see I had forgotten how to make the classy knot that Mr. R. had showed me – and had tied a most ridiculous girls' knot. But Mr. Ewart insisted – and I was covered with confusion as he tugged away at my numerous knots and twists – joshing me about it all the time. Of course he told the Robinsons – and I shall never hear the end of it. I had a delightful ride home – I took the roundabout way – forded a stream crossed cane fields – and climbed hills. About fifty times I was sure that I was lost – but I went sublimely on, enjoying to the fullest the sunset and the singing of the birds – finally I came to the Government road, then I knew where I was and I proudly cantered home. I shall venture out alone again some time – I have more confidence now.

We have had a house full of company since Tuesday – two house guests – and many extra people in for lunch and dinner each day. Mrs. Putman from Lihue (the other side of this island), and Miss Harriet Hatch from Honolulu – in whom Sinclair is *desperately* interested. They are *awfully* nice girls, both of them – about my age or a bit older. So we have been amusing them all week – afternoons especially. School went on just the same in the mornings, except Friday, when we were gone all day.

One afternoon we went thro' the Makaweli Sugar Mill – and I shall now endeavor to explain to you ignorant (?) people, the process of making sugar from sugar cane. It was intensely interesting to me – but of course I cannot make you see it as I saw it. I'm thankful tho' that you didn't have to *smell* all that I did. It is *too* sticky sweet. To proceed -- the cut cane is hauled to the mill in cars by an engine. When it

---

[*] Margaret Lindsay (Mrs. Fayé) of Kaua'i was the sister of Mrs. Ewart, and her brother Alexander was Attorney General of Hawai'i at that time. She was the wife of Hans Peter Fayé.

[†] George Robert Ewart, Jr. was the manager of Gay & Robinson's Makaweli Sugar Plantation from 1906 through 1912.

reaches the mill it is dumped on to moving chains – and carried way up into the mill. Here it comes down – goes thro' an immense cutting knife, which cuts it into about foot long pieces – then it passes on, going through four huge crushing mills, one after another. The juice pours off through a sieve in the bottom, and the pulp goes on. After the fourth mill, the pulp is so free from juice and so dry that it is dropped down to the furnace room and immediately used for fuel. This waste cane furnishes all the fuel that is needed to run the *entire* mill – and the ashes are used for fertilizer in the cane fields. Not much waste is there? When next you see the juice it is almost like syrup, after the first boiling this is. Then it is boiled again – and appears like molasses, almost. It then passes thro' lime – this neutralizes any acids – then again it is boiled, and the crystals form. Then into huge tubs it is poured – and by centrifugal force, any remaining liquid is forced out and only the sugar remains. Along goes this brown sugar and is poured into the sacks, which are weighed and sewed up, and piled on a car – shipped to San Francisco and Boise and you buy it – and Dordie eats it in syrup and bread. They were grinding Gay & Robinson cane that day – which made it the more interesting. We tasted the juice and sugar, at every stage in the process. Do you wonder that dinner did not look appetizing? And now after all this, I don't believe that you are any the wiser as to how brown sugar is made. Well, you'll have to come & see for yourself.

Yesterday (Friday) was the glorious day. We were in the saddle practically all day. The Knudsens came over, and went with us up to Makaweli House. Mrs. R. wanted her guests to see it. Instead of taking the road we took a delightful new route – right up ridges, and down valleys until we reached the house. It is much more fun to climb a rocky cliff and zigzag up ridges than to follow a beaten trail or road. Something very exciting happened yesterday. We were all twelve of us riding rather close together – climbing a rather steep hill. Miss Hatch and Eleanor were listening to a thrilling cliff story which Sinclair was telling them – and watching him as he pointed out the *very* cliff. They were all looking in the distance – and Eleanor did not realize that she was near a tree – suddenly a branch struck her and swept her from her saddle to the ground. Her astonished horse turned and faced her, and snorted – not knowing whether to run or not. When Eleanor fell – she startled Miss Hatch's horse – it jumped back about six feet, leaving Miss Hatch on the ground. Then her horse bolted – simply tore off down the mountain. Fortunately neither girl was hurt – for they luckily fell in a relaxed way – and did not catch their feet in the stirrups. It might have been a *very* serious accident. I was close behind Miss Hatch – and when her horse shied – my own horse jumped, but I soon quieted it. You cannot imagine how *quickly* this all happened – it was a revelation to me as to the rapidity with which such accidents can happen. I thought that we had all been struck by lightning, when the two in front of me fell – I was sure that my turn was coming. The horse that ran away was soon caught – and we went on our way. It was a very careless accident – we have been warned and *warned so often* – to be careful of trees and branches & even twigs – for sometimes that which appears to be only a twig can throw you from your horse if you are going at a good speed. Poor little Eleanor was covered with chagrin – she is such an unusually splendid rider for a child – and so prides herself upon that fact, upon her careful riding.

We had a delightful lunch at Makaweli House – after which some of us walked over to see the swimming pool. While there it suddenly began to *pour* – you have to come to Kauai to understand the meaning of "*pour.*" We sought shelter in the bath house – squatted in a circle on the floor – and Mr. Knudsen amused us by telling of his recent adventures & experiences in the Orient. We hoped it would stop raining, but it did not – and no one came to rescue us – so we had to go home in the rain – and we were drenched. I put on a little dressing sack under a huge oilskin raincoat – and went merrily home on horseback in the rain. Everyone was wet before we reached home. But it was a *delightful* day.

They all staid to dinner – after which we played with the youngsters new toys and games. Then some billiards & music before they departed.

But if I don't hurry I shall not have time for my bath before dressing for dinner. I love you *all* just *heaps*!

Your loving Hettie

Sugar production was synonymous with Hawaiʻi for many years. The plantation system had expanded during the American Civil War when products from the southern states, including sugar, were unavailable in the north. The commerce grew with the Reciprocity Treaty of 1876, which allowed Hawaiian sugar and other products into the American market duty-free.[32] The plantation system was established by and for Europeans and Americans. The crop was planted on tropical soil with capital from abroad, and the benefits went to the white planters, who employed low-paid labor.

The nineteenth century plantation era was a time of transition for both Hawaiians and immigrants. Hawaiians moved from their ancient system of rule by chiefs toward a modern world of individual autonomy, and the plantation owners were the "new *ali'i*" or royalty.[33] For immigrants, the plantations were their entry ticket into a new country and society. Workers labored ten to twelve hours per day, six days a week. Plantations developed camps with services for their workers, yet it was a system that today would be considered benevolent paternalism, since the workers were dependent on the plantation store, clinic, and the largesse of the owners. Still, there is some nostalgia among them for these simpler, well-defined times, and among European/Americans who enjoyed many privileges.

The Gay & Robinson, Inc.'s involvement in the sugar industry began in 1889 when a Scottish firm leased 7,000 acres at Makaweli to form the Hawaiian Sugar Company (Makaweli Plantation). When Hettie Belle was living on Kaua'i, Gay & Robinson, Inc. still retained 4,000 acres for planting their own cane, and this was processed at the mill owned by Hawaiian Sugar Co. (Makaweli Plantation) where she observed the transformation of cane into raw sugar.

The sugarcane fields were burned before harvest, an amazing blaze viewed by Hettie Belle. This process got rid of the leafy material, increased the amount of sucrose that could be recovered at the mill, sweetened the acidic soil with ash, and removed vermin from the harvest. In addition, it saved on the amount of material that had to be hauled out of the fields for handling at the mill. Portable tracks were laid in the fields to move the cane to the mill by rail. These narrow-gauged railways were first used in the 1880s. At Hettie Belle's time in Hawai'i, the sugar was packed in 100-pound bags and shipped to refineries in the states.

Gay & Robinson, Inc. was the last family-owned sugar plantation in Hawai'i.[34] The yield in 1999 was the highest in the world. The mill closed in 2010. At this writing, the last sugar plantation on the island of Maui has closed, ending the run of sugar production in Hawai'i.

Crushing plant or mill rollers for extracting juice from the sugar cane stalks, from Henry Waltz, Jr.'s 1931 album for the 50th anniversary of the Hawaiian Sugar Company at Makaweli. (Courtesy of the Kauaʻi Museum)

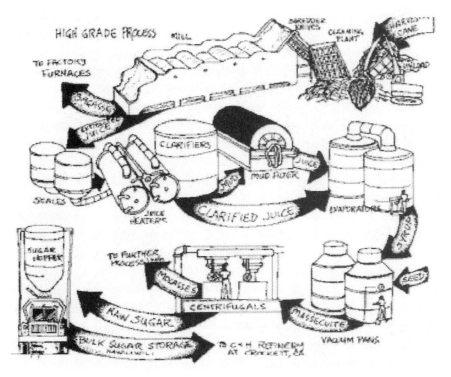

Illustration of sugar processing steps from after 1950s.
("Kauai Sugar Plantation Tours: History of Sugar at Gay & Robinson, Inc,"
courtesy of artist Christine Fayé)

CHAPTER SEVEN

FLOWER PARADES

"Kapalawai"

Jan. 22, 1912.

Mother, dearest –

Have just come home from a lovely dinner party at Mrs. Hofgaard's* and as it is late, you can have only a wee note tonight. We had a most delightful dinner – after which your humble servant, the "Governess," played for about an hour. These people are simply *starved* for music – you can imagine that it must be so – when they keep *me* playing by the hour. But I love to play, when *they* love it.

I nearly died laughing at the children today. It was rather rainy, so they played indoors. One had a ramshackle old tricycle – the other an Irish mail coaster – and around and around the court veranda they raced. It was *far* more exciting than Ben Hur's chariot race – for they had a collision at each corner. They are awfully cunning but *awfully* funny. Things are not stupid here, for very long at a time.

On Saturday Mrs. R. and I, played with the youngsters all day – helped them feed their chickens and pigeons – chased chickens – crawled away up into all the hay lofts in search of nests and eggs – searched for them in the tall grass and in the rubbish heap, even. Mrs. R. and her "governess" are noted in the "district" for their *dignity* – but people would be surprised, could they see us crawling thro' fences, chasing chickens – or lying flat on our stomachs on the floor, playing with the cat – as we do some evenings. This delicious freedom is due to the fact that "the men

---

* Marie Mahlum was the wife of Christopher Blom Hofgaard, a prominent member of Waimea business and society.

are *all* transported far beyond the northern sea"– and being on Niihau are at a safe distance.

German Club on Wednesday – and a lawn party on Thursday – and the weeks fly past – *too* quickly to suit me.

Lots of love – Your Hettie

Irish Coaster like the one used by the children to race along the lanai.
(http://www.geocities.ws/rcgilmore3/Child_rowers.htm)

"Kapalawai"

Jan. 29, 1912.

My Mother, dearest –

Yesterday afternoon, (Sunday) I started the children in on their Bible study courses – I got those splendid graded lessons for them, and they seem *much* interested in them.

Saturday was a "lazy" day – we just did anything that came into our heads to do – chased chickens – Mrs. R. and I played duets for a couple of hours – and by the way we are thinking of having a concert tour, shortly – we are truly becoming quite proficient, we play duets for a couple of hours every day. Mrs. R. plays *very much* better than I do, you know – we play lots of Haydn, Mozart, Beethoven & some lighter. Lots of those Andantes & Minuets that you love we play.

Saturday afternoon we donned our bathing attire and ran down to the sea for a dip. Ah! The water was fine and warm – we staid in more than an hour. We are building a bathhouse down there now – that will make it more convenient, you see.

Friday night was "Aaser" night – there seems to be such a night each week, now. He brought me some more shells, nice ones. We talked and played billiards – and had a nice quiet harmless time. Mrs. R. is *quite* troubled over the fact that he always comes in a hired automobile – which means $5.00 per – she says that there won't be anything left to keep house on. Isn't she horrid? And I could tell you some worse things that she said – but I won't. She has to keep up the good work – while Mr. R. is away, and cannot tease me. Friday afternoon last, Mrs. R. & I made some formal calls – the kind where you wear white kid gloves and leave your cards. There are some terribly nice people in this "district."

Thursday afternoon – Mrs. Baldwin* had a *grand* lawn party – everyone in the country appeared in their "gladdest rags" and longest plumes. The Hawaiian band played, the autos spun in and out – the men stopped work, and appeared in their white or pongee suits – and the ladies were quite gay looking. We marched about on the great lawns, and thro' the gardens – met people – gossiped – drank tea & ate a hundred indigestible goodies – then left, with profound bowing and scraping. Mrs. Baldwin is a most gracious hostess – and it was a charming affair. People have such marvelous homes & gardens – and such *wonderful* views of mountain & sea.

Last Wednesday was German club afternoon – I went on horseback and "Gopher" was *terribly* frisky. I guess that that is all of importance since last I wrote. Perhaps they do not seem of great importance to you – but they are the things that are happening in my life – and therefore I know that you are interested.

Enjoyed Father's letter *so much* – shall answer *very soon*. Goodness, it is getting late – I must say goodnight and "aufwiederschen."

Love, to *each* dear one –

Your loving Hettie Belle

---

* Louise Theresa Voss (Mrs. Baldwin) was the wife of the plantation manager of the Hawaiian Sugar Co. at Makaweli.

During the 1890s and early 1900s, just as proper Edwardians in America and Europe did, white settlers in Hawai'i had the custom of making formal calls and inviting others for tea. This was an important social event among women who could afford the leisure time. Besides being a chance to share gossip, these calls and gatherings served many purposes. They were a way to introduce new members of the community or visitors to the district. They were an occasion to announce engagements, births, and even deaths. They allowed performers the opportunity to sing or play instruments. Some were very formal affairs, and others were more relaxed with funny stories told and tealeaves read.[35]

"Kapalawai"

Feb. 5, 1912.

Mother, dearest –

For the first time since my arrival – I am left tonight in charge of the children – in fact I am "Mistress of the Manse." Mrs. Robinson has gone to a big dinner party on the other side of the island – and will remain all night. The men folks are still on Niihau – so I am left in charge of the old ladies and the youngsters. I feel quite important.

I must tell you about the perfectly *elegant* time I had spending the week-end out at Waieva [Waiawa] and Hoea with the Knudsens. Soon after breakfast, Saturday morning, Oahi, the chauffeur, took me out in the auto – along with bag and baggage. I did a thing that Governesses are not usually supposed to do – sat in front with him – *not* because he is nice – and I didn't want to sit alone in the back seat – *but* – because I am learning to run an automobile! Yes, indeed! So when I come to visit you – you must of course have one – that I may show off.

I went right to Mrs. Voldamar [Valdemar] Knudsen's – she is the *senior* Mrs. Knudsen & a sister of the *two* grandmothers here. I believe that I explained before that she has living with her, as a companion, a Miss McLaren, a trained nurse from Berkeley – a very lovely girl (tho' she is slightly off on the tangent of "new Thought"–"Science" etc.) Miss Creedler, an Illinois girl and now the trained nurse at Waimea Hospital, was also a guest. Miss Creedler rode out from Waimea on horseback, reaching there just before I did. The plan was that we three girls take a horse back ride out to "Waielile" [Waiele was a bath shelter for changing near the beach] at the Knudsen beach home – have a swim, and then return for a late lunch.

As it happened, we had both ride and swim – but not in just the way that we had planned them.

Mr. Eric Knudsen and Hans L'Orange, helped us on the horses, and then announced that they were going with us. Of course we were delighted. We started out bravely – but they had given me a small horse, with a *very* short gait – and if there is one thing that I *cannot* stand it is a very short gaited horse. I was trying to stand it – but they noticing my discomfiture – insisted that I make a change – so I was given Hans' horse – a *beauty* – and *terribly* lively. As for him – he liked one horse as well as the other. So we went merrily on our way – *but*, suddenly it began to *pour* – and the wind to *blow!* The rain came so hard and fast, that it stung as it hit our faces – felt like hail. The horses were snorting, and cringing under the force of it – we could scarcely make any headway, so we sought shelter under a tree. In just those few moments, we were all wet to the skin. Then the storm somewhat abated – we started on again – for we were feeling cold from the lack of exercise. However we did not go as far as we had intended – nor did we go in swimming – we were already wet enough, but we went to the beach and watched the surf for a little while, it was *perfectly marvelous!* The waves were raging in at a *terrific* rate – the sea was pale green – with mountains of foam – and a lovely mist over all. Great flicks of foam were flying down the beach. We made our horses walk along in the edge of the waves – and we enjoyed the surf. On the homeward way – the sun broke forth – and I had a bright idea – and suggested that if we let our hair down, the wind and sun would dry it by the time we reached Waieva. Luckily we all had our *own* hair – so we didn't take it off and tie it to the pommel of our saddles – but it hung down our backs in pure Indian style. We really looked quite charming – Hans took our picture. As you may imagine we had to change everything to the skin, but it was *stacks* of fun to ride in the rain – and I don't think that one of us regretted the experience.

We had a delicious luncheon, after which Mrs. K. went off for a wee nap – and we three girls, armed with books, piled on to a bed – but we got to talking, and of course did no reading. Later in the afternoon we played some billiards – then talked with Mrs. K. Then we had to get ready for the big dinner party at "Hoea"– Mrs. Eric Knudsen's.

There were sixteen young people there – and the dinner was a *tremendous* success. We had stacks of fun – I was her guest of honor – being her house guest – you see I left Mrs. K. *senior* at dinnertime, & took dinner, spent the night & Sunday with Mrs. Eric K. After dinner I played, of course – then we all sang songs around the piano. Later we went into the den, cuddled down on couches – set the phonograph going – vied with each other in telling stories – and Miss Lee [the principal at Makaweli School] read our palms. Being youngsters, they didn't have sense enough to leave until midnight – and went singing away in their autos at that hour.

People are *so* good to me – they are always doing lovely things for me.

Tell Gertrude that she can expect a little birthday package in a few days – and "spank" her for me.

Changes are always going on aren't they? They don't even wait for me to come back.   Love, Hettie

Keith Robinson recounts that his father Lester remembered Hettie Belle's hair as being so long that she could tip her head back and step on her hair with her heel. In her letter she notes proudly that none of the ladies had fake hair padded to create bulk in the Edwardian pompadour style. During that era, some women used a "rat," (a matted roll of hair) or a pompadour wire frame hidden under their own hair.

"Kapalawai"

Feb. 8, 1912.

Babe, dearest –

In this same mail – I am sending you a wee package containing a tiny birthday gift for you. I'm sorry that it is late. Is it *possible* that you are twelve years old this year? I can't believe it. My! I feel like a very old lady indeed. You must stop growing – for you are making me grow old too rapidly.

Perhaps you will wonder, when you open this package – what on earth it contains. Well, it contains two place cards from dinners that I have gone to lately – (I thought you'd like to see them.) And a lei (pronounced lay) to wear around your neck. It is made of little seeds, called "Job's tears." They grow on little weed-like shrubs, on the banks of the stream that runs thro' the garden. I picked them and strung them for you. You can wear them double around your neck, or just single, with a knot tied in them. If you wear them, they will bring you

Job's Tears

(J. Burtner, 2018)

good luck – no misfortune of any kind will come to you – and you will never have cause to weep.

Must go to tennis now – so goodbye, dearie. Love to *each* dear Matthew. Please write. Your Hettie

"Kapalawai"

Feb. 14, 1912.

My own dearest Mother –

If you *only* could know how I loved your dear, fat letter – yes, loved every word of it – but it is really impossible for me to tell you how dear to me your letters are – they are my treasures.

It was really unkind for Father to send that "pictorial sermonette"– what does he infer? Won't you remind him that I am as yet *only* 23 – and there surely must be some hope for one at that age. And I haven't turned down more than a dozen, surely *the* man will be in the next dozen. Also remind him that the hopeful thing about me, is – that I *have seen him!* He is not merely an ideal. And I'll *get* him – you just wait and see – even tho' the Fates are against me. He surely doesn't want me to do anything rash – surely he wouldn't want an "Aaser" or a Kanaka in the family.

I want to explain a bit about the sugar – you asked about the "white" sugar – of course you know that white sugar is simply brown sugar refined still more, don't you? Very little of that refining is done here in the islands – almost *all* the sugar is sent away brown – and made white in the U.S.

About dear Mr. Aaser – yes, I have been *most* gentle with him – nevertheless I really believe that he is "*cracked*"– not *my* fault, mind you – he was in that condition when first I met him. Why is it that I attract all the Aasers in the world? And the *one* man in all the world will not look at me.

Mrs. R. just came in to say goodnight to me – so I showed her the "sermonette" – *she* says to tell my Father that I'll have to work *mighty hard* against the powers that here exist – if I am to return to my family in the state of "single blessedness." So *there!* Listen I want to tell you something – you won't believe it so I'll just whisper it. On this island where only cannibals and exiles exist – *I am considered a "raving beauty"*! There – I knew you wouldn't believe it. But if you want to be appreciated, come to a desert island.

Knowing this – you probably will be all the more worried about my wandering alone on horseback over this island. But once and for all time – be assured of this one fact – situated as I now am with this family, it is *absolutely impossible* for me to do anything that would be in the least unsafe or improper – I have never before been, and probably shall never again be – as careful about everything that I do, and every movement that I make, even to the way I hold my head and to the way I blow my nose. (Improvement in the latter, will no doubt please you.) Goodness – *don't* read my letters to anyone.

Thank you *so* much for the financial statement – I did really want to know. Why should I be ignorant of such matters? I am glad that I understand now. Really, it is astonishing how rapidly *time* and *money* both go – and I am beginning to realize, I think, the value of them both. Some lessons are hard to learn, though.

Now what do you think? Mrs. R. has suddenly decided to go to Honolulu for a week – to take in the big floral parade Feb. 22 and *perhaps* take a trip to the volcano and do much shopping. She *insists* upon taking your humble servant the "Governess"– I always feel like the "prize package" when I go to Honolulu – the way I am "shown" off, and looked up and down. But we'll have a *terribly* good time – we did when she took me just before Christmas, you remember. Eleanor and Sinclair shall probably go – so there will be quite a merry little party of us. More about this you shall hear later. In the meantime I am trying to keep all my clothes clean – am going about in rags. We shall go either next Saturday or the following Tuesday.

Today was German Club day – we are truly becoming *quite* proficient.

Monday night we had a grand dinner party – the entire tribe of Knudsen – junior & senior, & the minister. Said minister is a bachelor, as I may already have mentioned – and how my maternal heart longs to brush him off and smooth down his coat collar, at times. Poor man! We had a very hilarious time at dinner – and more hilarity followed it at billiards etc. No, they never have any strong drink at the table – water and grape juice are their limit.

I have a little piano student. A little Ruth Knudsen˙ begins tomorrow – they begged and begged me to take her, as a special favor – and the Robinsons said that they would be most happy if I only would take her (being a relative of theirs it was also a favor to them) so I consented. I think that she will be a *splendid* pupil – she seems so bright & musical.

---

* Ruth was a granddaughter of Mrs. Valdemar "Annie" Knudsen, sister of the two grandmothers in the Robinson home. Her parents left her in her grandmother's care.

In Gertrude's letter I mentioned Mrs. Eric Knudsen's dinner – did I also mention the "Aaser" episode? If so *don't* read it again. He tip-toed up to me and whispered "Miss Matthew, have you a pocket?" I enlightened him by informing him that ladies did not usually have pockets in their gowns. He was thoroughly "squelched." But when I said goodnight to him, he left in my hand a tiny bottle containing some "very rare shells," so he said. I'm really getting a lovely collection – Mr. R. and the boys returned from Niihau last Friday – and Mr. R. brought me some beauties, large beautifully polished ones.

The last time that Mr. Aaser called, he said before leaving, "Tell me Miss Matthew – do I call too often?" I intended to be real coy and say, "Does it seem to often to you?" And what I *did* say, was –"*Doesn't* it seem too often to you?" He hasn't called since – and Mrs. R. is positive that he is not simply "cracked"– but that he is now *broken*. What do you think – I'll leave it to you.

But I must retire – tho' it is just about this time in the night that I begin to receive my inspirations – does this letter seem inspired?

Gute Nacht und Aufwiedersehen, meine schone, liebe Mutterchen!

Your loving Hettie Belle

Hettie Belle never reveals in the extant letters who the man is that she thinks is her ideal. She may have removed that letter later in life in deference to her own husband.

Alexander Young Hotel
Honolulu

Feb. 22,1912.

You dearest Mother –

As you see – we *did* go to Honolulu – and such a trip! Believe me, a person is brave to journey from island to island at this time of the year. *Rough* doesn't adequately express it – it was terrible. Oh! I was *so* sick – everything came up but the moon – and I longed for that to come up. But I have almost forgotten all about it – for we have had such a *wonderful* time since our arrival.

Today was *the* great day – Washington's birthday. And it is the day in all the year when Honolulu celebrates. People came from all over the world to be here on this day to view the wonderful Floral Parade this afternoon – and the lantern parade which took place tonight. I am writing between events – we are about to go up to the roof garden – some of our party to look on, and some to take part in a grand ball.

The ball is half over – and being half dead, we have returned to our rooms. Now you must hear all about today.

This morning, soon after breakfast, we went out to see the navy, army & cavalry parade – it was most interesting. After this we went out to Poonaho [Punahou] College and saw a splendid field meet – people from the various islands taking part. Then a huge luncheon party at the hotel this noon, after which we rushed out to see the grand Floral parade. And it surely was a thing of beauty.

First a float representing the king & queen, as they once were – then a princess & her retainers from each island. These were all on horseback – and such *stunning* horses as they did ride – and how beautifully they rode. These are called the Pau [pa'u] riders – because they wear a long peculiar drape about their legs that hangs away down and floats in the breeze. Each island had a different color – so the pau would be either purple, yellow or some other color – with leis about neck and on head, to match. They were *lovely!*

Then came float after float – *hundreds* of them – so original and so beautiful. Each seemed handsomer than the last. I have never seen such beautifully decorated automobiles in my life. It would be impossible to *try* to describe them – I can only say that it was all wonderful. After the Floral Parade, came the lovely "Battle of Flowers" – such fun, and pretty, too.

Then we went to a very swell tea – met any number of handsome army and navy officers, who poked various varieties of sandwiches, cakes and hot and cold drinks, into your hands – and longed to have you drop your bag or "hanky" that they might show you how gracefully they could pick it up. I must remark that with all their suavity and good looks – officers *fail* to interest or fascinate me.

Tonight Mrs. R. presided over a dinner party for ten of our Kauai people – we had a terribly jolly time – and a lickin' good dinner. Then came the *loveliest* feature of the day. We had seats with the "big bugs" on the marble porch of the Executive Building, from which place we viewed the lantern parade. Hundreds and even thousands of Japanese carrying torches and lanterns of every size, shape and color. Then float after float brilliantly lighted and *so* unique in design. Really, I marveled as they passed by – they are a remarkable little people those Japanese. It had rained – and the reflection of the lights on the wet sidewalks made it doubly attractive.

Then back to the hotel we came – dressed in our grandest togs, and went up to the ballrooms & roof garden. Many people were in costume tonight, several in very clever ones – for which prizes were given. It is fun to watch them dance for a while, watch the pretty clothes, the way they hold them up, etc.– but it grows tiresome – and I would rather talk to my Mother – even tho' it is past midnight.

Tomorrow will be full of shopping, with a luncheon party at noon. Then in the evening we will probably see "Pinafore" played on one of the Cruisers, and the water parade. We leave for Kauai at midnight.

Aloha nui – to each one of you. It isn't strange that I am nearly maki [*make*] tonight – my opu has been bothering me – I need a lumi-lumi [*lomilomi*] Being a malihini and living makai it is to be expected I suppose – but when we return to Kauai, we are going mauka almost immediately – then I shall be a kamaaina once more. This all makes sense – tho' *you* wouldn't believe it. Explained at some future date. Just for fun, tell me what you think it means.

Love, love, love to *all* – and to all a "goodnight."

Your loving Betty

The big celebration in Hawai'i one hundred years ago, when the islands were a new territory of the United States, was held at the time of Washington's birthday, celebrating the Father of the Country. Hettie Belle attended the 7th and 8th Annual Mid-Pacific Carnival and Floral Parades along with many of the European/American elite. This mid-Pacific fete was known worldwide and was considered a showcase for the "Paradise of the Pacific."[36]

Pā'ū riders were selected from each island. They were queens and princesses accompanied by ladies-in-waiting and paniolo out-riders. A pā'ū was a wrap-around skirt costume made with voluminous material. The ladies did not ride sidesaddle but straddled their horses. The horses were decorated with lei that matched their riders' costumes.

Every island had both a color and flowers that represented it. For Kaua'i, the color was purple with lei *mokihana* (small, anise-scented fruits found only on Kaua'i). Ni'ihau's color was white, with lei *pūpū* (lei of shells) decorating the riders' costumes.

Pāʻū riders. Notice the voluminous cloth in the dress of the women riders who rode straddling the horse, not sidesaddle. (Hettie Belle, 1913)

CHAPTER EIGHT
HINANA AND HORSEBACK

"Kapalawai,"

Feb. 26, 1912.

Think what an appetite your big sister is acquiring, Johnny Boy – when besides many other things she eats several thousand fish in three days. Laugh if you wish, this is the solemn truth. Yes, and I'm yet alive to tell the tale. My one regret is that you people are not here to also enjoy thousands of these fish. At this time of the year, there is a delicious tiny fish about the size of the tine of a fork which is found in Waimea River. Being so small – you take at least 25 at one mouthful – so count up, and you will easily see how two plentiful helpings could take you into the thousands. We had them twice a day – several days last week – and my! They were lickin' good – so sweet and tender and of course no bones. They are called hinana. When I settle down here – and you come to visit me – you too shall have your fill. In fact, I think that you would enjoy going out on the River and fishing with mosquito netting for them – wouldn't you?

In the absence of the regular organist, your friend the "Governess" played the organ in church yesterday – to the huge amusement of herself – and the huge enjoyment (so they declared) of the congregation. The minister said that my music was an inspiration to him. I really enjoyed playing thoroughly.

Today we had a grand swimming party, down below the house. You should see our swell new bathhouse! It's a beauty. I'm crazy to learn to really swim – and you see, I'll learn yet.

Tell mother, if she is still there, that I am sending all my letters to her, to Berkeley now. Sent a *fat* letter the other day, telling all about my wonderful time in Honolulu. She can forward them to you people, when she is thro' with them.

Did enjoy your letter, dear. Why don't you write oftener? I'm indebted to you for the new crop of slang which you send me each time. Love – from Hettie

A letter which Lester sent me while I was in Honolulu – it possibly might amuse you, as it did me.

> Dear Miss Matthew
> It was very lonely after you all leaft.
> Today Grandmother and Grandma Papa Eleanor and I went for a drive in the Auto at eleven and got home at twelve.
> Eleanor and I went down to the chicken house and we saw 3 little white leghorn chicks the hen was still setting 11 Eggs.
> One of the pigeons is setting up in the bean loft.
> Much to you all.
> ever your loving
> Lester

Hinana are the spawn of the ʻoʻopu fish and were a delicacy at the time, a very dainty and popular fish. They were netted in the river by two women securing nets in the middle from opposite sides of the river. Stronger men then lifted up the net like a hammock. These fish were called *ke iʻa ili kanaka o Waimea,* (the fish of Waimea that touches the skin of man.) Once numerous, their numbers have dwindled, and it is now unlawful to take them by traps or weirs.[37]

The Robinsons kept numerous birds and animals on the grounds of their houses. Once, on a walk, Hettie Belle recalled coming to a sty with a mother pig and her piglets. Lester began to beg his father for a piglet. This was granted, and to Hettie Belle's surprise, Lester taught his piglet to play "hide and seek." The pig would stay at a given spot. Lester would run and hide, then call, and the little pig would run squealing around until he found him. "All too soon, Little Piglet was all too big."

Pigeon roost door Kapalawai. The pigeons were a form of communication with the island of Ni'ihau. (J. Burtner, 2013)

The family had imported doves, peacocks, chickens, and pigeons. Homing pigeons, sometimes called carrier or messenger pigeons, have an innate ability to fly home. These working birds were the method of communication between the people on Ni'ihau and the Robinsons on Kaua'i. Carrier pigeons served the Robinsons until early in the 1960s.[38] Even today, one of the pigeon lofts still exists at the Kapalawai house.

"Kapalawai"

Feb. 29, 1912

You dearest Mother –

By the heading of this, you will of course know that I am again on Kauai – school and music have started again – and all goes well. Did I tell you that I have a new little pupil. Tho' asked several times, I have of course refused to teach any outside pupils before this. But a little Ruth Knudsen, who is a cousin of these people – wanted lessons – these people really wanted me to teach her, and her people begged so hard – that I consented. I haven't been sorry, for she is a very very musical child – and is doing remarkable work. Really she has been such a success, that other people are begging – but I shall refuse all – for I feel that I am doing *quite* enough as it is.

Last Sunday the regular organist was absent – and your humble servant and daughter, the "Governess," took her place – at least tried to fill it. Apparently, I was successful for I received scores of compliments. They said, "Oh! If we could only have music like that every Sunday"! The minister declared that I was an inspiration to him. It was a splendid organ and I did enjoy playing it hugely. One of these days I am going to study pipe organ – you see. Am to play again next Sunday – as she has not returned yet. Went in today on horseback & practiced for a bit on the organ in preparation.

We have been swimming three afternoons this week – you know we have a swell new bath house – which makes it awfully nice. I am really learning to swim – am surprising myself in fact. Today we had a lovely swimming party. The Knudsens all came over – we were in for almost two hours – then home we came sipped tea, ate sandwiches, fresh strawberries with cream – and cake. It was jolly good fun.

Tomorrow we are going on a "horse drive" – a thing that little Hettie Belle has been looking forward to for months. Do hope it doesn't rain.

My! The weeks are flying past. Must seek my virgin couch now. Love you all so much. Your Hettie

[Written approximately March 5, 1912 to her sister Sally in Berkeley where her mother is visiting. The first pages are missing.]

....but a bit overcast. We rounded in all the horses from three valleys – drove them all down into a pen at the foot of one of the valleys. Believe me – it was exciting – for they are not so easy to drive as you might imagine. Again and again, one or more would turn round and tear up the mountains again. Then we would have to tear after it, and finally getting ahead of it, turn it down the valley again. I was quite proud of myself – for they declared that I made a splendid and fearless cowboy. I begin to think that I missed my calling in life – it should have been a cattle range, instead of a studio.

Just fancy me tearing up and down hills, (clinging to my pommel once or twice it may be), but tearing nevertheless. Many a ditch and rock and tiny stream, I jumped that day. These are such splendid mountain horses, that it is perfectly safe – they are so accustomed to it all. Once or twice the other peoples' horses went down on their knees – but not my sure-footed Gopher.

Well, when we had finally driven them all (some two or three hundred) into the pen – we ate our lunch. The things that happened after lunch, I'll admit did not interest me especially–such as branding, breaking-in etc. But when that was pau – came more fun and excitement. We drove some fifty horses clear down here to the lowlands. They simply tore – and we tore after them – cantered the *entire* ten miles down – stopping only for the big streams. Now I guess that at last you people will believe that I know how to ride. These people say that I could *never* have a harder ride than that – it wasn't along a road you understand – but down hill over rough, rocky country. My! but it *was* fun! And I wasn't the least bit stiff – tho' I truly expected to be. We reached home a little after five – and down we all went to the sea, and had a swim. You can imagine how refreshing it was, after riding in a cloud of dust.

Sunday, I played the organ again in church. All went well – until the benediction – then when the church was as quiet as could be, I dropped one of the clothespins that I use to hold my music with. I was terribly mortified – but the minister forgave me. Sunday is such a lovely quiet day in this home – before church we sing hymns for an hour or so. In the afternoon we all scatter to our rooms – I usually give the children their Bible study. Late in the afternoon we all walk in the garden or along the sea beach and watch the glorious sunsets. Then in the evening we sing hymns again and have prayers. Sometimes I used to think that our Berkeley Sundays were a mad whirl of church going – with no time to read or think. Here, there is time for both.

After school today – for it is evening as I return to your letter – a girl, Gertrude Hofgaard came over to play tennis with me. We played three hard sets – she won them all which was to be expected, as she is a splendid player – and I am but a beginner. But I am learning.

Tomorrow the Robinsons ℰ the Knudsens are giving a joint riding party to the lovely Hanapepe Falls. About twenty are going – the guests of honor are a Miss Harding (visiting the Knudsens) and Miss Matthew, of whom you may already have heard. I am looking forward to it eagerly – they say it is a wonderful trip.

Oh! Sally dear – if *you only* knew how I did enjoy your dear letter. I wouldn't mind a bit if such a letter came from you *often* – even tho' it was scribbled off at the Post Office. Your letters are *so* refreshing, dear. I love them.

I've just been wishing that you could keep Mother in a glass case – that she might *really* rest. I just hope that you will be good and severe – and not allow anyone to touch, taste, handle or *look* at her. But I am *so* afraid that she will want to go to church and to see people and to do things. And *more* afraid that hundreds of people will want to call on her, and entertain her – and so take her time and strength. You must keep them off – even if you have to keep a pistol handy. How long is she going to stay? If I come home this summer she must wait there until that time, *sure*. Love you *all heaps*.

Your Hettie

There was a regular ritual on Sundays at Kapalawai. First, the family drove to church in a lovely three-seater carriage with a yellow fringe on top, drawn by two horses with a cowboy driver. However, Hettie Belle remembered, Mr. Robinson preferred to take the reins. The ladies wore large hats with long scarves to keep them in place.

After church they came home to Sunday dinner. And next, "after dinner, all retired to their rooms for a long Sunday rest in utter quiet. Late afternoon, suddenly all would appear, for a walk in the garden. This was amazingly beautiful. Trees from all over the world were collected by Mr. Aubrey Robinson. The family might sample a ripe cherimoya or star apple, or perhaps a ripe pineapple would by magic be cut into slices and enjoyed." Finally, on Sunday evening the family would have "prayers." Someone would read from the Bible, and then each would choose a hymn with Mrs. Robinson playing the piano.

"Kapalawai"

March 7, 1912.

You dearest Mother –

I didn't go to tennis today – my conscience sort of pricked me when I tho't of letters that should be written – so here I am at work.

We had a funny time after German yesterday – a whole crowd of us were riding with a Mrs. Shultzy [Schultz] in her auto. As there are only women in the club, she stopped her auto in a place where to start it again she wouldn't need to "crank up" – but could just start coasting down hill. When it was time to go home, five of us all piled in – but it refused to start to coast – so three of us got out, the driver was one of us – and we got behind and pushed. Suddenly the car started down hill, and she had to run, jump & grab the wheel – the rest of us jumped in as best we could. It was awfully funny. Goodness! I shouldn't have told you, for I can hear you saying, "It might *not* have been funny."

Tuesday we had a most *wonderful* day. No school – away to the mountains we went, twenty of us on horseback. All this family, all the Knudsen family, and several guests. We went way up Hanapepe Valley – a valley owned by these people, and considered the most beautiful on the island – which is saying a *great* deal. Our destination was a magnificent waterfall – Koula Falls, at the head of the valley. The trail crosses the river *twenty two* times – and it was surely fun – tho' we *did* get wet. You cannot imagine how much fun it is for a whole party to go riding like that. The scenery up the valley is more than beautiful – I have never seen anything half so lovely. Great cliffs two to three thousand feet high on each side – not bare, but *covered* with verdure, beautiful trees, ferns & moss. We reached the falls at noon – and I was speechless – I couldn't find words to express my feelings. This great foaming mass of water, falling from a height of many hundred feet was to me a most marvelous sight – the first great waterfall that I have ever seen. Both before and after lunch, I lay on my back on the grass and gazed up at it – it seemed to be ever changing, and ever growing more wonderfully beautiful. I can still see it, if I close my eyes – and can still hear its thunder. I was certainly loathe to leave that spot – but they promised me that I should see it again many times. It was in sight of these lovely Falls that Mr. & Mrs. Robinson spent their honeymoon. Think what an *ideal* spot! A little below these Falls – down the valley a bit, you can see from one view point *seven* smaller falls – it is a charming sight, I can tell you.

All we Californians know the beautiful Pillsbury pictures – photos of Tahoe, Muir Woods, Yosemite, Shasta, Big Basin etc. – and I remember Sally speaking of a picture of some redwoods, taken by him – that she loved. Well, our trip was made doubly interesting on Tuesday – by Mr. Pillsbury, himself, going with us. He is here in the islands taking pictures. He took many, many pictures on Tuesday – was more than enthusiastic about the country, and mad about the valley. He is a very quiet, but extremely interesting man – has had some remarkable experiences. By the way – by mistake *I* am in one of his panorama photos. Hope I will be small enough to look like some sweet wood nymph or elf.

Postcard of Kō'ula Falls (Manawaiopuna Falls) sent to Hettie's mother

Hug Billikin and Sally and Phil, little Helen Marion, Daisy and Allan, and my "Boy Dear" *extra hard* for me – and kiss all those who will allow it. I'm kind of lonesome tonight. Hope you all still love your Hettie

[Undated postcard to her mother]

Do you remember that I told you about our lovely trip to these wonderful Koula Falls? This is a good picture – but doesn't give you really an adequate idea of their tremendous size. Your dear letter shall have an answer very soon.

Much Love,
H.B.M.

Hettie's writing on the postcard.

"Kapalawai"
March 15, 1912

Mother, dearest –

Tomorrow we are planning a horseback ride along the beach, to Shell Beach. They say that there are very beautiful shells there – so I expect to add to my collection. Somebody (probably Mr. Aaser, tho' the box did not contain any card) made me wonderfully rich this week by sending me thro' the mail a large box full of the most *exquisite* shells. They are surely *beautiful*. As yet I do not know who to thank. I'll have to buy another trunk in order to bring home all my shells.

Am so anxious to hear how Raymond came thro' his operation. Poor boy! He had a hard time, I'm afraid.

Had you been here this morning, I might have shared my treat with you. Mr. R. brought me in from the garden a huge mulberry leaf full of lovely black-ripe mulberries, and delicious red-ripe strawberries. I tell you they were *lickin'* good.

Tuesday afternoon Miss Hofgaard came over to play tennis – we played four sets – after which we went down and took a dip in the ocean. It was fine.

Wednesday was German Club as usual – we had lots of fun. You know we have to tell in German, of our daily doings. I convulsed the class by telling about my hair being washed – and several other crazy things. But it is all splendid practise.

Mrs. Eric Knudsen has a *darling* wee boy, Voldemar [Valdemar], about a year and a half old. He is almost as sweet as Billikin, which as you know is saying a *great* deal. Although he is rather afraid of most people – he likes me – we are fast friends. I take him down and show him the wee pigs & chickens – that is really the attraction, I think. The other day – a whole crowd of people was here. I was down on my knees playing with Voldemar and we were the centre of an interested circle. His mother told him to kiss Miss Matthew. This he promptly did – then looking up at the many people, his big blue eyes just shining, and smacking his lips (so they all declared) he said, "Candy." My! How those people teased me! They begged me to pass around the candy, declaring that they hadn't dreamed that it was so sweet. It was funny – I was covered with confusion.

Now I must write Dordie a wee birthday letter. Dear little youngsters, they must be awfully lonesome without their mother. They are awfully brave I think.

For goodness sake! Someone write to me *soon*.

Packs of love.
Your loving Betty

"Kapalawai"
March 25, 1912.

My Mother, dearest –

Am feeling terribly puffed up and proud of myself – because I beat Eleanor at three consecutive *sets* of tennis this afternoon. She is a keen little player, I can tell you – and I have never won before, when playing against her. Later in the afternoon, Mr. R. & I won at croquet, against Mrs. R. and Ethel Gay. Should I not have the swell head?

The family are all excitement tonight – and I fear that your humble servant is the most excited of all. For we start early in the morning for the mountains. We are to have a cattle drive on the way up – stay tomorrow night at "Kahana," their mountain house away back in the mountains, come down the next day, driving horses all the way down. As you can imagine it will be terribly exciting and *stacks* of fun. I fear that I shall not be able to sleep tonight.

Saturday afternoon we had an awfully nice bathing party – a few friends came over – and it was jolly. We took our rowboat from the fishpond and use it in the ocean now. We do a good bit of rowing, then dive from the boat – tip each other out, etc.

I felt awfully badly today – I had to punish Eleanor. She was having her lesson before breakfast this morning – and she got stubborn and wouldn't play a certain measure. So to punish her, I made her play that one measure for *half an hour* this afternoon. I really think that *I* was the one who was punished – for I was trying to write & her incessant playing of that *one* measure nearly drove me to drink. But such is the life of the "Governess." Really I have nothing to complain of – for I have only had to punish her *twice* since I have been here – & Lester once. And Mr. & Mrs. R. told me, as have the children and Miss McDermott – that she, Miss McD., the last teacher, had to punish them nearly every day. She evidently did her work thoroughly, for I have had *no* trouble with them. The previous time, I punished Eleanor for cleaning her nails with a knife in school. I told her once before that she mustn't do it – and explained why. When she insisted on doing it the second time, I sent her to her room and made her scrub her nails until school was over for the day. In the meantime her mother delivered a lecture. Lester, I punished for something a bit more serious. I gave him his Spelling lesson while sitting in a far part of the room where I could not watch him. To my surprise (for Spelling is his weak point), his lesson was perfect. So 15 minutes later I gave it to him again & watched him. He missed 2/3 of the words. Then he confessed that he had cheated, & after talking to him, I sent him & the 2 papers to his parents. I think that it will never happen again. But my clothes must be tied up in a bundle – so goodnight you dearest mother

Your Hettie.

Hettie Belle later reminisced about strong-willed Eleanor's reading *pilikia* (trouble).

Mr. and Mrs. Robinson believed that to read aloud well, was an excellent talent. So—each day Eleanor read aloud to me. It would be from an interesting book such as "Ivanhoe," "Lady of the Lake" and such.

One day I said, "Eleanor shall we read for a while?" She replied that she did not care to read that day. I insisted — Eleanor insisted. I handed her a book — only "mumblings" ensued. These mumblings delighted both Eleanor and Lester. I insisted that she relate this episode to a parent. Nothing more was said — but I noticed at dinner that Eleanor was a bit hoarse and red-eyed. Much later Mrs. Robinson told me that they had kept Eleanor reading the entire afternoon!

"Kapalawai"

March 29, 1912

Mother, dearest –

The trip to "Kahana" was wonderfully ideal – I enjoyed each and every second. The weather was *perfect* – we started early Tuesday morning, this entire family and six native men, and a cook.

Kahana valley is kept very private – there are several locked gates on the way up, and these together with the inaccessible cliffs on either side keep people out. I told these people that they were frightfully selfish to keep all of that marvelous beauty to themselves, for it is a very wonderful valley. We saw many, many wild goats on the way up – Sinclair killed one, and we enjoyed it for supper that night. The scenery all the way up is indescribably beautiful – the more I see of this island, the more I marvel at its tremendous cliffs, beautiful streams and dense verdure.

We reached the cottage at about noon – had a delicious lunch – soon after which we went down to the river and had a delightful swim in the clear cold pool. There is quite a pool there – and a lovely waterfall feeding it. We got under the fall – and had stacks of fun playing in it.

Later in the afternoon we each took a rod and line and went fishing for oopu – a *delicious* tho' quite small fish. Mr. R. found a dandy pool for me – I sat out on a huge flat boulder – and I must have had beginner's luck for I pulled out one fish after another. Mr. R. was awfully good to me – he sat on the bank, took my fish off the hook, rebaited it, and into the water I would throw it again. You see, he did all the disagreeable work and I had the fun – it surely was fun – and I was *so* proud as I strutted home with my string of *sixteen* fish, mostly all of which were *extra* large. I got more than anyone else of the whole party. They were all so jealous that they said that my success was due to the fact that I had the best man, the best pool, the best rod – and the *fattest* worms. Anyhow I *did* get the *most* – and the *biggest*.

The Kahana cottage is the cunningest wee affair – five tiny rooms, a veranda in front and a cookhouse near by. At night we were packed in like sardines – but it was fun. Ethel Gay and I had a room together – next to Mrs. & Mr. R's. I distinguished myself by talking in my sleep. After supper at night we amused ourselves by telling the most horrible tales and gruesome ghost stories – then we tried lifting each other by breathing – and all sorts of weird stunts. We went to bed quite late, and slumbers were disturbed by rather mixed dreams – ghosts and flying fish intermingled. Ethel and the Robinsons declare that I suddenly shrieked out, "Eleanor, Eleanor, Ether!" They hurried to my rescue – but couldn't waken me.

In the morning, we went on a cattle drive – tho' we women folks keep pretty well to the rear. I must confess that a cattle drive is too dangerously exciting to quite take my fancy – I rather enjoyed it, but I was scared stiff all the while, for fear that a wild pipi would turn and charge me. After the drive there was time for another swim in the pool – then came lunch – then we locked up the wee cottage, picked many oranges & peaches from the trees about the cottage, and started homeward – driving horses all the way down. We stopped at a pen, to brand some wee colts – and when they threw one, it fell and broke its neck. This put a damper over our trip – tho' we tried to forget it as soon as possible – poor little fellow. Ethel and I were simply *sick* about it – we had to leave the pen – she nearly fainted, and I forgot myself in working over her. We reached home at dusk.

Lots of love. Your Hettie

George Vancouver introduced the first cattle to Hawai'i in 1793. The steers soon became wild, numerous, and hard to handle. In 1832 King

Kamehameha III* invited vaqueros from Spanish California to come to the islands and train Hawaiians in their skills. The word paniolo probably originated from *espanol*, meaning Spanish. The Sinclair/Robinson family imported short-horned cattle from England to New Zealand and then to Ni'ihau and Kaua'i. As Hettie Belle related, these, too, became semi-wild, and rounding them up was an exciting and dangerous undertaking.

During trips into the hills, sitting around a fire at camp prompted much storytelling, especially ghost stories. Hettie Belle may have heard about Eric Knudsen's encounter on a moonlit night in the Kōke'e Canyon with the ghost of Papu. Old Papu, carrying a pack of dried fish, had been murdered on the trail many years before, and it was believed that his ghost returned one night each year, sat beside the trail with his pack of musty dried fish, and avenged Papu by murdering the first man who passed. Eric's mellow mare certainly knew something strange was nearby when she snorted and bolted at top speed, and Eric smelled fish that Papu was said to have carried when he was murdered long ago. The experience was scary enough that Eric never ventured again up that canyon trail at night.[39]

"Kapalawai"

April 1, 1912.

You very dear Sally –

Had the *craziest* dream just before I woke up this morning, and as I'm not hardly any more than awake now, it is still quite vivid. I dreamed that I was playing tennis with some men, away up in some cliffs. I thought that the men were all dressed in dress suits. The funniest part of it was that Bishop Hughes was there – and tho' he didn't take part in the tennis, I kept him busy. I would throw his hat over a huge cliff – he would clamber down, rescue his hat and come back wearing a broad grin. Then I would throw it once again. This went on until I woke up. Did you ever hear of anything more silly? And yet you can't imagine how very vivid it was.

---

* King Kauikeapuli Kamehameha III was the longest reigning monarch of the Hawaiian Kingdom.

The Rices are visiting us now for a few days – Mrs. Charles Rice & her two sweet little girls [Edith and Juliet]. I love Mrs. Rice – better than any other woman on the island, I think. She is so very sweet and loveable.

Saturday evening we four young people – Ethel Gay, Aylmer, Sinclair & I – all went to Mr. Aaser's party. Yes, my quiet little Mr. Aaser had a grand moonlight riding party, and supper on the sands, for *forty* of the young people of the island. We went on horseback from here & joined the crowd at Kekaha. It was a wonderful night – and we had a *great* time. My! he had the most elegant "feed"– tamales, chicken sandwiches, coffee, salted nuts, olives, cake, pineapple, candy, & *everything*. It was *sumptuous*, indeed. He quite outdid himself. This afternoon we are all going to join the Knudsens in a riding party, supper on the beach, following. Nearly breakfast time, so adieu.

Lots of love, Hettie

CHAPTER NINE
BACHELORS AND TRAVELING MERCHANTS

"Kapalawai"

Easter Sunday

You dearest Mother –

We had such a beautiful service in church this morning. The usually bare little church was beautifully decorated in greens and Easter lilies. We had special music – and a splendid sermon. I tried to keep my mind upon it – but it just *would* wander as far as Berkeley – and I tried to imagine what you were all doing.

We people are just over a siege with the dentist. A Dr. Derby comes from Honolulu, about every six months, and usually stays in this home a week or so. He was here all last week. He goes from one place to another on the island here – tortures everyone, then returns to Honolulu. I like him – he is so *quick* – and tho' a bit rough, perhaps – the agony is soon over. He found my teeth in splendid condition – I just had three tiny fillings put in and my teeth polished. This is quite a change from my usual siege.

Last night Mr. Brody [Brodie]* (a bachelor who resembles Ichabod Crane, but is very nice) and Mr. Hime† (a grass widower, wealthy, good-looking and about forty years of age) called. Don't worry, for I haven't designs on either of them – but they are calling very often of late – every week, almost. Mr. Brody is very musical – played

---

* Alexander H. Brodie was Superintendent of Kaua'i Schools.

† Arthur Gilmour Hime was employed by the Kekaha Sugar Company.

the moonlight sonata for us last night, & several other pieces. He brought a lovely book of duets, & we played together. Also, he presented me with a lovely volume of Chopin.

Mr. Brody & I, played billiards against Miss Gay & Mr. Hime – and beat them at three games. Perhaps the duetts accounted for the splendid teamwork.

Friday night we four young people – Ethel Gay, Aylmer, Sinclair and I – went to a supper and dance at the McBrides' [McBryde]' beautiful beach place. We went in the auto. The road is all lovely – following the sea most of the way. At one place we pass what is called the "spouting horn"– about ten feet from the water's edge is a large hole in the rock – as each wave comes in, the water is forced thro' this opening and shoots up into the air geyser-like – to a height of perhaps 50 ft. It is lovely – and so strange and fascinating.

We reached the beach place at dusk. Such a picturesque place it is – the most tropical place that I have yet seen in the islands. It is just the sort of place that you picture in your mind before you come to the islands. It is near the water's edge – in the curve of a little bay. Hundreds of old, old cocoanut trees surround the house. Behind rises a cliff covered with brilliant purple flowering beauganvellia. The house itself was once the beach place of one of the old queens'– so it is quite a historical spot. We had a delicious luau (feast), sitting on the floor in true Hawaiian style (which by the way, is not particularly comfortable for long-legged people). After the luau – they danced. We started home early – just as the moon was rising over the sea, and we had it full in our faces all the way home. There were more than 50 there.

The other day – a woman & man came, selling laces, embroideries and linens, and sundry articles. Besides two elegant embroidered robes, Mrs. R. bought quantities of table linen, cluny doilie sets, etc. Ethel bought an evening dress and some towels. I looked on – and gave sage advice. The only thing I wanted was an embroidered gown $125.00 – but I wouldn't allow myself to be so extravagant (even considering a trousseau). Well, I helped Mrs. R. decide upon all her lovely things – finally she put three Irish crochet collars in my lap – and asked which I thought prettiest. One was

---

* Alexander McBryde owned the lower valley and held the fishing rights at Lāwaʻi.

† Queen Emma, wife of Kamehameha IV, spent time on Kauaʻi at Lāwaʻi in 1871 after the deaths of her son and husband. Her cottage was on the bluff, later lowered to the beach area by McBryde in 1899.

$7.00, one $11.00 & the other $28.00. Naturally the $28.00 one was the loveliest – and I told her so. After the people had left, she gave me the collar, saying that she wanted to give me a little something – and wanted it to be something that I *really* liked. Imagine my weak feelings! But the collar *is* beautiful!

This week has been crammed full of affairs – as I told you, the Rices were here – and that meant dinners and luncheons both here & elsewhere. Mrs. Sandow had a delightful luncheon for us. Mrs. Knudsen had a lovely beach party for us – both for children & grown-ups. We had a swim in the afternoon, then a delicious supper. It was April Fool's day, and we took a beautiful-looking but cotton-filled cake – had lots of fun about it. After supper we played games in the sand – then rode home– many of us on horse-back. I raced one of the autos and kept ahead – only stopped because I lost my gold back comb. It was a gorgeous moonlit night – my! But the moonlight *is* wonderful here.

Very, very lovingly –

Hettie

In the late nineteenth and early twentieth centuries, the Robinson family's home was a busy place with frequent visitors. Hettie Belle, who came from a large family, relished the hustle and bustle of guests. Many visitors, such as Ethel Gay, were members of the extended family. Others were neighbors in the district, suitors, or people from the other side of the island, such as the Rice family. A preferred and frequent guest at dinner was the Reverend Milliken. According to Hettie Belle's recollections, he was a brilliant man. "He preached an excellent sermon — rode his bicycle about the district — played the best tennis game — and was a most delightful dinner guest, much in demand."

Grass widower was a term used for men who were without their families. This expression may have started in India in reference to the British men who would send their families into the hills, where the grass was still green and not parched, during periods of insufferably hot weather. Hettie Belle speaks of Mr. Hime as a grass widower, but he was in fact a divorced man.

Spouting Horn (J. Burtner, 2018)

The Spouting Horn phenomenon is along the southern coast of Kaua'i and is caused when the ocean water rushes under a lava shelf and pops up through an opening in the surface. Another large opening near the Spouting Horn blows air and makes an eerie, groaning sound. According to legend, a large *mo'o* (water dragon), with an enormous appetite that would eat anyone fishing along the shore, guarded this coastline. A boy named Liko wanted to catch fish for his grandmother and went into the water. The mo'o tried to attack. Liko escaped through a lava tube (a hollow pipe formation left by lava), but the mo'o got stuck in it and moans to this day.[40]

The McBrydes' beautiful beach place is now part of the National Tropical Botanical Gardens. Visitors can take a walking tour in the McBryde Garden or a guided tour of the Allerton Garden, wandering the numerous paths that reveal garden "rooms" with sculptures and water features. Birds flit through the vast array of tropical flora, including plants and trees endemic to the islands, as well as some brought to the islands by canoe from distant parts of Polynesia, and others transplanted later by settlers from around the world. The cottage Hettie Belle admired was, for a while in 1871, the temporary residence of the Dowager Queen Emma, wife of Kamehameha V.

McBryde house by the bay. The hillside behind is covered with purple bougainvillea. (J. Burtner)

The dentist appeared regularly with all his paraphernalia, including a red plush chair, which he would set up in a private room. According to Hettie Belle, Dr. Derby was not only a competent dentist, but also a delightful conversationalist at the table.

At times, traveling salesmen, such as lace solicitors, would arrive coming all the way from Honolulu on the interisland steamer. Fine European lace was popular for household linens, collars, jabots, and evening gowns. Sometimes, by appointment, a merchant would arrive from Wichman & Company, Honolulu's great jewelry shop. Hettie Belle remembered the beautiful displays set up for perusal. Mrs. Robinson purchased much jewelry, often for Christmas gifts. Hettie Belle said, "Imagine buying jewelry by the $500-worth!"

At other times, large boxes would arrive from Honolulu with hats, scarves, and gloves. Hettie Belle would be invited into Mrs. Robinson's suite, along with the grandmothers, to serve as an audience as the hats were modeled. Mrs. Robinson always insisted that Hettie choose some hats and scarves for herself.

Hettie Belle had arrived in Hawai'i with short-sleeved dresses, most of them with V-necks or round collars. Mrs. Robinson, however, always dressed in "lovely white linen — pleated skirts — shirtwaists with long sleeves — cuffs and collars of embroidery and lace. A jabot was at her throat, with a brooch — a gold watch chain, with watch tucked in to her belt." Hettie Belle learned later that Mrs. Robinson's linen nightgowns had long sleeves, with cuffs and a collar.

Mrs. Robinson admired Hettie Belle's simple (and undoubtedly cooler) nightgowns, which were low-necked and sleeveless. Years later, on Hettie Belle's trips back to the islands from California, Mrs. Robinson suggested that she shop for her while in Honolulu. For Mrs. Robinson, Hettie Belle wrote, "I sent, on approval, great boxes of exquisite French 'intimate' wear. I had arrived with lisle [fine cotton thread] tan stockings and 'pumps.' Mrs. Robinson wore long black cotton hose. But liking my hose — she insisted that I send to Berkeley for some for her." Mrs. Robinson then wore silk hose even when on horseback!

Alice Gay (Mrs. Aubrey) Robinson (courtesy of Susie Somers)

Other visitors to the Robinson household were adventurers, world travelers (such as the Cropps), artists who might even capture a young woman's fancy, or photographers, including Arthur C. Pillsbury who was a photographer of natural wonders.[41] All of these guests were taken to see the wonders of the folded hills, waterfalls, and rivers on the family property.

Robinson family with Hettie Belle and Ethel Gay. Standing: Hettie Belle Matthew, Aubrey Robinson, Alice Gay Robinson. Seated: Eleanor, Alymer (or Sinclair), probably cousin Ethel Gay, Sinclair (or Aylmer), Lester

"Kapalawai"

April 12, 1912.

My dearest Mother –

Since yesterday evening we have been an awfully sad household – the news came of the death of Ethel Gay's Mother. I believe that I have spoken several times of her (Ethel) in my letters lately. She came to the Islands in December with the fleet, as the guest of Admiral & Mrs. Thomas – since about the first of February she has been here with us – intending to remain on thro' the summer. In May, she expected her Father, Mother & sister – they were all to be here during the summer. But now, of course – all is changed.

Poor Ethel is just broken hearted – I feel so badly for her – but there is so little that one can do to show sympathy at such a time – you somehow feel so helpless. She will return at once to her home in Coronado – she starts for Honolulu tomorrow, catching a vessel for the coast on next Tuesday. I packed her trunks this morning and did all I could to help her. All this sorrow coming to her has made me feel decidedly far away from you, and very lonely and homesick. I feel so sorry for this poor family – they all knew her so well and loved her so dearly – they seem to feel her death almost too keenly. Besides being a sister-in-law of Mrs. Aubrey Robinson, and, of course, the daughter-in-law of Mrs. Gay (Mrs. R.'s mother), she was for years in this home as governess for Mrs. Aubrey Robinson when she was a girl. Later she married an older brother [George Gay] – and lived here for years – then on Niihau. Oh! They are all so sad – and there is such a deathly silence throughout this home. If I only could do something. Mr. & Mrs. R. were away yesterday when the wireless came – so I had to receive it of course – and you cannot imagine how very hard it was to tell these two dear old grandmothers. I knew how terribly they would feel – and besides I was afraid as to how they could stand this news – they are both so very frail. They were quite brave, however – and I was thankful for it.

Wednesday we took the children to Mrs. Rice's where she had a children's fancy dress party. Lester went as a sailor boy – and Eleanor as a little Spanish girl. She was so attractive – perfectly lovely, really. Ethel and I had such fun on Monday & Tuesday planning & making her dear costume.

Oh! dear! I have come to love Ethel so – and it has been so delightful to have a girl about my own age in the house – I shall certainly miss her.

I don't suppose that I should have burdened you with all this – but my heart is so full of it that I could write of nothing else. I love you all so dearly – and I'm longing for another letter. Your very loving Hettie

April 15, 1912

You dearest Mother –

Have just given little Ruth her lesson – and she has sped away in her auto, her Japanese nurse beside her. She is making such splendid and rapid progress that I am getting the name of being some kind of a kahuna (witch) [Hawaiian priest connected to the spirit world or an expert skilled in a profession.] I'm terribly proud of her, it is really a pleasure to teach such a child.

Ours is certainly the desolate house – all three men away and poor Ethel on her homeward journey. Sinclair and Mrs. Eric Knudsen went with her to Honolulu – it wasn't best for Mrs. R. to go with her and thus leave the two grandmothers – they are so frail and are feeling so sad just now. But poor Ethel – it seems too dreadful to think of her having that long trip across the water all alone.

Really, my head is so tired that I can scarcely think – it seems that I have had no exercise for days – just been thinking incessantly. Guess I'll have a game of tennis with Eleanor. Aloha nui loa - which, being interpreted, means *much dear love!* Your Hettie

Mrs. Valdemar Knudsen with Ruth Knudsen (Hanner) and "Sandie" Alexandra Knudsen (Moir) at Waiawa, circa 1910. Hettie Belle wrote that her piano student Ruth was a vivid, most interesting child. "Soon she began bringing me her 'compositions' – all about nature." (courtesy of the Kaua'i Historical Society)

CHAPTER TEN
FIREBRANDS AND SUFFRAGETTES

"Kapalawai"

April 18, 1912.

Meine liebe Mutterchen –

A letter from Babe has just delighted my ear – and given me a refreshing laugh – for at the end she sent "much love to her little Hettie Belle." To think that my baby sister, whom I am expecting to go home and cuddle, has grown up enough to call me "little." Woe is me – I can feel the grey hairs sprouting – and the lines deepening in my once rosy cheeks. She enclosed some sweet violets – and I can just imagine what they must mean in Boise – after a long hard winter of ice and snow. To think that I have been enjoying both blossom and fruit – during *all* these past months. I feel kind of selfish.

Yesterday I went to German – the first time in a month. You see going to Hanalei, to Kahana and to Lihue – made me miss three lessons. But I wouldn't have missed the trips – I can easily make up the German. Yesterday I went on horseback – and halfway there I was caught in the tail end of a thunder storm. You can imagine what I looked like when I reached Mrs. Brandt's. This thunderstorm was coming down the valley – and had been so tremendous in the mountains – that a *tremendous* freshet came down the river – overflowing its banks and discoloring the sea for about a mile out from shore. Luckily I missed it – when I crossed the river going to German – I met only the rain – and when I came home late in the afternoon, the freshet had passed, and the waters somewhat subsided. The rainfall is indeed tremendous when it comes. But they have had an unusually dry winter

– no Kona storms, the *heaviest* winter storms – they *count* on them – they need them. They are having a rather serious time on Niihau because of the lack of rain – sheep are dying by the thousands – and they are having to cart water for the natives, even. I do hope that rain will come soon. We hope that yesterday's shower visited Niihau – but do not know.

Sinclair is back from Honolulu – reporting that Ethel is off safely. People were very, very kind to her in Honolulu – did everything possible for her.

Am finishing this letter after Mr. Aaser's call – yes, he came tonight and brought me some more lovely shells – and some new music. Goodness! I wish he would go home to Norway and get married! I feel such a kind of responsibility about him. He is very nice – and ought to marry an awfully fine girl – but *I* wouldn't marry him to save him. We talked about earthquakes, tidal waves, water spouts, thunder storms and all *sorts* of dreadful things tonight. I'm feeling scared.

I'm surely the only one of my kind – who could write a *longer* letter with *less* in it? Anyhow there's *stacks* of love for *everyone*. Your loving Hettie

Freshets or flash floods in Hawai'i can be frighteningly powerful. Water from the rainy tops of the mountains finds its way down the streams and rivers in a torrent. If Hettie Belle had arrived at the peak of the storm, she would have had to turn back. In her memoir, Hettie Belle recalled a terrific rain during one mountain trip, which caused high, rushing water at one of the streams they were to cross. Mr. Robinson saw her dismay and said, "Do not be fearful. Just draw up your legs, give your horse his head, and he will easily swim across." And he did.

Hettie Belle mentioned her trip to Hanalei just briefly in a letter, but she later wrote about it in her memoir. On the northern coast of Kaua'i, where Hanalei is located, there are strong wind updrafts from the cliffs. She wrote:

"The Rices* had a very beautiful Beach home at Hanalei [Hā'ena] — for vacations. We were invited there at times. A great jagged mountain

---

* William Hyde and Mary Waterhouse Rice were prominent figures in the Kaua'i and larger Hawaiian community. He was active in the royal Hawaiian government under King Kahmemeha V and governor of Kaua'i under Queen Liliuokalani.

range ran along the lovely bay. At night — Mr. Rice sometimes had the natives climb these mountains — set fire to light weight pieces of bark and cast them into the air. They would slowly float out over the sea. A spectacular sight!"

William Hyde Rice, Mary Waterhouse Rice, and new mother Emily Rice Sexton (1889-1975) and her baby Lloyd Sexton Jr. (1912-1990). Emily was the youngest of eight Rice children. (Hettie Belle, 1913)

Edward Joesting writes about this firebrand-throwing ceremony. Men climbed a steep trail to the 1,600-foot level of a mountain named Makana. They clung to the near-vertical cliff, carrying shafts on their backs of dried *hau* and *pāpala* wood. After dark, they would light the shafts and throw them into the wind coming off the cliff, where they sailed down to the sea, trailing tails like comets. The downy flower spikes of the *kului* sparkled like fireworks. People watched below from the beach or in canoes. The ceremony was only for very special occasions, often related to the hula school in that area.[42] In recent years, this ceremony has been reenacted, as Hawaiians are bringing back their valued traditions.

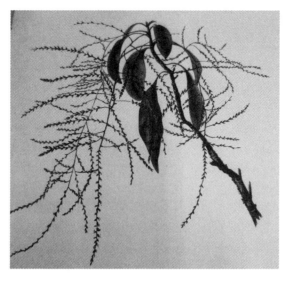

This photo is from Plate 44 in Isabella Sinclair's book *Indigenous Flowers of the Hawaiian Islands*. The painting is titled *Pāpala*. The plant is endemic and endangered, found only in gulches of the Nāpali district on Kaua'i, and used for the ancient torch ceremony on Makana. (Limahuli Garden)

"Kapalawai"

April 22, 1912.

Dearest Mother o' Mine —

If *you only* could be here today — you would see a most wonderful sight. In the front garden is a huge Algiroba [algaroba] tree which is covered by a huge vine. Today that vine is one *mass* of pale yellow blossoms — the most exquisitely beautiful bloom that I have ever seen, I believe. Great swinging arms of the vine — covered with blossom — hang away down nearly touching the ground. The whole vine seems like one huge sunburst. It is indeed a "thing of great beauty"— I wish that it could be a "joy forever"— but Mrs. R. says that it will not last more than a week. I wish that *you* could see it.

It is Monday noon — I am writing while waiting for lunch. We have just come down from Makaweli House where we spent Sunday. It is so delightfully peaceful and quiet up there, you someway feel entirely away from the world. I wish we could live up there for a while — as we did when I first came — you know. I love it. We went up Saturday afternoon — the Grandmothers, Mrs. R. and the maids, went in the auto — Sinclair, the children and I went on horseback. We had a very quiet Sunday

– had a little service in the morning – then read, and slept and took a little walk in the afternoon. When we awoke this morning – we found that there had been a little shower during the night – making everything especially green – and everything smell *so* fresh. It is so restful to have such a day as yesterday.

I haven't heard from Margie for a *long* time – wish that you would send me a letter from her – once in a while. Couldn't you?

It is lunch time now – and there is nothing more of importance to tell you – except that I love you *very*, *very* dearly.

Your very loving Hettie

"Kapalawai"

April 25, 1912.

My Mother, dearest –

My! How I danced up and down when your 28 page letter arrived! You wouldn't believe me if I told you how many times I have read it – so I shall not tell you.

It makes me as jealous as a *cat* – when you tell me that Amy, Pard & Eleanor [friends of Hettie Belle] have all seen you & kissed & hugged you. The *idea*! And here I have to sit patiently in the middle of the ocean. Never mind – soon I'll have you *all* to myself!

Mrs. R. and the two grandmothers are off for an auto ride. They wanted me to go – but I had many letters to write, so refused. Am I not conscientious? If you could see my pigeon-hole stacked *full* of unanswered letters – you would think that it was about time that I was becoming conscientious. Tomorrow Mr. R. & Aylmer return from Niihau – this means fresh crawfish – plover – salt beef – and lots of lickin' good things – but it also means that I will have two weeks business correspondence & checks to write for Mr. R. So it behooves me to write all necessary letters today – of my own. You know I do all of Mr. R.'s secretary work – am a private secretary, in fact. You should see how rapidly I can write on the typewriter now. I write all his checks & do all his booking. This all takes a few of my spare moments, as you can well imagine – but I enjoy it *very* much, it is a pleasure to work for him. This work is not compulsory – but the other governesses have done it – so why shouldn't I? With all that I do – my work is merely play.

Lots of love.

Your loving Hettie

"Kapalawai"

April 28, 1912

Mother, dearest –

Soon I must give the children their bible study – for it is getting late in the afternoon.

Mr. R. & Aylmer returned from Niihau on Friday – bringing us all kinds of goodies to eat. Really if you could *hear* your lovely daughter eating a crawfish, cracking bones etc. you would be sure that she was turning *cannibal!*

Mother, these people are becoming very *persistent* in their oft repeated question, "are you going to stay with us next year?" Now I *must* answer soon – it is only fair to them – and I *must* know on account of booking for passage across the ocean – for travel is *very* heavy during the summer months. And the *main* reason why I must answer soon – is because of the vast difference it will make in *their* plans.

On *only one* condition will they remain here next year – said condition being that the present governess will *also* remain. If I refuse – they will all start for Boston in August. So you see it *is* imperative that they know *at once*. I must say that the children have done remarkable work this year – I am *more* than pleased with the results. I should dearly love to teach them another year – for it has been *most* enjoyable to me – as you well know.

Now this is the proposition – I *have* to teach, anyhow, next year – so why not *here* – where pupils, environment and all, are so congenial and the salary is bigger? It seems almost foolish to give it up.

Now, what do you say? As for me – I should like to go home for a visit this summer – then return here for another year. That seems the wisest thing to me. But *do* tell me what *you* think – and tell me *soon* – for I *must* know? But *don't* tell other people. I don't want them to know anything yet. Love to all. Your Hettie

"Makaweli House"

May 3, 1912.

You very dear Mother –

As you see by the heading – we are again at the mountain home, "Makaweli House." Not for a day, only – this time – but for at least two weeks. In fact we expect to remain here until Mrs. Welcker arrives.

You know how dearly I love this place – and so you will know how very happy I am to be here once more. It was fun coming – you should have seen the luggage. Someone suggested that it looked as if an expedition were about to start out for the south pole. But then we were reminded that people going to the south pole wouldn't carry so much!

The Grandmothers, Mrs. R. & the maids – came up in the auto & carriages – while the children, Sinclair, Aylmer, Mr. R. and I came up on horseback. We came up yesterday afternoon, and before sunset everything was in its place and in running order. They surely have remarkable servants. We had school this morning – and company for luncheon this noon – Mrs. Gay and her friend Mrs. Spaulding. They spent the afternoon – and we had a delightful time. They are both charming, without a doubt. Soon after they left, Lester found a *darling* wee pheasant chick – the weeest thing – and cunningest that you can imagine. We were unable to find its mother – so Sinclair and I have been foraging for food for it – we came back with a choice selection of earthworms, saw bugs & wee centipedes – a collection guaranteed to please the most fastidious pheasant chick. He gobbled them all with amazing rapidity – but he looks kind of sick, now – I fear that he will soon be maki.

I have been awfully provoked at Sinclair for the last couple of days – you see he had a birthday, is now twenty-six – and with his nose in the air, he now insists that I am a *mere infant!* The disgust & disdain in his voice are the things that hurt. Don't you think that he is really unkind?

I loved your letter, Mother dear. I wish that every one of your children could have the experience of going to a strange and new country – that they might feel the *real* joy of receiving one of your letters.

Yes, Mother dear – I do feel more thankful each day for the marvelous beauties that our Bountiful Father has placed about us – and each day do I feel more thankful that he has made it possible for me to see the many wonderful things in these islands. It often makes me feel *very* humble – for I can't understand why all these blessings should come to me – when I am *sure* that many of my girl friends are more worthy of these opportunities that I am now enjoying. But as this good fortune *did* come to me – I am trying to be duly grateful – and striving to make the most of it.

I understand perfectly how you must have held your breath as Mrs. Welcker spoke of doing things such as taking trips – and buying gifts – for really when I first came here and began writing Mr. R.s checks – I would turn cold when he asked me to write check after check for hundreds and even thousands of dollars. I kept thinking, "Is there *no* limit?" And I guess that there is no limit and no end of his money – for month after month I write checks for *thousands* of dollars. I have written such immense amounts on checks that you would scarcely believe me if I told you their size. You know they consider Niihau their *smallest* possession – the main money of course comes from sugar on this island – & other investments. You know of course that *incomes* are taxed – well this year's income tax on Niihau was $75,000.00. You can judge for yourself as to what the income from that *one* island must be. Mr. R. must be a multi-millionaire – I say he must be – but I do not know. For all that he has told me – he hasn't a dollar in the world – for tho' I have been here almost a year – and tho' I am *most* intimate with Mrs. R. & Mr. R. – and tho' we have discussed every possible problem & subject – I have *never* heard *money* mentioned. I have *never* had cause to feel that they had *one cent* more than I had. I have never heard them boast as to property – and had to ask before I found out what property was theirs. But of course, altho' it is never mentioned – there is daily evidence that there is tremendous wealth – for they have *every* luxury – never have to think twice about taking a trip. In fact Mr. R. said the other day – "Alice, if Miss Matthew has to return to California to stay next year – let's take the children and make the trip to Japan with her." And the only possible thing that stood in the way – was where to leave the grandmothers. But as wealthy as they are – it would surely delight *your* heart to see Mrs. R. upholstering an old couch & chairs – turning an old dress inside out and upside down – retrimming an old hat, etc., etc. She *loves* to do such things – as unnecessary as they are – and has been brought up most carefully under old Scotch-English by-laws, therefore she cannot get away from the "saving" idea. And Mother dear – she too has an "*attic.*" I laughed when I saw it. Yes, *you* and Mrs. R. are truly "kindred spirits." But I can tell you more about her when I come home – for I am coming soon. *Hurrah!* For all that I was waiting for – was your decision, as to what you thought it best for me to do. Now that you really feel that it is best for me to remain – that decides it.

The mail must go – and your little Hettie Belle must go to sleep so Goodnight, Mother dear. When shall I begin writing to Boise? Don't go home *too* soon. My *dear* love to *all.*

Your Hettie Belle

In her memoir, Hettie Belle wrote that after her arrival on Kaua'i she was soon asked by Mr. Robinson to prepare his business letters and checks. "I remember my shock when I first wrote a check for $40,000.00 for guano fertilizer! However, such became a routine. I had not learned shorthand or typing — but soon found that 'piano' fingers can learn. The typewriter was in the school house — I prepared letters in triplicate, first taken in long hand."

The Robinson family did not flaunt their wealth, but simply lived their belief in the Bible's promise of plenty. However, Hettie Belle must have been aware that goodness and riches do not go hand-in-hand. She occasionally refers to financial troubles in the Matthew family. A Methodist minister father with a family of twelve children found the budget tight at times. She was happy to be able to help her family back in the States by sending them money.

The society among the European settlers in Hawaii was genial. There was a sense of plenty in the Robinson household. Hettie Belle was impressed by the abundance of the Robinson's resources, yet amazed at the result. They showed neither pretensions nor display of these riches but instead, openness to housing and feeding others in warm hospitality. Isabella Bird noted this attitude a half-century earlier when she visited the islands. She observed plantation owners' pride in knowing how to live rather than in making money, handling social occasions with understated grace. "All this lavishness was placed at the disposal of guests without ceremony," she wrote.[43]

"Makaweli House"
May 6, 1912.

My dearest Mother —

You surely haven't finished reading my last impossible epistle, so I'll have pity and write a wee short one today.

The children have just announced that a mysterious string of fish has arrived at the back door. Mr. & Mrs. R. are nowhere to be found in the house — so putting two & two together, we think that they are down the river fishing. This is a very favorite Robinson pastime — I'm catching it — (and some fish also).

Sad to relate – the wee pheasant that I mentioned in my last letter, died – and there were copious tears spilt over him. Poor wee Lester – he was such an attentive mother – but his wee child died in spite of his numerous efforts.

Love to all – Your Hettie

"Makaweli House"
May 9, 1912.

Dearest Mother –

Lester has just picked a great pan full of delicious mountain peaches – we are going to stew them – and make some little cookies, later on this afternoon. So you see wee children and a governess can sometimes supply the dessert for even a fastidious family. Up here, we have our own wee kitchen, stove and pantry, as you know – and the cooking is *great* fun. Yesterday we made pop-overs just before dinner time – they were *most successful* – *really popped!* And *three* dozen of them were gobbled by this family – before you could say "Jack Robinson." Oh! I tell you – they think we are *terribly* clever! When I come home – you are to teach me to make your brown bread – *then* I'll make something for them that is *worth* eating!

Altho' started yesterday – it is now the 10th – Mrs. Welcker, Miss Andersen and Selwyn are on the ocean now – sailed today. These people are all excitement in anticipation of their visit. We'll surely have a jolly house-full this summer.

Your loving Hettie

"Kapalawai"
May 13, 1912.

Mother dearest –

We came down today from "Makaweli House" and will remain here until after next Sunday. We must be here to welcome Mrs. Welcker and her party on Saturday. Mr. R. and Sinclair are going to Honolulu tomorrow to meet them. We will probably all spend next week at "Makaweli House" again – *then* to Niihau we go and then Home! Yes, Home!! Do you hear? And it's *true*! I'm *really* coming home!

Saturday, last – we all came down on horseback in the morning – spent the day here and returned to "Makaweli House" in the late afternoon. We had more fun going home – Sinclair and I *raced* Mr. *&* Mrs. R. all the way home. It was certainly exciting, to say the least – and stacks of fun to tear up and down hill.

Your loving Hettie

"Kapalawai"

May 15, 1912.

Mother, dearest –

My! How I enjoyed your dear letter, and Margie's fat one and the snap shots! Gertrude seems the same little Gertrude, in the pictures – but John seemed *so* entirely changed – I hardly think that I shall know him when he comes to meet me at the station. I hardly dare *think* of really coming home – for my heart begins to beat *so* hard that it nearly jumps out of my body. I dreamed the other night (all my dreams are about Boise now) that I decided to surprise you people – didn't tell you when I was coming. Well, I reached Boise all right – but I *couldn't* find you people. I went up hill and down hill – and couldn't find you. (I was riding a bicycle, by the way.) Finally I found John – he said, "go on in that direction (pointing) and you'll find 'em." So I went on my way – weeping – but awoke before I found you. Never mind – dreams *always* go by contraries. I'll find you – and Johnnie will come to meet me, probably.

But I must get some beauty sleep – or you'll think that I'm not looking well – when I come home. All I'm waiting for now – is to hear your summer plans. *Love to all!*

Your Hettie

"Kapalawai"

May 15, 1912

[Written to her father]

So my dear Father is a *boy* again – playing baseball with all the other boys! Well, I *am* surprised and delighted! And to think that his *picture* appeared on the sporting page! My! But I am *proud.* I'll certainly have to turn a suffragette or something – to be worthy of such a Father. Did you notice the article that was directly *under* your picture – it amused me vastly. I immediately caught the words "a new movement against corsets"– and wondered *what on earth* my Father was advocating. Ha! Ha!

Your sermon I enjoyed *tremendously!* To think that I am very soon to *hear you!* It is too wonderful to be true. I am intensely interested in this new movement – Men and Religion Forward Movement – I wish that I might hear more about it.

By this time – Mother is again with you, of course – and you are once more a happy family. I think you were awfully good to spare her for so long – it must have been awfully hard and lonesome. But if she is *really* better, as they all say she is – you of course feel more than repaid for any sacrifice on your part. Hope the letter containing the check reached you safely. *Much* love to you, dear Father. Hettie

As the Edwardian Age came to an end, educated women like Hettie Belle were beginning to break out of their traditional roles and sometimes chose to remain unmarried. However, Hettie Belle's letters indicate that she becomes more and more concerned about the fact that she cannot "fall" for any of her suitors. She is determined to have a choice in the matter, and she writes her mother that she seems to attract strange men. She sees herself as different from other young women, preferring older, confident men to those she calls "boys." Apparently she had been courted by men in California and then sought after by men on the island, but she is particular, waiting for that special person. She does not say directly, but she was probably disappointed when she did find someone on Kaua'i and the feeling was not reciprocated. One of her father's letters may have scolded her for discouraging marriage prospects, and she began to call herself a "spinster," "old maid," and "school marm." Still hoping to find that special someone, Hettie Belle doubted that she would be able to fill the expectation of wife and mother, so she half-joked about other plans.

During the same time period, women also began to shed restrictive clothing like corsets that constricted the waist. Hettie Belle reflects this trend, as she loved dressing for tennis or swimming in the "togs" that allowed her more freedom.

When Hettie Belle was in Hawai'i, the suffrage campaign in the U.S. was advancing quickly. In fact, California granted women suffrage to vote in state elections in 1911. Women were parading, forming associations, being jailed, and causing a general ruckus. In 1920, the Nineteenth Amendment became the law of the land.[44]

The Men and Religion Forward Movement, of interest to Hettie's father, gained ground when gentlemen became aware that there were three women church members for every man. The movement's desire was to "restore the requisite masculine element to popular religion."[45] The Men and Religion Forward Movement aimed to bring men and boys into the US churches using the same business methods employed in making a fortune.

"Kapalawai"

May 18, 1912.

My *adorable* Mother –

Of course you know that there is *great* rejoicing in this home today – for they have all arrived safely. Sixteen at the table this morning – seemed natural to me. Besides this family all being home – Mrs. Gay's children are all here – the first time in *years*. One son from California [George], one from Lanai [Charles], and the other from Oahu [Francis]. [The other daughters, Elizabeth Gay Welcker and Alice Gay Robinson were already there.] It was an affecting sight to see the joy of that dear old lady this morning.

Mrs. Welcher and her party had a splendid trip – and she sends love to you. Isn't she dear? Lots of love to all.

Your own Hettie

"Makaweli House"

May 24, 1912.

Mother, dearest –

The men are all out on a cattle drive today – had it been a horse drive, we women folks might have gone along – but the cattle drives do not appeal to us.

We had such a delightful day last Tuesday – we all went to Mrs. Knudsen's for lunch – a beautiful elaborate lunch it was, too – after lunch, we went in autos and on horseback out to the "Barking Sands," that I have described before – and listened to them bark – and they were certainly *yelping* that day. Then we rode to "Waiele," her beach place – and had a glorious swim – after which we feasted on fresh cocoanuts and mangoes. I have ceased to wonder that "Little Black Quibba's" mother got well

– when she had mangoes to eat. They are *unspeakably* delicious and refreshing. We rode home by the early moonlight – it was a delightful day.

You know it seems rather useless to write to you now – for I feel that I am to see you so soon, and talk with you. A postal came from Margie, begging that I come to her this summer instead of next – but I can't – my heart is too Mother-hungry – and family-hungry. I'm just counting the days now.

Your loving Hettie

"Kapalawai"

Hurd's birthday.

Mother dearest –

It's early to bed – for this family tonight – for we must be up at one o'clock in the night, and off in automobiles to the steamer by two o'clock – at eight we land on Niihau. They sail at this unearthly hour because it is less rough – and it is a rough trip at best. I can't tell you how terribly excited I am! You would have howled could you have seen the loads *&* loads of baggage that went off today. But perhaps it was not too much, considering that there are sixteen of us going – besides six Japanese servants and eight or ten native men, and we will stay six weeks, about. I had a great time packing today, for besides packing my steamer trunk for Niihau – I started to pack my big

Dr. Dukes (San Francisco Call, Volume 111, Number 81, 19 February 1912)

trunk for coming home. You see after we come home from Niihau, I have just a day before I start homeward – so I mustn't leave everything for then. I am coming home on the "Korea" leaving Honolulu July 9ᵗʰ *&* landing in S.F. July 15ᵗʰ and shall be with you dear people before the following Sunday! Shall stay just a day or so in Berkeley – just long enough to have my laundry attended to – and to say "hello." It seemed best to wait for the "Korea"– for then I will not be all alone –

Dr. Dukes˚ can take care of me – and besides, some *lovely* people, Dr. *&* Mrs. Putman are going at that time *&* have promised to chaperone me – (as if I'd need it!).

Stacks of people have been here during the afternoon saying "goodbye"– we had an elaborate tea for them – and a walk in the garden afterwards. By the way, during tea – we played the lovely new "Graphanola."[46] It is indeed beautiful and wonderful! She [Mrs. Welcker] brought some *splendid* records with her for it – and we have had continual music since she came.

Dear love to you *all!*
Your loving Hettie Belle

Little Black Quibba by Helen Bannerman tells how a small boy with a blue basket goes hunting for mangoes to bring his sick mother back to life. He meets a selfish elephant and a treacherous snake that finally fight each other and die before Quibba can collect the life-saving mangoes. Aubrey Robinson was particularly fond of mangoes.

The Robinsons bought a graphanola during Hettie Belle's stay. In the 1910s, these early record players became popular among the wealthy, who could afford the fancy new machines.

---

* Dr. Harrison Columbus Dukes worked as physician and surgeon for the Pacific Mail Company. Hettie Belle was fond of Dr. Dukes who befriended her as she traveled back and forth between Honolulu and San Francisco.

Ni'ihau Summer

CHAPTER ELEVEN
THE IDEAL LIFE

Niihau –

June 2, 1912.

My dearest Mother –

Tho' I am a bit farther away from you than when last I wrote – I feel just as close as ever – and even *closer* for the time is always nearing when I shall be with you.

As you see – we are on Niihau – and more than my fondest expectations are realized, it is a beautiful, *beautiful* island, and I am charmed by all that I see and by the novelty of everything.

We had a *glorious* trip over – got up at one o'clock – coffee was ready for those who wished it, then to the wharf we went in autos – reaching the steamer by means of row boats at about two o'clock. It was the most *glorious* night – full moon and as bright as day – the ocean was as smooth as glass. Most of the way over we sat on the Captain's bridge – listening to his funny experiences, Irish stories (and swearing)), and watching the moonlight on the water, and the glorious sunrise when it came –the flying fish and the bright red & white sea birds. We reached Niihau about seven o'clock. It is the *prettiest* island to look at as you approach it – so green & lovely and undulating. You know, they have no wharf – so we were carried from the steamer in row boats, and when they go in as far as possible, you gracefully (not gracefully the *first* time, I fear) climb into the arms of two waiting natives, and are carried ashore. It was a *thrilling* experience for me – I was so excited that I wanted to put an arm around each neck – but as I had to hold my hand bag – and didn't want to be partial to *one* native by giving him my free arm – I discreetly held my hands in my lap, and was carried safely ashore.

Just think of it! We are the *only* white people on this immense island – the rest of the population is made up of about 500 natives, 50,000 sheep, and I know not how many cattle. They say that these natives are the most primitive in all the islands.

We are to live in our bathing suits and riding skirts here. This is the *ideal* life. Yesterday we started in by having a swim & going canoeing & surf boarding – and eating two kinds of shellfish, which we pulled from the rocks. Now the excitement begins – about which I will write later. You can only have *one* letter a week now – for the steamer only comes once a week to this desert island. And isn't it quite extraordinary to hear from a marooned maiden *that* often?

I haven't heard from you since you left Berkeley – but am sure that a letter will come *soon*, now.

Today is Eleanor's Birthday – she is fourteen years old – and proud of it.

The manager's home at Kiekie, Niihau. This island, private property, is used as a big sheep ranch. The population, except for the resident foreman and a few Oriental servants is entirely native Hawaiian.

The family Niʻihau home, "The House," Kiʻekiʻe, first built in 1864, was added to and improved by Aubrey Robinson. (Photo courtesy of the Kauaʻi Museum)

June 6 – For certain good reasons, I haven't joined in the swimming and boating for the last few days – while the other folks have been indulging in such sports, I have been searching the beach for shells, am adding to the collection already given me by Mr. Aaser. This is surely the place for shells – millions and millions of them – the beaches are *covered* by them – and such *beauties!* It is certainly fascinating to gather them. How *you* would enjoy it! One of my earliest recollections is following you *along a beach as you gathered mosses & shells. We all went to the beach yesterday afternoon – on the way home we stopped in an old garden & feasted on mangoes and cocoanuts – delicious!*

Stacks of love to you all! Hettie

The island of Ni'ihau lies across the rough Kaulakahi Channel from Kaua'i, seventeen miles by boat. It is an island shaped like a foot, comprising about 72 square miles.[47] In 1864 the rains came to Ni'ihau, leaving it green and lush. The Sinclair family found it was a large enough parcel of land for their family to grow and to ranch, and there appeared to be enough rain to support a ranch. Further, it was not divided up by many tracts of land claimed by Hawaiians during the Great Mahele (the land distribution of 1850s) but was still almost entirely royal land. They arranged to purchase Ni'ihau from King Kahmehameha IV. The family soon built "The House" at Ki'eki'e near Nonopapa landing and began ranching.

According to Tava and Keale, Ni'ihau, the farthest west of the Hawaiian archipelago, had close ties to Tahiti, the ancients even traveling back and forth by sea in early days. A rich song and story culture flourished. Many people there were noted for their size and strength.[48] Hettie Belle, with her Edwardian viewpoint, thought of them as the "most primitive," meaning that they were least affected by the European/American influence. Even today, the residents of Pu'uwai live the quiet life on this privately owned island away from the more hectic Kaua'i with its tourism and traffic. Pu'uwai is a small village where the Hawaiian language and traditions are still alive.

"The House" was surrounded by plantings of olives, Norfolk pines, citrus, monkey pod, century plant, mesquite, ironwoods, palm, and pandanus. It had been expanded over the years, the family bringing in three pre-cut building additions. It could accommodate a large party of family and friends.

While the men were often busy attending to ranching business, they also joined the guests in croquet games, fishing expeditions, and horseback rides. The young men of the family were accomplished surfers. Guests climbed the rocky coasts, walked the beaches, and explored in canoes. Besides Ki'eki'e, there were other smaller houses on the island for overnight outings, even a grass hut near Keanahaki Bay.

Hettie Belle loved the entourage for this holiday on Ni'ihau and in her 1973 memoir said,

> At the appointed time — the Ship was at our Makaweli landing — and on board we happily and excitedly went — the lovely grandmothers and their Japanese 'amahs'— the cooks, butler, yes — all of us!! In front of the home is an excellent croquet court — and there was always a game after our early dinners. Mr. Robinson was the champion — we never could beat him! One evening we were playing, and Mr. Robinson said, 'Miss Matthew, look over your right shoulder!' For the first time I beheld the vivid, gorgeous Southern Cross!

The topography of Kaua'i, with the central mountains rising over 5,000 feet, causes condensation of the trade winds' moisture, producing hundreds of inches of rainfall. But as the air flows to the leeward side of Kaua'i, the moisture is drastically reduced. By the time the winds reach Ni'ihau, the moisture is almost depleted. Hettie Belle finally truly was on a desert isle. She was fortunate to be able to make the visit at this time, because after 1915, probably due to drought conditions, a period of isolation began on the island. More people from Ni'ihau had to move to Kaua'i for work. Hettie Belle stated that there were 500 people there in 1912, but other sources say approximately 208 were living on Ni'ihau in 1910. Today, due to water shortage and the decrease in productivity of ranching, the Ni'ihau population is even smaller.

The Sinclair/Robinson families did bring some changes to the island of Ni'ihau, particularly by enforcing common nineteenth-century Christian taboos. But the Robinsons' overriding aim appears to have been (and continues to be today) a desire to allow the people living there to preserve their way of life and their language. The Robinsons' resources and time have been invested for many decades in supporting this goal. The pristine waters surrounding the island are a testament to this dedication, as the health of the ocean is tied to the well being of the island's occupants.

House Party, July 6-13, 1908 to Ni'ihau. Mrs. H.P. (Margaret Lindsay) Fayé, was on this house party to Ni'ihau given by the Aubrey Robinsons. Note Captain Gregory of the "Kinau" seated on the ground with Francis Gay. Aubrey Robinson's back is to the camera. Included in group: Alice Robinson, Lily Gay, Margaret Faye, H.P. Faye, 3 Robinson sons Sinclair, Alymer, Selwyn, and Eleanor. Of Captain Gregory, Hettie Belle wrote, "a small, stout man – but loud-voiced and efficient." (courtesy of the Kaua'i Museum)

Niihau –

June 10, 1912.

My dearest Mother –

Since lunch – we have all been playing croquet – Selwyn was victorious, but we all enjoyed it immensely. This morning, immediately after breakfast, we went on a horse drive – and I have already told you how tremendously I enjoy them – this one, however, was especially enjoyable – for we had such a vast stretch to drive in – and so many horses – it was very exciting with none of the horrid part (branding, etc.) for we just drove all the horses into a certain pen – and then separated them – sending some to the mountains, some to this pen, and some to that. There were some dear wee colts today – and we each chose "ours."

Yesterday was Sunday, and one of the most enjoyable Sundays that I can remember. We all went to the native church – and tho' I couldn't understand a word, I was deeply impressed. The minister seemed so in earnest – and the people listened

145

so attentively, nodding their heads at times – and saying to each other "Ai, ai" (yes, yes). The singing was beautiful – they have no organ – but their voices are so rich and powerful & melodious – and you feel that they *mean* what they are singing. I joined in the singing – for I knew the tunes and could read the words from their hymnal – tho' I couldn't understand them. After the service the people all, great and small – shook hands with each of the "white people" in turn – and after Mrs. R. told them that my Father was a minister, they looked at me with a kind of awe. The church is lovely – large, clean & airy – and practically *every* native on the island goes to church every Sunday in the year, both morning and evening. Here you see the results of Christian influence.

You should have seen me swimming, and better still, out in the canoe on Saturday. Oh! it was *great* fun – I enjoyed it *immensely*. I can paddle, some. Must write Mr. R's letters now. Four weeks from tomorrow I start homeward. Love to all – Hettie

Moving cattle off Niʻihau (Hettie Belle, 1912)

The Robinsons' carrier pigeons went to work when communication was necessary between the Robinsons on Kauaʻi and the islanders on Niʻihau. Hettie Belle reminisced in 1973, "Communication between Niihau and Kauai is unusual and interesting and completely satisfactory, apparently. They use carrier pigeons. Interesting to watch the preparation — see them off — and the quick return. In case of real pilikia (trouble) on Niihau — a fire is lighted on a certain point — and help hastens over."

While visiting Niʻihau, Hettie Belle observed how Mr. Robinson handled a local issue. In her 1973 memoir notes she wrote:

If the people of Niihau had any disputes they could not resolve — they brought them to Mr. Robinson, when he was with them. There had been an 'episode'— and the Niihau parents did not know how to handle it. It seems that several of the teenage boys had disappeared, and been gone several days. They had taken with them a very lovely young Niihau girl. So — Mr. Robinson called them all together.

'Is it true,' he said, 'that you all disappeared, and were gone for many days — without permission?' They admitted it.

To the young girl he said, 'Were they unkind to you? Were you mistreated?'

'No,' she said, 'they were all kind to me — it was very nice.' And so — the verdict. Mr. Robinson said that she must choose one of the group — and be married immediately. And so it was.

This story Hettie Belle related to her family is an illustration of the status the Robinsons held as owners of the island. Their ability to make such decisions and have them honored can be likened to the position of aliʻi in the ancient Hawaiian tradition. In this case, Aubrey Robinson acted as chief.

Niihau –

June 21, 1912.

My dearest Father –

The steamer is in, and soon the mail will be here – and I'm hoping for a letter from Boise – and don't think that I shall be disappointed. Only *two* more mails from you people before I leave – so don't send any more mail to the Islands after this reaches you.

Last week was a *glorious* week! We spent it at Kii at the other end of the island. It was one round of fishing, swimming, horse-driving etc. You cannot imagine what a good time we had. The first day that I went fishing, I caught *eleven* fish – *beauties!* Am I not a worthy daughter of a splendid fisherman Father? The fish here are such *gorgeously* brilliant colored fish – and have such strange & beautiful markings – that it is especially fascinating to catch them.

One night we went Kupei [*kupe'e*] hunting — the Kupei is a small delicious shell fish that comes out of the sand and on to the rocks at night — the meat is good and the shells are *beautiful* — especially if you were as fortunate as I was to find a beautiful bright red one. When we went after these kupeis we were a strange looking procession, each armed with a lantern in one hand, and a cup in t'other — trotting along the beach in our bathing suits — stubbing our toes on every other rock — but enjoying it all *immensely* — and coming home tired but happy.

One night we all went crawfishing — that was the exciting time! All the natives (at least about 12) went with us carrying flaming torches. We waded along in the water up to our waists — by the light of the torches we would see the crawfish [spiny lobsters] on the bottom and pounce on them. I caught five and let three go — no, not on purpose — but they wriggled so horribly that I was terrified. You probably heard my shrieks even in Boise — didn't you? We got two sacks full of crawfish — my, but they are delicious when broiled. Wish you could have tasted them.

The mail has come — but no foreign mail — so little Hettie Belle is disappointed. Now I'll have to look forward to next week's mail. A great deal of love to you all. Your loving Hettie.

Preparing to fish at Lihua, Ni'ihau. The Hawaiian men are pounding up crawfish and crab for bait. Hettie is standing next to Mr. Aubrey Robinson in the white blouse on the right. The couple of left are Eric & Cecilia Knudsen.
(Hettie Belle's photos, 1912)

148

One of the traditional Hawaiian tales passed down from one generation to another is set on Ki'i. The beach was a renowned fishing place, but the problem was that supernatural beings, called *akua*, would sneak up and eat the fishermen sleeping on the beach after a long day's work fishing. A brave man finally decided to put an end to this carnage. He built a long house with only one door, carving many *ki'i* (wooden models of people) putting them inside. He made their eyes of *'opihi* (limpet) shells. The akua came as usual. They were tricked, assuming those ki'i inside the house were people sleeping with their eyes open. The akua's teeth got caught in the wooden images, and the brave man closed the door and burned down the house. There was no more trouble fishing on Ni'ihau, and the place is still called Ki'i.[49]

Hettie Belle fishing on Lihua, Ni'ihau (Hettie Belle's photos, 1912)

The kupe'e (an edible marine snail) were tasty little sea creatures that, according to the present day Robinsons, are all gone. They were hunted at night because they hid in daylight. They were used in Japanese cooking. Hettie Belle also recalled that the natives on Niʻihau taught her which sea anemones were edible, cracking the anemones open to show the visitors how to find the sweet, tender parts.

Hettie Belle later expanded on her description of the spiny lobster hunting expedition and wrote in 1973:

> One thing that we would do on Niʻihau was altogether delightful! On a moonlight night, we would put on our bathing suits and tennis shoes. Over our hands would be tied square canvas bags. We would wade in the shallow water, at low tide. The natives would carry flaming torches — and we would learn to see the crawfish lying between the shore rocks. We would learn to grab a crawfish and pop it into an open sack held by a native. Of course they wriggle and fight — throwing back the long rasp. This is why the hand must be protected. When enough have been procured — the natives would roast them over a great fire and we would have a feast!

Kiʻi Landing house July 1908. Hettie Belle wrote, "Last week was a *glorious* week! We spent it a Kii at the other end of the island." (Photo courtesy of the Kauaʻi Museum)

Niihau –

June 27, 1912.

Mother, dearest –

This is the *last* letter that you shall have from me until I mail one from San Francisco with *my own hands*! Maybe you don't see anything wonderful in that – but I do. It is surely *too* wonderful to be really true.

Mr. & Mrs. Robinson & Eleanor have decided to go to Honolulu with me and see me safely off – won't that be lovely? Then I won't have to stay at the hotel alone – and they will see me safely into Dr. Duke's care. They are *more* than good to me – I feel so indebted to them.

Today we finished school for this term, and to celebrate, I made a ponger [*pongee*] traveling dress [pongee was a soft Chinese silk fabric] – which you shall presently see. Tomorrow morning the steamer brings Mrs. Welcker & Miss Gay back from a week in Honolulu, and also, Mr. & Mrs. Eric Knudsen who will spend the remaining week of our stay here with us on Niihau. This means one grand jolly week to end our beautiful stay here. We start for Kauai next Friday, reaching there sometime in the afternoon – then I shall have to do some *hustling* – pack my trunks – on to Honolulu the following afternoon – sailing from Honolulu Tuesday, July 9th.

I *loved* your letter, Mother dear – and the sweet, sweet roses enclosed. You know I have been having an awful fight with myself – during this past year *hundreds* of letters have come to me – all letters that I *love* – from my dear blessed family – and dear friends – of course I cannot carry them all home with me in my trunks. I realize that I *must* destroy them – but every time I get them out to burn them, I begin to read them – and then straight way begin to weep at the thought of burning them.

What *shall* I do? Shall I just dump them *all* in without reading them – and try not to realize what I am doing? Oh! how it *hurts* me to destroy letters!

Oh! I love you all *so, so much*.

Your loving Hettie.

[Mailed from Berkeley, CA
on July 31, 1912]

Mother o' Mine –

At *last* come definite plans. I leave here on the Western Pacific, Thursday morning, August 1st. Am going via Salt Lake City, reaching there Friday afternoon and remaining there until Saturday afternoon – then on to Boise, reaching there at four o'clock Sunday morning. Now *don't* be angry – for I'm not traveling on Sunday, merely reaching Boise on Sunday. I can't arrange it any other way – for I am going home thro' Portland, and I *do* want to see Salt Lake – and I *can't* wait until next week – I want to sit with you in church on Sunday. *Hurrah!*

Now, tomorrow I shall send along my baggage checks – my trunks should reach Boise on Saturday – and you can please have them sent up – so that I can be clean for church.

You will know at what station to meet me. All letters answered in person *soon*.

Your Hettie.

Hettie Belle decided to spend another year as governess with the Robinson family on Kauaʻi. Her decision undoubtedly was influenced by the wishes of the Robinsons themselves to spend another year on Kauaʻi before heading to the East coast for Eleanor and Lester's formal schooling in the Boston area. Her enjoyment of the teaching post, her parents' agreement, and the monetary rewards were other considerations in her decision. Though she still planned to gather a trousseau, her hopes of marriage in the islands faded, and she was willing to get back to her work after a short visit with her family in Boise. Her agreement with the Robinsons allowed travel to see her family during the summer.

Leaving the idyllic Niʻihau life and the district high-society on Kauaʻi, Hettie Belle joined the small-town life of Boise, Idaho for a summer month. It was her first visit to Boise, and she became aware of the struggles faced by a pastor and his family in the society of small-town America. Contrasting with this new awareness of provincial American life, she had become a world traveler, and her confidence took her by train to Berkeley to see family and friends, to Salt Lake City to view the Great Salt Lake, and to The Dalles and Portland, Oregon to visit her married brother and small nephews. She would never again settle for the middle-class restrictions.

During this summer when Hettie Belle returned to backwater Boise, the United States was bustling with change. Suffragettes were parading, and Jim Crow laws in the South were nullifying civil rights gains for African Americans. There was new interest in the southwestern United States as desert states New Mexico and Arizona entered the union. The Republican Party nominated Taft, and dissidents who supported Teddy Roosevelt withdrew, forming the Bull Moose Party. Woodrow Wilson gained advantage as the Democratic Party nominee.

Air travel advanced with cross-channel flights and the first parachute jump from an airplane. Baseball was wildly popular; new stadiums opened for the Tigers in Detroit, and Fenway Park was completed in Boston. A strange new type of jukebox was gaining popularity. "Phonograph parlors," like Internet cafés of today, opened in most major cities. The customer could sit down, pay a nickel, speak into a tube, and order music to be played. The disc jockey, unseen by the patron, was often in the basement under the shop.[50]

Hettie Belle, a young woman aware of all these exciting changes, sat on the vine-covered porch with her mother in Boise, absorbing the comfort of family. After a long talk with her father, she felt rested and loved. With growing confidence, she contemplated another year of adventures on Kaua'i.

SECOND SCHOOL YEAR

Chapter Twelve
Back in the District

Sept. 27, 1912.

Mother, my dearest –

Here I am at Makaweli House once more – and it hardly seems possible – but it seems *terribly* good to get out of trunks and live in closets once more. You may think it strange – but these people seem *awfully* happy to have me with them again – and I am happy to be here. It was good to see the people of the "district" once more – and they said that they were awfully glad to see me again – and that I looked *very* well indeed. That's what my beautiful summer did for me, you see.

Everything seems more beautiful than it ever did before. We began school yesterday morning – and had music lessons in the afternoon – so that everything is in smooth running order once more. Tomorrow I have my first horseback ride – we are all going to the lowlands to spend the day – among other things I am to unpack my belated hat trunk – which was lost someway – and didn't reach "Kapalawai" until today. The trip from Honolulu to Kauai was *unusually* smooth Tuesday evening. For the *first* time, I ate supper on board and *enjoyed* it – suffering no after-effects. Quite a crowd of us came down together and had an awfully jolly time. Mr. Brandt,' Mr. Eric Knudsen, Miss L'Orange – Mr. Eric's sister [-in-law] from Norway – and Hans, her brother from Honolulu – Mr. Francis Gay and Mr. Waterhouse. So you see, I was well taken care of. Mr. Robinson met me at the wharf in the auto – and Mrs. R. and the children were awaiting me at "Kapalawai."

---

* Thorvald Brandt managed the Bishop and Company Bank in Waimea.

Mrs. R. says that mail *must* go – so that long letter must be put off one more mail – but you *shall* have it.

My *dear* love to you all.

Your own Hettie

Makaweli House

Sept. 30, 1912.

Mother dearest –

Here beginneth that long-promised and promised-*long* letter!

I had intended to do a great deal of sewing (finish embroidering my morning dresses & *mark* my underclothes) reading and writing on the "Mongolia"– but I met so many delightful people and had such a gay time that I didn't do any of the things that I expected to do. The six days were all too short – I hated to leave that steamer. We had a most congenial little party, and we had such good times. At table, I sat at Dr. Duke's right hand – he was very good to me – often I went to his room and had long talks with him. At our table were at least *eight* missionaries – most of whom were returning to the foreign field – several of them knew Margie, spoke *beautifully* of her and of her splendid work. Miss Maud L'Orange, a girl of about my age – and a sister of Mrs. Eric Knudsen, of whom you have heard me speak, came on the "Mongolia"– we were together most of the time – she is *so* sweet and refreshing – is just out from Norway & Germany, will probably be here all year visiting her sister – that will make it awfully nice for me. Mrs. Danford, a Honolulu lady – very clever little English lady – called herself our chaperone, and she did her duty – was awfully good to us – and really took care of us. Among others, Mr. Brandt of Kauai was on board, also a most fascinating Scotchman with an accent and a pure white pompadour. Our wee party walked the decks together, played games, swam, joked, ate candy, and had a good time generally. Being a large passenger list, there was something going on all the time that was either interesting or amusing or *both*. The officers were very agreeable and nice – we went in bathing almost every morning with the Captain at about 6:30. He's the youngest Captain in the service, and rather conceited over it. The Chief Engineer took us all thro' the engine rooms – we went 27 ft. under water – it was intensely interesting, but *intensely* hot.

When I got my ticket in S.F., Piggy & Puggy [Hettie's school friends] were with me, and they laughed when the agent gave me his card and told me that if I presented it to the Chief Steward that I would be well taken care of. However, it meant more than I dreamed – It meant that the Steward *couldn't* seem to do enough for me – he sent grape fruit every morning to my room at seven o'clock, served tea for myself and friends every afternoon at four, and the last evening gave me a lovely dinner party for eight of my friends – we had a table to ourselves, all decorated, an elaborate menu and were served an hour later so that we had the dining room to ourselves. Then the last afternoon we had a big "spread" as he called it – and all because I had a card from a friend of his, a Mr. Eins! It made it *awfully* nice.

When I went on board first, I found myself in a room with an elderly woman (a regular Aunt Samanthy) and a frail young woman with a baby two months old – she said that she had to feed the baby every hour during the night which meant a howl from said baby, the lighting of lights, the sterilizing of bottles, the warming of milk on an alchohol stove – and no sleep for a certain little Hettie Belle who was tired to begin with and at any time enjoys her sleep. So I skipped out – got an outside splendid room with a dear frail little old maid who had just discharged two actresses who had been occupying her room with her and smoking and drinking meanwhile. We lived quite peaceably on the whole – she buttoned me, and I hooked her and tried not to shock her. Yes, the trip was lovely – the stay in Honolulu equally so – but that is another chapter. This must go with great love to you all, *all*.

Your loving Hettie

Forgive any mistakes – no time to read over.

Like many American passenger ships, the *Mongolia* was later pressed into duty during WWI. Just three years after Hettie Belle's voyage, the ship was shifted to the Atlantic and equipped with Navy-manned guns. In 1917, her crew fought off a German submarine, the first US engagement in WWI. After that, the USS *Mongolia* became a military transport ship, taking troops to war and then home after the armistice in 1918. Her sister ship was the *SS Manchuria*.[51]

SS Mongolia (courtesy of Department of the Navy)

Makaweli House
Oct. 4, 1912.

My dearest Mother –

With this mail – I am sending beside this letter – a small package – which you are not to open until Oct. 24th! Now mind! There is a wee giftie inside for you – and with it goes Oh! *so much* dear love. Then I am sending the Niihau pictures – I have written explanations on their backs – these you will find in the box, also – you may keep the picture of me – but after you have seen the others as long as you like – kindly return them – I will put them into my album – I haven't duplicates of them.

Do you think me an ungrateful wretch when you realize that I haven't as yet thanked you for your beautiful letter which reached me before I left Berkeley? I wasn't ungrateful tho', Mother dear – I was so, *so* grateful – you cannot imagine how I *love* that letter – I have read it again and again – altho' busy, I had time to read it many, many times before leaving Berkeley – it was such a comfort on the steamer, when each moment was taking me farther and farther from you, and these first few weeks here, when I have had no letters from you – I couldn't have stood it if it hadn't been for that letter, with its assurance that you love me dearly – and that you *are* loving me, thinking of me – and praying for me. I need all the love and all the prayers that such a Mother as you can give – for I'm not what I ought to be – nor as strong as I want to be. So I really *did* appreciate your letter, dear, and thank you *very* much.

Let's see – where did I leave off with my narrative? Was I safely across the ocean and in Honolulu? I didn't have time to read my letter over – as Mrs. R. said suddenly that the mail *must* go – but I think that I finished telling you of the sea trip.

Because there were no boats to Kauai during that time, I had to remain in Honolulu from Friday morning until the following Tuesday afternoon. I anticipated a most stupid time – but was most happily disappointed, for many Kauai friends – Mrs. Knudsen, senior, little Ruth, Mr. Eric Knudsen, Mrs. Danford,* the Sandows and the Gays – besides my steamer friends, were in Honolulu – it was one very *gay* time, and the moments flew – I was loath to leave on Tuesday.

I had some meals and some delightful visits with the Knudsens – and saw them off on Saturday afternoon. Mrs. K., Ruth & Mrs. Danford went to California – Ruth is to attend school there. Mrs. Francis Gay had a gorgeous dinner one evening for 24 people at her valley home, Wailele. The dinner was wonderful – tho' I didn't approve of some features – I was noticeably the *only* woman at the table who neither drank nor smoked – but I was *not a bit* ashamed of that fact – and don't think that people thought any the less of me because of it. After dinner there was dancing – lovely to watch – and Mrs. Gay danced a hula – one of the most beautiful and graceful dances that I have ever seen. It was a gorgeous moonlight night – between dinner and dancing, some of the native band boys went in swimming in the pool, diving from the house verandas – it was very picturesque in the moonlight.

One day we all had lunch at the Moana hotel – with a dip in the surf afterwards. Also some delightful moonlight auto rides. One day we went clear around the island in an auto – a trip that I have longed to take – and which proved more beautiful and marvelous than any one could dream of. It is wonderfully beautiful *all* the way – but such varied scenery – always different and ever more beautiful. We had dinner at Haliiwa [Hale'iwa]. One day we went to a bachelor's beautiful place – it was fascinating to see a bachelor's ideas and ideals carried out, a Scotchman's at that.

---

* Jean Harwood was the wife of William Danford, assistant manager of Kekaha Sugar Company.

It was a most charming place. But I wouldn't have wanted the place if I had had to have taken the bachelor with it – he was too apparently "sot" in his ways – and there were too many pipes, cigars, matches & glasses to suit me.

The "Kinau" left on Tuesday afternoon – and I caught it – and as we sailed off towards Kauai I found my arms full of wonderful American beauty roses – and some new steamer books. I have quite a library now. I believe that I told you of my trip to Kauai – of the things that we have done here since my arrival I shall tell you in my next letter.

Tell Father, Marian & Babe that their dear letters shall soon be answered.

Someone loves you just *heaps* and *heaps* – and that someone is

Your loving Hettie

Makaweli House

Oct. 7, 1912.

Mother, dearest –

You know I have just been thinking how I have been sending your mail all to 1020 State St – and as yet I don't *really* know that you are still there. Of course, Father's telegram said –"Reappointed"– *but* your postal which followed said, "I'm not crowing yet."

Yesterday was a quiet Sunday – we remained up here all day, for church doesn't open until next Sunday. On Saturday morning we all rode down to Kapalawai on horseback – had a lovely day down there – a sea bath in the afternoon, which was *most* refreshing. They complimented me on my swimming – said that I had improved mightily – I was pleased to know that at least I hadn't lost any by lack of practice. In the late afternoon we had a delightful ride up to Makaweli House again. Half way up the road, when it was beginning to get dark – I said that I wished we might meet a ghost or have some excitement. My wish came true in the form of some wild bulls and cattle which we soon met on the road – had it been lighter we might have had a serious time – as it was in the dusk – they were as frightened as we were – and when we rushed at them, they tore down over the bank.

We have had several guests up here lately – Mr. Francis Gay has been up several times – and then last week Mrs. Waterhouse˙ from Koloa – and her father-

---

* Mabel Palmer (Mrs. Waterhouse) was the wife of Albert Herbert Waterhouse,

in-law from Pasadena – spent some days with us. Mr. Waterhouse came down on the "Mongolia" with us – he is very, very funny. He was a schoolmate of Mr. R.'s when they were boys – you should have heard them "remembering" things. We had some nice walks and talks and played dominoes and billiards a good deal. I imported the dominoes – thought it would be good for Lester's mental arithmetic. In California I found everyone playing dominoes – even the businessmen hurry thro' their luncheon. It is an interesting game – and can be scientifically played. We play each evening now – are perfect fiends.

Such evil reports as we do hear, from Japan – I trust that our dear Margie is perfectly safe – and that reports have been exaggerated as were the big earthquake reports. I'm so anxious for more word.

And tell me – have you heard anything from Hurd – I wish that I could get in touch with him. You must forward that mail of mine to him, as soon as you hear from him.

I love to talk to you – I can almost pretend that we are again on the screen porch, together. Happy hours, those!

Your loving Hettie

Although Hettie Belle initially gives no hint to her mother what the "evil reports from Japan" were, it may have been the political upheaval following the death of Emperor Meiji in July 1912. However, Hettie Belle's "evil reports" were probably referring to a natural disaster, such as a recent typhoon, and concerned about the safety of her sister, Margie, in Japan.

Makaweli House
Oct. 11, 1912

My Mother, dearest –

I would like your commendation – and a sound patting on the back – for I have been doing something that should meet with your hearty approval – marking all my clothes – yes, burning the midnight oil, and marking my clothes – and the task is nearly completed – I really feel quite proud of myself. I realize that that should

---

company doctor for Koloa and McBryde Plantations.

have been done *long* ago – don't scold – but praise me now because it really *is* accomplished. Mrs. R. is quite delighted.

Tomorrow we go again to the lowlands (makai) – but we shall not return until Sunday afternoon – for church commences on Sunday – and we want to be there, of course.

Yesterday afternoon and Wednesday afternoon we spent making candy – turned out three beautiful batches – said candy has been duly appreciated by the masculine element of this household – and the feminine, as well, I had better add – for at this moment I have a huge "gob" of taffy in my mouth – that is why I cannot talk to you – but must write instead.

It has rained almost all day today and I glory in the smell of the wet earth, trees and ferns, that comes in at my open door. Don't you love that earthy smell?

Am going to write a wee birthday note to my little Winnie, now – so enough for this time. Wish that I could be with *you* on your birthday – but I shall be with you in spirit – shall think of you and love you *especially* hard, all day long.

Your own loving Hettie Belle

"Makaweli House" –

Oct. 14, 1912

Mother, dearest –

We *didn't* ride down to makai (Kapalawai) as we had planned on Saturday – because Mrs. Robinson's Mother was not feeling well – and Mrs. R. disliked leaving her – so I spent Saturday sewing and reading and had a most satisfactory day.

Sunday morning Mrs. R. and I rode down in the carriage – met Mr. R. and Sinclair at Kapalawai and all went in to church together. During the summer the church has been renovated – and I rejoiced to find the colors in the church *really* matching –and the hangings about the pulpit are now all the same tone of red. Really one can now hear the sermon with some comfort – and one's eyes do not ache all day after leaving church. We had a splendid sermon about the loaves and fishes – and I was hungry before we reached home.

It seemed good to see the people of the "district" once more – and they said that they were awfully glad to see me again – and that I looked very well indeed. That's what my beautiful summer did for me, you see. We had a cosy little dinner for fam, at Kapalawai – and in the late afternoon came up to Makaweli House in the carriage, Sinclair driving – we left Mr. R. behind, as he wanted to attend to some work down there.

Wednesday is my birthday – I approach it with sadness and bitterness of spirit – think of it! Twenty-four, and still a spinster! Not so sad, you say? No – not so sad if one had any prospects – but for an old maid with no prospects whatever – – However, I think that I shall live thro' the disgrace that that day will bring to me, if the mail brings me a letter from my own Mother – that will be my first letter from you since leaving Berkeley. You see I'm talking as if it came – 'cause I do expect it and am praying for it. If it comes, I shall be a very happy girl, and not a lonely girl on that day.

Lots of love – from your girlie.

Makaweli House –
October 16th

Dearest Mother o' Mine –

Lester has just thrown into my lap, a handful of pohas – a delicious, little wild mountain fruit – wish that you could taste them.

I fear me – Mutterchen – that this note and the little gift will not reach you in time for your birthday – and I am so sorry about it. But you see I embroidered this for you – since coming to Kauai – and it was not finished in time to catch the last steamer. You will try to forgive my tardiness, won't you – and remember only that each stitch was sewed in love. You will never know how glad I am that you were born – and how glad I am that you bore me – that I might come to realize the perfect love of the most beautiful Mother that God ever put on this earth. My one prayer is – that I may grow to be at least a little like you. It is a very wonderful thing to have a Mother who is a perfect ideal – an ideal that grows more and more perfect. And a wonderful thing to have a Mother whose influence is just as strong and just as real to the child that is thousands of miles away from her – as to the child that is under the home roof. The only hard thing is – that this child cannot express to her Mother the wonderfully deep love that she feels towards that Mother – the thankfulness that she feels for the innumerable things that that Mother has done for her – and the sorrow that she feels because of her seeming ungratefulness – and because there seems to be no way in which she can repay the tremendous indebtedness that she feels.

But, just because you are my own dear Mother – I shall try to believe that you understand all that I want to tell you. I just *hugged* your letter when it came. One has to be an exile on a desert island to fully appreciate home letters.

Do you know, Mr. Robinson keeps me supplied with stamps – leaves $3.00 worth at a time in my room. I protested – but it was useless – he said that he would feel like a stingy old man, *if* he allowed anyone in his home to buy their own stamps.

Kisses + packs of love. Your Hettie

"Makaweli House"
Oct. 18, 1912.

Mother, dearest –

I guess that we will never doubt your intuitions again – no wonder you didn't want to buy another ton of coal – new bed for the boys etc. etc. But *how* did you know? Father's telegram said "reappointed," and his letter a little later said that the "welcoming back" reception had been planned – so pray *what* has happened that you are now at Vallejo, California? I am the most amazed person that you can imagine – I really can't believe.

Of course you want to hear of my 24th birthday – don't you? The startling news of you people coming to Calif. reached me on that day – also many dear birthday letters and gifts. As usual these people heaped gifts upon me – early in the morning, Lester appeared at my door with a huge bouquet of roses – Mr. & Mrs. R. gave me the most *exquisitely* beautiful white embroidered scarf that I have *ever* seen – then a stunning jabot from Eleanor – weren't they *lovely*?

It is really good to be alive – even if you *are* twenty four and a spinster! Have nearly decided to turn a Suffragette – what think you?

But it's away past sleepy time – so good-night you dear, sweet Mother – do you realize that you are a *great deal* nearer to me now? That makes me happier. Love, love, *love* – and a great deal of it to you all – and don't dare write, until you *really* have the time.

Your own Hettie Belle

An exquisite example of a lace jabot, this one Edwardian c. 1901

(victorianaladylisa. blogspot.com)

Hettie Belle and Lester had a special connection. They really adored each other, and she was often amused by his innocent comments. Though she worried over her lack of marriage prospects, she could laugh over Lester's pronouncements. She wrote:

> I'm still laughing over Lester's last remark — we were all discussing marrying (a dangerous topic, I'll admit). Mrs. R. said that a person owed it to his family to marry well. Wee Lester sighed a long sigh — said he thought he would never marry — that he preferred to 'die a natural death.' Do you wonder that we all screamed? It makes me grin!

"Makaweli House"
Oct. 21, 1912.

Father, dearest —

Your dear letter made me weep — yes weep just lots — so much so that I had to go to dinner with very red eyes — and they all wondered what the matter was. Why did I weep? Why because you busy, tired, upset people had time to think of me away over here on my birthday and send me sweet birthday messages and write me a letter late Sunday night when I know you were tired. Now isn't that enough to cause any normal girl to weep — to know that she is loved as much as that? By the *dearest* people in the world? You will never know how much I really appreciated that letter, Father dear — thank you very, very much for it — and for all the love and good wishes.

I have always trusted implicitly in God's guiding us. I hope that you will have a pleasant home in Vallejo, Father — and that the church is all that you deserve. I have been so happy about you ever since our talk this summer and since I understand your attitude. Your spirit is *so* sweet and so unselfish — and the vast amount of good that you do wherever you go — can *never* be undone — no matter who trys to talk or in any way harm you. I was glad that a brief resume of your work was given in the paper — could any other pastor show such a record for two years work.

May everything go well from the start, Father dear — and may you be happier than ever in your work — and may you be more and more blessed in it — this is the sincere wish of your very loving

Hettie Belle

Judith Marion Burtner

I think of you especially hard each Sunday morning and evening – and pray for you.

Much love to you all.

Chapter Thirteen
The Axident

"Makaweli House"
(Win's birthday) – Oct. 31, 1912.

Mother, dearest –

If my hand trembles a wee bit – you must forgive it – for I have come lately from a tragic scene – and I cannot quite get it out of my mind, as yet. You see this wee boy has a passion for chopping down trees – and his Father is always telling him of certain trees and shrubs that he may cut down – cutting is his pastime – I couldn't count the trees and shrubs, medium and smaller, that he has cut down since we have been up here. Well, when Mr. R. went to Niihau, he left him enough to cut to keep him busy while he was away – one was quite a large tree. He has been hacking away on it for the last two days – using a brand new ax that Mrs. R. purchased for him in the lowlands this week – she burnt his initials on it – and he has been so proud of it – has kept it in his own room – and allowed no one to use it except himself. At luncheon today (Mr. Gay was here), Lester announced that the large tree was almost ready to fall – that two more strokes would bring it – and invited us all out to see it fall – out we went – crash went the tree – and we all applauded. We came back to the house, I went to my writing – and everyone scattered.

Suddenly outside my door, Lester called, "Oh! Miss Matthew *do come quick* – I've cut myself!" He had been back cutting up the tree into short lengths and in some way the ax had slipped. It was his right foot (he was bare-footed) and he had cut the big toe quite badly – the toe next was cut almost off – right through the bone – and just barely hanging by a thread of skin. You can imagine how it was bleeding. The child didn't even whimper or shed a tear. I picked him up in my arms – and carried

169

him along to the back veranda and put him down just outside his bathroom. Then I got Mrs. R. and Mr. Gay and the servants – and there was some lively hustling around, I tell you. The only hope of course – was to get him to a doctor and have it sewed on. So while the horses were hitched to the carriage – we bathed his foot in warm water and carbolic, and carefully tied it up. They have gone some time, now – but of course we have not heard the outcome as yet – a messenger will come up this evening – and then I shall tell you the result of their trip to the doctor. Of course, I hope that they will save it – but I doubt it – it was so nearly gone. We were so thankful that Mr. Gay was here – so that he could go down with Mrs. R. and Lester. You kind of need a man-body at such a time, don't you? (Yes, *other* times as well, of course) Perhaps I shouldn't have told you all about this – but I like to tell you everything – the pains as well as the joys! And that wee child's bravery was really remarkable – you ought to hear of that – never a tear – and he watched the whole performance – giving sage advice, meanwhile.

Oh! I hope it will be alright – altho' a missing toe is not such a frightful disfigurement – but we are better off to have them all, I think. Poor Mrs. R. was pretty white when she went away – she was quite worried – seemed to blame herself for giving him the ax – but of course she wasn't to blame. It was the very first time in my experience that I have ever seen blood—and worked in it, that it hasn't made me sick and faint—possibly I'll be a trained nurse yet. They won't come up tonight, of course—and perhaps not for a couple of days.

This, of course changes my plans of spending the weekend with the Gays – they wanted me to come tomorrow and remain until Monday. I'm sorry to miss it – but they will understand.

Even yet – I haven't heard from any of you dear people from California – but a letter from Jessie said that she had seen Marian and Gertrude – so I expect that at least *some* of you are there. I have been sending *lots* of mail to Vallejo – in care of the 1st M.E. Church – I trust that it will reach you safely – and not go astray.

Mr. Cole [Berkeley neighbor] sent me an "Outlook" with an article on Roosevelt by Lyman Abbott and also a lot of newspaper clippings about his being shot, etc. Wasn't that a frightful thing? How could anyone do such a thing? The Coles are such *staunch* Roosevelt people – they can't allow me to be anything else – and I don't know that I want to be, anyhow. I'm quite an ardent admirer of the big "Bull Moose." I even sent him a telegram of sympathy and love – at least I wanted to.

You shall have a postscript later about wee Lester.

With my dearest love –

Your Betty

You will be relieved, as we were – that a message came from Mrs. R. saying that they had returned from the Hospital – that Lester's two toes had been sewed on (the large toe was more badly cut than we thought) – and that he didn't take any anesthetic – but was very brave – and that he was resting comfortably, his Pussy amusing him. We were so thankful and relieved. By the time you get this – the wee boy will probably be walking about and begging to cut another tree. Axes are dangerous things – guess he'll be forbidden to use one for some time.

I slept in Mrs. R's bed last night – and Eleanor in the next room. It was the most uncanny thing to hear her jabbering away to herself in her sleep. Twice she woke me by calling one of the servants – and I had to speak to her.

But I must hurry –

Very Lovingly –

Your Hettie Belle.

Theodore Roosevelt, campaigning for presidential candidate of the Progressive Party (Bull Moose Party), was shot in Milwaukee, Wisconsin on October 14, 1912. Roosevelt was seeking to win a third term in the White House, and apparently a saloonkeeper felt that was too many years. John Schrank shot Roosevelt at close range. However, the Bull Moose had his glasses case and a speech manuscript bundled over his chest under a heavy coat.

Roosevelt went on to deliver his speech, pulling the bloodied manuscript from his coat. Afterwards, he was treated at the hospital. Roosevelt reportedly said, "You see, it takes more than one bullet to kill a Bull Moose."[52] Although Hettie Belle admired Roosevelt, the Matthew family favored Woodrow Wilson. Wilson, a Democrat, ultimately won the election, largely because Roosevelt's third party had split the Republican vote.

"Kapalawai"

Nov. 4, 1912.

Mother, dearest —

First I must tell you that as far as can be known the wee boy is getting on famously — has slept well, eaten quite well, had no fever or temperature — has seemed normal in every way — and as jolly and comical as ever. Of course we cannot know positively that the toes have healed all right until the doctor takes off the bandages — that will not be done until tomorrow or next day — but we are all praying for the best. The cut was worse than we at first thought — *both* the large toe and the next were cut clear thro' the bone. Lester has been so brave and so dear — the doctor calls him a little *Hero!*

Mr. R. received the news on Niihau early Saturday morning — and came over immediately in the launch. He reached here shortly after noon on Saturday. He was *terribly* worried — he seems to doubt that the toes will heal. Poor Mrs. R. was *so* relieved to have him come — she felt the responsibility *tremendously.* Aylmer was left on Niihau to finish up the business — he'll be rather lonesome, I fear.

Lester has had lots of company and sympathy — people have been awfully nice. He lies in state in his gorgeous lavendar pajamas — and smiles at everyone.

Mr. R. Sinclair, Eleanor and I went to church yesterday — and were *late!* An unheard of thing in this family — and really unpardonable yesterday — as we were all ready and sitting around for an *hour* before church time — gossiping.

Well, I must have at least *one* more game of Flinch with the wee boy. We have exciting games, I tell you.

My *dear* love to you all.

Your loving Hettie

Kauaʻi society enjoyed catching up on all the gossip or *nuhou* (news) of the district. In the Edwardian Era, gossip was like Facebook today, the social networking of the times. A half-century earlier, Isabella Bird wrote about gossip. She stated that gossip was

> the canker of the foreign society on the islands. Its extent and universality are grotesque and amusing to a stranger, but to live in it, and share in it, and learn to enjoy it, would be both lowering and hurtful, and you can hardly be long here without being

drawn into its vortex. By *gossip* I don't mean scandal or malignant misrepresentations, or reports of petty strifes, intrigues, and jealousies, such as are common in all cliques and communities, but *nuhou*, mere tattle, the perpetual talking about people, and the picking to tatters of every item of personal detail, whether gathered from fact or imagination.[53]

Hettie's letters indicate that "spicy" gossip was a normal part of any gathering. It's clear that she and Mrs. Robinson did some gossiping about some of the men who came to court Hettie Belle, poor Mr. Aaser in particular.

To amuse Lester during recovery from his injury, Hettie Belle interested him in Flinch, a lively card game invented in 1901 by A. J. Patterson. The game is based on "Spite and Malice" but requires a special deck. If one player failed to see a play made by the other player, the other yelled out "Flinch!"[54]

"Makaweli House"
Nov. 4, 1912.

Mother dear –

This is merely a post-script – and to let you know the "latest." The doctor came in late this afternoon and removed the dressing. This is the first time that Lester's foot has been touched – and the toes are *all right* – have joined nicely – and look very healthy. And Lester made them wiggle! So we are a *very* thankful household tonight. After we had seen them – Eleanor and I came immediately up here in the auto – so as to be with the old people tonight. They were *so* thankful for the good news that we brought them. They have been *terribly* worried about it. Guess we'll all sleep well tonight now that we *know* that all is well. Of course I had to tell you this – as long as you heard all the rest – and knowing also that you will rejoice with us.

More love –

Your Hettie Belle

Judith Marion Burtner

"Kapalawai"

Nov. 8, 1912.

Mother, dearest –

For a change – Eleanor and I didn't ride up to "Makaweli House" this evening – we will remain down here until Sunday afternoon, I think – then probably next Tuesday we will all move down from the mountains. Aylmer came back from Niihau today bringing tales of most interesting experiences – and a lot of delicious crawfish, akakaiki (small bird) [either the ake'ake or 'akekeke] and fish – he will spend the night at "Makaweli House" and so protect the dear old Grandmothers in our place. Last night Sinclair rode up with us girls – it was night, too – 'cause many things detained us, and we got started late. Before we were a quarter of the way up – it got dark – no moon – but millions of *glorious* stars! It was nice, and we didn't need a chaperone – you needn't worry about that, you know – for we are too proper to even *think* of a chap! However, last night after dinner up there, we did need someone to put us in an insane asylum – we all got silly – unutterably silly! Sinclair said the *craziest* things – and Eleanor and I went into hysterics! However I'm a sensible Christian again today – spent the day playing with poor wee Lester, writing checks and letters for Mr. R. and some of my own. It is very seldom that I have a silly fit – and perhaps silliness is a safety valve, don't you think so?

Tuesday we had a luncheon at Makaweli House – just a family affair, of course – the Knudsens were there – Mr. & Mrs. Eric – and Maud L'Orange and wee Alexandra. They came up on horseback – we had a delightful luncheon, some music – and some nice walks – and heard all the "district" gossip. They are nice people – especially do I love Maud.

Mr. & Mrs. Francis Gay have departed for New York and Paris – for the winter – when saying "goodbye" all around the family, Mr. Gay *almost* kissed me by mistake – talk about narrow escapes – nicht wahr?

Wee Lester is slowly improving – but has reached a bad stage – he is beginning to be *so* tired of everything and everybody – and he is looking pale and worn. It isn't any fun for him or for us, either.

Now I guess that that is all the news that I have to tell you – and now I am going to try to tell you how very much your beautiful letter meant to me. Your new home sounds lovely! Remember one bedroom is for "Bargie" & "Betty" when they happen in in a few months – I'm glad that the home is large and for your sake glad that you have a large basement – now you won't have to build a store room.

Say, don't worry about disposing of your furniture – and *don't* have an auction – for there is no telling but that *I* may need some furniture myself next year. Kindly bear in mind (our trade mark.)

So your car arrived safely – made good time, didn't it? And were many things damaged – and did the 502 wee bottles [of Hettie's shells] arrive safely or did Babe sell them in Boise to a Rags-bottle sacks man? I'm glad to hear that the children are again in school – they are plucky to begin late – but I'll wager that they are doing *splendidly* – I'm proud of them.

I'm *so* anxious to see your home and church – I shall be there the *first* Sunday after I return, remember, and Raymond & I will sing in the choir – a duet, maybe, to celebrate. Won't that be *supergobslapshus?*

Now Mother dear – *don't*, I pray of you – work too hard. Do be careful and *go slow!* How glad I am that you have heard from Hurd! I shall write him *immediately.* Send my mail when you think best – and *if* you think best.

Now, listen! You people don't need to write me for a *month*, unless you have too much time on your hands. 'Cause now I know that you are safe, and in a lovely home – and I can just picture you there and be very happy about you – and what you haven't told me, I can imagine.

Father's postal shall be answered *very* soon, tell him. Love to you all.

    Your Hettie Belle

        "Kapalawai"

        Nov. 15, 1912.

Mother, dearest –

Here we are in the lowlands to *stay* – came down on Thursday, bag and baggage. For the first time in two weeks Eleanor and I had a days schooling on Tuesday up at Makaweli House – Wednesday morning we packed our personal belongings and school books and music – and came down, reaching here about lunch time.

Then Thursday Mr. R. brought the Grandmothers down in the auto – they were pretty tired after the trip, especially Mrs. Gay who has been quite ill, you know, for several weeks. But they seem rested now – and are very glad to be here where they can see the wee boy – and really know to their own satisfaction how things are going. I'm glad to be here – although' you know how dearly I love Makaweli House and its surroundings. But everything is together here – whereas

when we are at Makaweli House – some things are here and some there. We expect
to start school in earnest again on Monday – I'm going to read Lester's lessons to
him – so that he won't get so far behind. He mustn't lose any more time – as he
expects to enter Voltman's [Volkmann] school in Boston next year, you know. His
foot is doing very well – but there is no telling how long he will have to remain in
bed – it has been over two weeks, now. Poor boy! He's getting *awfully* weary.

You are the dearest family that I have ever known or "met in all my travels"–
and I can hardly wait to be with you all again. Have you heard more from Hurd? I
wrote him last mail – Love to you all – you dear people. Yours Betty

Hettie Belle could not help but compare her cozy family life to her
time with the Robinsons. Dinner was a formal affair at the Robinsons'
home. There were always about ten people for dinner, and often many
more because of frequent guests either from the district, Honolulu,
or houseguests from abroad. Dinners were jolly, filled with delightful
conversation and much jesting.

Never, in two years, did Hettie Belle recall seeing any Robinson man
sit at the dinner table without his jacket, even on the warmest evenings.
The grandmothers joined the family at dinnertime. Katzu, the butler,
rang a gong, and two Robinson men would go to the Grandmothers' suite
and escort them to the table. Mrs. Gay sat with a smiling face dressed in
severely plain long black gown with a simple gold pin at her throat and
a plain gold wedding band. Both Grandmothers wore beautiful lace over
their heads that fell to their shoulders. Hettie recalled, "Mrs. Robinson
Sr. wore long black gowns heavy with *passementerie* [trimmings] and
many heavy jewels." With her wit and repartee, she was a match for her
brilliant son who was a great raconteur.

Hettie Belle continued:

> There was always the same routine after dinner. Mrs. Gay said
> 'goodnight' as did the young men who had been in the cane
> fields by 4 AM. Mrs. Robinson, Sr., on her son's arm, proceeded
> to an exquisite little inlaid table in the living room where they
> enjoyed a game of backgammon. When Mr. Robinson out-did
> his Mother, there was a roar of joy.

The children and Hettie Belle would go into the library following dinner. She read aloud to them for a while, which they seemed to love. They read such books as *The Secret Garden.* Although in charge of their education, Hettie Belle was not responsible for the personal care of the children. Their rooms were near their parents' suite. Always, before she said "goodnight," the Robinsons asked Hettie Belle to "please play a bit," which she happily did.

"Kapalawai"
Nov. 18, 1912.

You dearest Mother –

Monday morning – and Eleanor is practicing an hour before we start school – so I'm improving the shining moments – then we shall go out and have school. I had hoped that I could begin today reading Lester's lessons to him, but the Doctor said a very firm "*no*" when I even suggested it – says it may be two or three weeks yet before he can use his brain – he wants all the blood force to go to his foot – and not by any chance to go to his brain. In the meantime the poor wee boy is getting sadly behind – I fear that he won't make Voltman's next year – but his parents declare that they care not about that – if only the toes are saved. Things have looked *most* encouraging the last few days when the doctor has dressed his foot – so *much* splendid new healthy flesh – I think that there is no possibility of his losing his toes now – the doctor is most confident also. But this waiting game is slow and tiresome – most of all, for the wee boy.

Yesterday I went to church with *three* men! Mr. R. Aylmer and Sinclair – Eleanor didn't feel well and backed out at the last moment – so I was the popular young lady.

Saturday evening Aylmer, Sinclair and I went to the Schulze 5th wedding anniversary. There were about fifty there – and it was an altogether delightful affair. Being their wooden wedding – many funny gifts were given them – you should have seen the Knudsens and Danfords come in, laden down with brooms, large and small – a mop – a chopping bowl – spoons etc. She or rather *they*, received many useful as well as funny things -– lovely trays, all shapes and sizes – some beautifully carved

---

* William K. and Mabel B. Schultz were a young European-born couple. He was head *luna* (overseer) for the Hawai'i Sugar Company.

– and salad forks and spoons, and many other practical gifts. We had a lovely buffet supper out on the great lawn under the trees – the moon was shining – and overhead to help out were strung pretty lanterns. We had a jolly table full – the Knudsens (Mr. & Mrs. Eric), Maud L'Orange, Mr. & Mrs. Charles Rice, Mr. Aaser, Dr. Sandow, Sinclair and your humble servant. After and during supper there were many clever toasts and responses – especially did I enjoy the groom's response – he is a German if there ever was one – short and fat – with the roundest, redest, shiniest, happiest face that you ever saw. He looks just like a ripe, red winter apple. He has a decided accent – and I wish you could have heard him and seen his happy expression as he said, "As you know we have been married five years – and I must say that it doesn't seem more than five weeks, our honeymoon is not yet over – I hope that it will continue for five years, and yes, for *twenty five* years after that!" But to appreciate it – you really had to hear *him* say it. We applauded long and loud. Then we sang some German toasts and other songs and then left the tables – some wandering about the garden, but most of us went into the house. Mrs. Truscott sang several solos, also Mrs. Sandow – I accompanied them. Mrs. Truscott sang *magnificently* that evening.

We got home about eleven – but talked for an hour or so with Mr. & Mrs. R. We three young people all agreed that it had been a *delightful* evening – even Aylmer admitted it – so it must have been. You know he is a woman-hater – and especially despises any kind of social event.[55]

Guess we won't be so gay this week, as I know of no invitations so far – but people do certainly go a "pace" even in this country – so ridiculous – when they could be leading the truly "simple life." But human beings are queer things, even if *I* am one – and I cannot altogether understand them.

The cane is all in lovely purple tassel – cutting is beginning – the mill is running – and soon all these lovely fields of green & purple will be bags of sugar – and you'll be buying them. So it goes – each thing blooms and then fades – but not until it has served the purpose for which it was created – and served the world. If you serve you don't die – that good that you have done lives on forever and ever – that is why I resent the saying and hate it, that people so often quote –"the flower that blooms forever dies"– it isn't true – not a bit of it! Do you think it is?

Selwyn is coming home for Christmas – possibly Mrs. Welcker with him – he will only be here *five* days – but that seems worth the two weeks trip to him – and to his family.

Mrs. Hofgaard just sent in a box of cookies to wee Lester –– he was quite delighted – and you know Norwegian cookies *are* lickin' good.

Here is *stacks* of love *to you all.*

Your loving Hettie Belle.

"Kapalawai"

Nov. 21, 1912.

Mother dearest –

We have just been out seeing the men folks depart in peace – Sinclair and Aylmer and Mr. Charles Rice and his brother-in-law Mr. King, together with four of the native men, have gone up Kahana valley on a hunting expedition – will return tomorrow afternoon. I only wish that we were *all* going – you remember, perhaps, that I wrote you of our trip up Kahana last year – and of the horse and cattle drives. We had *such* a glorious time – a kind of time that one cares to repeat. No doubt we all would have gone this time – had it not been for poor wee Lester. He is still in bed – *but* the stitches were all removed yesterday, and the Doctor assures us that he will be walking about in two weeks time. So all is well with him apparently.

I suppose you want to know what these hunters expect to get? Wild goat are plentiful in the cliffs – and there are many quail and pheasant – so they ought to get plenty. Then they will probably fish – as the streams are *full* of mountain trout and black bass. I can just hear Father and the boys smack their lips. I'll remember them as I'm smacking mine tomorrow.

I was writing some checks for Mr. R. yesterday – among them, servants' checks – he counted up – and it may interest you to know that these people have *thirty-two* servants at work every day. This number includes household servants, gardeners, stable men, etc.– of course it has nothing to do with the plantation hands. Aren't we a little city in ourselves? However all these servants *seem* necessary – it does take so many to run a large establishment such as this is. When your home covers an acre – other things must be in proportion. Sometimes I have to smile as I think how I take all this for granted – it doesn't seem different to me, some how – it seems that I have always been accustomed to this. I have never felt in the least strange and out of place, here – not even at first – and of course now, it has become just like a second home.

Mr. Dougherty from Honolulu is coming in this morning to show us his wares – more jewelry – I love to see these people buy it by the *quart* – wonder how much they will get this morning.

The other night, Mr. Milliken came to dinner and spent the evening – I disgraced myself by making two awful breaks [social blunders] during the evening – but he seemed charitable enough to forgive me, as he took me for his partner in billiards – and we were victorious in three different games. I tell you I'm becoming a "shark"!

Was so excited to hear about the 3 to 3 score of the big California - Stanford game – altho' I haven't had the accounts to read as yet – I'm sure it must have been a *terribly* exciting game – only wish that I might have seen it. Am crazy to have Raymond or someone tell me about it. Perhaps I'll have a letter soon – as he owes me one. Love to all. Hettie

Hettie Belle continued to maintain an interest in what was going on back at home in the States, yet during her second school year on Kaua'i, she felt at home on the island with the Robinson family. Likewise, the Robinsons began to adopt some American customs. They had not celebrated Thanksgiving until Hettie Belle's first year on Kaua'i, but by 1912 the family planned to celebrate without any prompting from their American governess. The American influences on Hawaiian customs were becoming acceptable.

The Robinsons, being of British origin, were undoubtedly more comfortable with the European cultural influences on the islands. Many of their associates and employees were of Scottish descent, and several of their friends were Norwegian. In addition, the manager of Gay and Robinson, Inc., the local doctor, the foreman at Ni'ihau, and the Honolulu agent were all British.

During the nineteenth century, a heated rivalry had developed over trade in the Pacific. The British did not want to concede Hawai'i to the United States. American traders began to assume a dominant role in the 1820s. The Hawaiian monarchy was caught in the middle of this power dispute, trying to balance competing interests for their own kingdom's benefit.

180

In 1837 Davida Malo* made this analogy: "If a big wave comes in, large and unfamiliar fishes will come from the dark ocean, and when they see the small fishes of the shallows they will eat them up."[56]

There is no information about how the Robinsons viewed these political changes, but it is known that in 1874 Francis Sinclair became a citizen of the Hawaiian Kingdom. (Some of the businessmen who overthrew the kingdom also held Hawaiian citizenship.) Aubrey's generation that grew up on Ni'ihau were thoroughly "Hawaiianised," as Isabella Byrd said. They spoke the language, were natural cowboys, and could surf like Hawaiian royalty.

"Kapalawai"

Nov. 25, 1912.

Mother, dearest –

Mr. Rice just returned from California and he brought us a basket of delicious big bright red apples! And they tasted and smelled so like California that tears came to my eyes as I ate them. They were "Spitzenberg" or whatever you call them – anyhow Father used to go down to old brother Salzberger and order a box – and we used to have them on Thanksgiving Day. Which reminds me that next Thursday is Thanksgiving – and I think that this household will celebrate with a vengence this year – so thankful we all are about dear wee Lester. Last night they carried him into the living room so that he could be with us during hymns and worship – it sounded so good to hear his voice join in once more in the singing. Today the doctor dressed his foot – and it has nearly entirely healed – the deep cut is filled with new flesh – and the skin has almost entirely grown over. Isn't that *splendid*?

Yesterday morning we went to church as usual – Mrs. R. going with us for the first time in many weeks. Aylmer, Eleanor and I went, also. The sermon was rather good – but I enjoyed it more the first time that he gave it. The jist of it was – that you cannot measure the *truly great* things of this life with a yardstick. Good thought.

Saturday morning I had a great race – on the typewriter. Sinclair was supposed to have written a letter in the early morning – but failed to come in from the plantation even to breakfast – so after breakfast I took this seven page list of seeds etc. and type-

---

* Davida Malo was a leading Native Hawaiian historian.

wrote it. The mail closes before nine – and so I had to scurry – for it was a difficult letter to write. Every word was an unusual one – latin or otherwise. But I finished in grand style, and it caught the steamer!

Friday evening the hunters returned – tired but happy – they got seven goat and four pig.

I must tell you something – you must get out your coral bracelet – it is the very latest thing – all Mr. Daugherty's bracelets were the same style – jewels or coral, set in gold or platinum and linked together as yours is – so now is the time for you to wear it. I must tell you of a bracelet that these people nearly took – a sweet platinum bracelet, with diamonds set in – and a wee watch. *Such* a pretty thing – we all admired it so – Mr. R. asked Mrs. R. if she wouldn't like it – she thought sometime about it – and then refused it – it was only $450.00 but that wasn't the cause of her refusal – she merely liked something else more – he got it – and I think it was twice the price. Can you imagine it? But I don't envy them in the least. I just feel happy for them that they are so fortunate – and happy that they know *how* to use their money – so that it brings happiness to so many – and apparently no misery and worry to them.

Oh! Mither, Mither – I loved your letter so – one letter from you – lasts me a long, long time – and makes me so wonderfully happy. You will probably laugh and call me foolish when you hear that I very often sleep with your letters under my pillow – right next my head – where I can reach out and touch them. That is what I get for being a sentimental, romantic girlie, but I'm not sorry, for my foolishness – *if* it is such – brings me much happiness.

Here is a great deal of my love – enough for *each* one of you – especially my dear Mother and Father.

Your loving Hettie.
My latest nickname is Cynthia – do you approve? (I have a *new* lover)

Hettie Belle never revealed in her letters the name of the man who called her Cynthia, nor did she divulge who the man was that she hoped to marry. In some ways, she is outspoken, but in true matters of the heart, she only hints at possibilities or jokes as if unimportant, leaving us, the readers, wondering.

"Kapalawai"
Nov. 29, 1912.

Mother dearest –

Such a *gay* day as this one has been! Mrs. Charles Rice and her two small daughters came from Lihue in time for luncheon. You know I *adore* her – and enjoy every moment that she is here.

Last evening Mr. R. and Aylmer went to Niihau – will be gone a week – and hope that no "axident" will call them home this time. Today the doctor peeled yards and yards of skin from Lester's foot – and behold! He has two lovely new pink toes – and a respectable white clean foot. Also, Lester hobbled about four steps with the doctor's aid and support. His crutches came today – and soon he'll be using them. Making splendid progress, isn't he? He was pleased to learn that you felt sorry about his "axident." He had a *grand time* today with the Rice, Danford & Knudsen children.

You must really forgive this abominable letter – I promise a *real* one next mail. *So much* love to you all.

Your Hettie

"Kapalawai"
Dec. 2, 1912.

My dear, *dear* Mother –

Eleanor and I had almost finished our second set of tennis this afternoon – when suddenly the rain poured down in sheets – and we fled to the house, I can assure you. They say that this afternoon's rain is probably the beginning of a *real* "Kona" storm – and I am hoping that that is true – you know I have been longing to see a *real* "Kona"– and was cheated out of that pleasure last year – I *must* see one this year.

You should see wee Lester, walking about on his crutches! He is making tremendous progress these days – soon will be his normal self, I think. And he is happier than he has been, for the last month – so are we!

Saturday Maud L'Orange rode in on horseback. I love Maud so – (even tho' she *did* cut me out with Mr. Aaser – yes, she now holds his heart and receives his wee bottles of attention, in the form of shells) but I love her *dearly* all the same. She is the only girl of my age here that I can say that about – most of the others are anything but lovable.

Aren't men the strangest "critters"! I *can't* understand them – the older I grow the more I marvel at their queer ways. And I have been put in this world, apparently, to experience strange experiences – you shall hear the strangest and most romantic of them *all* when I can talk to you. In the meantime you needn't worry, however, for nothing will ever come of it – save a little more worry for me perhaps. But *why* do they all come to me, so many of them – and why doesn't someone come that I *can* love? If you can answer these questions, pray do – but I fear they must remain unanswered. You did a funny thing when you made me – someway I seem sort of different from other people. Anyhow you gave me a tremendous amount of love – that's why I can love you *all so* hard!

Your Hettie.

Hettie Belle was disappointed when she could not begin Lester's lessons during his recuperation. She learned that the Robinsons and their doctor honored the old Scottish belief that rest and careful feeding would promote healing. Another accident had occurred back in New Zealand with the Sinclair family ancestors. Anne (Mrs. Valdemar Knudsen) had been burned playing with gunpowder. Her mother Eliza Sinclair was certain that she had been healed by quiet nursing, by "rest and careful feeding."[57] Similarly, Mr. and Mrs. Robinson gave Lester plenty of time and attention for his recovery.

A Kona storm is an impressive sight. These leeward storms are low-pressure systems developing in the subtropics high overhead and dropping toward the ocean, bringing heavy rain.[58] During the winter months, this southwest wind may come to Kaua'i, creating enormous storm waves and swells. This is called a Kona system, bringing crucial moisture to the southwestern part of Kaua'i and to Ni'ihau. Hettie Belle never got her dream of seeing a Kona storm.

Chapter Fourteen
Christmas in Waimea

"Kapalawai"

Dec. 6, 1912.

Dearest Mother o' Mine –

Mr. R. and Aylmer returned from Niihau this noon – and it's good to have them back – they leave a great hole. They brought the usual delicious supply of crawfish and birds – adding delicious grape fruit and wild duck, this time.

You will be pleased (?) to learn that Mr. Aaser has not forgotten me – for he called last evening and was dearer, sweeter and gentler than ever. However he is gaining assurance – he doesn't "tiptoe" any more – but puts his whole foot down – and sometimes even makes a sound! We talked about accidents, last evening – and when things grew too red and bloody – we changed the subject to billiards. For some unearthly reason – Sinclair and I began to act ridiculously – and soon became almost hysterical – altogether I tell you we had a beautifully hilarious evening. Mr. Aaser has issued cards for a big ball in two weeks – and declares that he will not accept my regrets – that I *must* come. Really, he's an *awfully* dear man.

We had *lots* of rain during the early part of the week, especially in the mountains. So much so that there was a tremendous freshet in the Waimea River Tuesday afternoon – we went down in the auto to see it – stopped on the bridge and watched it. My! It was swift and fierce – fairly *boiling!* And carrying down great trunks of trees and boulders *&* parts of the bank. I had never seen such a sight before in my life. It was too dark, unfortunately, to take any pictures. They might have been interesting.

You must forgive and excuse me for the nonce – as I am sadly in need of some beauty sleep – so goodnight!

My dear love to you all.

Your Hettie Belle.

"Kapalawai"

Dec. 13, 1912.

My own dearest Mother –

Today Mrs. R., Lester and I went into Waimea – and all but bought out the store – then we went into the city of Waimea Bank – and ran into a whole crowd of men from Lihue – Mr. Charles Rice* etc. This I didn't appreciate – as I had on an old hat – and a crushed dress. Moral – always dress up before going into the city of Waimea – you never know whom you may meet.

Tuesday afternoon I scooted up in the auto and called for Miss Bannom (Mrs. Schultze's sister) and brought her down here to play tennis with me. I need practise, you know – and she is a *splendid* player. We had three lively sets – then stopped for ice-tea – after which Sinclair and Aylmer came out – and we had two more sets – Sinclair and I were victorious in the first & Aylmer & Ethel Bannom in the second set. Don't be surprised if your daughter is a tennis champion, a second Hazel Hotchkiss yet.

This may be in time to say Merry Christmas again – and send a *heap* more Christmas love to *each* one of you.

Your loving Hettie.

Tennis on grass courts was very popular for Kaua'i families at that time. There were courts at the Fayés, Knudsens, and Gays, as well as at their mountain houses. Hettie Belle relished her growing abilities in sport: horseback riding, swimming, rowing, fishing, and especially tennis. She admired Hazel Hotchkiss (1886 to 1974), who dominated women's tennis before World War I, winning the US Championships in 1909, 1910, and 1911.[59] Hettie may have felt a special affinity for

---

* Charles Rice of Līhu'e was a member of the Territorial Legislature. He was a powerful figure in the political life of Kaua'i.

the tennis star because she was also from Berkeley, graduating from the University of California in 1911.

Hettie Belle refers facetiously to the busy metropolis of Waimea. Though small compared to San Francisco, California's largest city, it was a bustling town on Kaua'i during its boom period which lasted from 1890 to 1927.[60] There were several stores and churches, small hotels, restaurants, mills for rice and sugar, stables, a lumberyard and a dairy, a courthouse, jail, post office, and schools. A railroad brought agricultural products from the fields to the port.

Hettie and the Robinsons probably traded at C. B. Hofgaard* store, the main mercantile establishment at that time. Today the Big Save/ Times Market sits at that location. Another large store in the area at that time was the Makaweli Store.

Hettie Belle never mentions the numerous Chinese and Japanese merchants. The Fah Inn Building was a Chinese restaurant and herbal store. The Wing Sing Kee was a gathering place for the working classes. The Ako Store was situated where the Wrangler's Steakhouse is today.

Hettie had an account at the Bishop Bank & Company, the first bank on Kaua'i. The Kawano Inn, perched high on stilts to guard against flooding, was located on the corner of Kaumuali'i Highway and Ala Wai Road. Waimea Stables, owned by Mr. Hofgaard, was behind the present day bank.[61] An Ice and Soda Plant was built in 1912.

In *The Garden Island*, Waimea Stables advertised a three-hour trip from Lihu'e to Kekaha on their "Automobile State-Line."[62] Visitors to the island were also able to arrange for transportation there by carriage or horseback to go exploring in the wilderness of the canyons or ride to the Barking Sands. In 1913, *The Garden Island* included in each issue Tourist Attractions, "Some Descriptive Pointers." These included the Waimea Canyon, accessible by horseback; Olokele Ditch, by carriage; the Russian Fort; Hanapepe Falls or "Manawai'opuna." Travel there, to the head of the Hanapepe Canyon, was halfway by carriage and then by easy horseback trail.

---

* Christopher Blom Hofgaard was a prominent citizen of Waimea, member of many organizations and owner of the store.

First tennis court on Niʻihau, probably at Kiekie
(Courtesy of the Kauaʻi Museum)

The Garden Island page with an advertisement for Hofgaard store. The newspaper was established in 1904 and priced at $2.50 per year. This ad was placed in the December 2012 issue, Vol. 8 No. 50.

"Kapalawai"

Dec. 16, 1912.

Mother dearest –

Sinclair and I just beat Mrs. R. and Eleanor at billiards – and feel justly proud of ourselves – as Mrs. R. is the best player in this house – and one of the cleverest in the "district."

Mrs. Brandt came over – and we had three sets of good *strenuous* tennis – we were both red in the face when the games were pau. Then after she left – Lester and I had a set – so you see I don't lack exercise these days – and Oh! Such an enthusiast as I am becoming! In fact – so much so – that I was out early this morning practicing my serve – It's going to be a *beauty* some day – is quite deadly at times even now. Tomorrow we are going to have tennis day again – about twenty of the elite are coming in. And I play now, you know.

Yesterday we had a full car going to church – and filled two pews after we got there. Mr. & Mrs. R. Aylmer, Sinclair, Eleanor and I, all went.

In the afternoon, this was a dead house – we all slept – about 5:30 coming to life and all going for a refreshing walk in the garden. Why were we all so sleepy? Because the night before – we young people Aylmer Sinclair & I went to a dance & "At Home" at the Hansens" – and didn't get home until midnight – the older people staid awake awaiting our return – for of course we always go in and tell them all about everything, and get unhooked before retiring. There was lots to tell about, too – 'cause it was a *most* delightful evening – about eighty people there – good music, dancing, eating – and plenty of nice people to gossip with. We had an *awfully* good time.

My *dear* love to you all – *You* and dear Father, *especially!*
Your own Hettie.

Friday evening –
Dec. 20, 1912

Mother dearest –

Mr. & Mrs. R. and Sinclair went clear around the island calling this afternoon –had luncheon at the Rices in Lihue on the way – then they staid to dinner at the Rices tonight – have not returned as yet. We expect them any moment. It is a *glorious* moonlight night and I envy them the ride. Mrs. R. had a stunning lavendar gown come from the coast recently – and she wanted a new hat to go with it – so she wrote to Honolulu for some – a *whole* box full came down on approval – among them a *stunning* big black straw and chiffon affair – with

---

* Gustav Henry W. and Helen Hansen lived in Kekaha. He was a timekeeper in the sugar industry.

bunches of wee pink roses & some pink ribbon on it – of course I tried on all the hats, as did Mrs. Rice who was here at the time. They all remarked that this big black one was especially becoming to me – but I had plenty hats as you know – however the box of hats has been returned – and here I find the stunning black one on my closet shelf. Could Mrs. R. *possibly* be more lovely? Answer me. I'm trying not to become spoiled. But she seems to be trying her best to spoil me.

Now I must write some postals – does this come in time to say "Happy New Year" to you all! I love you all so dearly. And thank you again for your *beautiful* letters! Your Hettie.

"Kapalawai"

Dec. 23, 1912.

Mother, dearest –

This morning I went into the little city of Waimea to do some last shopping – ribbon, cards, etc.– and even it was bustling with importance. Christmas is really coming – only two days off now.

Christmas eve I am invited to a tree and dinner at the Danford's,* out at Mana. Of course I am going – it will be stacks of fun – and I am to remain all night out there. Then early Christmas morning comes Mr. Francis Gay and Selwyn R. from California – also Aylmer and Sinclair, who went to Honolulu to meet them. Our celebration here comes at noon on Christmas day – we will have our gifts – and then a big dinner – about twenty guests. Mrs. R. felt that she didn't care to have a tree and large festivities this year on account of Mrs. Gay's death this year – so we will have a quieter affair than last year. However, I'm sure it will be very lovely.

Saturday the boys went to Honolulu – and soon after I packed my suit-case – for you must know that I spent the week-end with the Eric Knudsens. Went out in time for dinner.

Saturday evening – then we went to a dance at Waimea hall given by Messrs. Aaser, Oliver & Bailey – three fascinating and popular young bachelors of the "district." It was a huge success – the hall was lovely, music dreamy & rhythmical and the supper lickin' good – and I had a *most* interesting partner for the entire evening

---

* William Danford was assistant manager at Kekaha Sugar Company.

(a charming Mrs. Lindsay* from Honolulu – who was a wall-flower like myself – only a prettier one) and several quite interesting men condescended to sit out several dances with me.

Today Mr. Aaser was to be picked up on our way to church – but instead he walked from his home clear out to our (Knudsen's) home and rode in the entire way with us. After saying "good morning", and asking carefully after my health – he handed me a wee bottle with *one* tiny pink shell in it – "the rarest shell that he has ever found"– he assured me. He is still faithful, tried and true, you see. He quite quivered with delight, poor man, when I allowed him to hold the edge of my hat in the auto, where I was trying to put on my gloves, and the wind was blowing hard. And when a fine mist was blowing, he covered me carefully with a great rug. And I forgot to tell you that he honored me with the *supper* dance – at his dance. Don't worry – he won't propose – and if he does I won't hear him – for he speaks so softly and low that I can scarcely understand him – and at times ask him to repeat a sentence three or four times. This is indeed embarrassing when it turns out to be a compliment.

Loads of love to you all.

Your loving Hettie

"Kapalawai"

Dec. 28, 1912.

Mother dearest –

Mrs. Rice and her two wee girlies are spending a few days with us – it is always so delightful to have them here. We have been having *such* fun. Last night after dinner we sang around the piano and the children all did stunts, playing etc.– then about nine o'clock we decided that we would go out to Knudsens'. So Mrs. Rice, Mrs. R. Selwyn, Aylmer, Sinclair and I – all piled into the auto and away we went on a "joy" ride. It was a gorgeous moonlit night – and the air was so fresh and cool. We reached the Knudsens about 9:30 and stayed an hour or so – just cutting up and rough-housing. They danced some charming Norwegian and German dances for us – Maud and Mr. Aaser (who had been there for dinner) Cecilia and Eric Knudsen and Miss Day. The funny part came when they tried to teach us! You should

---

* Mrs. Lindsay was the wife of the Attorney General of the Territory.

have seen Selwyn's graceful high kicks. Then home we came thro' the moonlight, dropping Mr. Aaser (gently) at his gate on the way home. It was heaps of fun.

And now I come to *Christmas* and my prolonged celebration of it. Let me inform you that I had *three* Christmas dinners – and *two* Christmas trees! You see Mrs. Danford invited me away out to her home at Mana Christmas Eve. I went out in the afternoon, bag and baggage – for I was to remain over night at the Danfords'. She had a huge Christmas dinner – all the Knudsens and Messrs. Milliken, Aaser, Hime & Broadie were there. We had such a jolly time at table – after which we had the lovely Christmas tree. On that tree old Santa gave me a lovely silver picture frame & a dear silk sewing bag. It was really "Merry Christmas" morning before the guest departed, and we got to bed. And as we peacefully slept – the rain poured down and the next morning the ungraded road from Mana into Kekaha was too muddy for our auto – so Mr. Danford took me in in their carriage. They nearly had to send a handcar or a train out thro' the cane fields for me. We could just barely get in with the carriage – awfully hard pulling for the horse – Mr. Danford and I are neither of us very light, which reminds me of what an uncomfortably tight fit we were in the carriage.

When I reached home I found a *very* happy family here – Selwyn & Mr. Francis Gay had arrived from the coast – & Aylmer & Sinclair had returned from Honolulu with them.

Then I tell you we bustled around – decorating the rooms & table – and assorting the huge Christmas mail that arrived Christmas morning – (nice of it, wasn't it?) Besides our huge family – we had Mr. & Mrs. Danford, Mr. & Mrs. Brandt, & Dr. & Mrs. Sandow for Christmas dinner at noon (my *second* dinner) and *such* a good time we had. After dinner we had our gifts on the lanai – the opening of them & exclaiming over them took the greater part of the afternoon – then our guests departed, & we young people scurried into our evening clothes and out we went to Knudsens to a Christmas dinner for 30 young people – followed by a Christmas tree. It was a *lovely* dinner – and altogether a most delightful affair – on that tree, I received a lovely little ribbon case from Maud – embroidered hankies from Mr. & Mrs. Eric – and a huge box of candy from Mr. Aaser. They danced during the evening – and had music in between dances – I played – and Miss Day sang, also Miss Dean. It was a gay evening I tell you – so *much* fun – but I haven't been able to eat a square meal since – as you can well understand no doubt.

That night Mr. Aaser sat out several dances with me – and among our brilliant conversation, listen to this sweet thought –"he doesn't like the idea *one bit* of my leaving the Islands for good"– I changed the subject.

Heaps of love to you all!

Your own Betty.

"Kapalawai"

Dec. 30, 1912.

Father, dearest –

This afternoon Mrs. R. and I made *seven* calls – almost New Year calls – and it reminded me of how you and dear Mother used to make New Year's calls. Is it still a custom with you – this New Year calling?

Yesterday was Christmas Sunday at church – with last year's Christmas sermon, not even freshly trimmed, or disguised with holly berries. But the church was decorated prettily – and I sang my head nearly off in the Christmas hymns – and thought of you all at church.

Father, dear, I want you to know how truly I thank you for your beautiful Christmas greeting to me. No gift that you could have sent could possibly have made me any happier – it is the *love* that really counts – and your love is so evident. *Thank you!*

I could have shouted and jumped for joy along with Little Black Quibba, when I read that you had traded 2009 Lincoln [house] for ranch land. How *perfectly fine!!!* I trust that the transaction has been completed ere this. This is just the sort of trade that you should have made, I felt – and sounds as if it must be quite satisfactory.

So here's to the "wee bit Ranchie"– the cow – the pig – the chickens – horse & phaeton – auto & airship – orchard & nut trees – books & papers –& do "have a pair of bees – so that we may have honey when we please." And do have it all soon – so that I'll have some incentive to get ..... but I can't finish that awful sentence. You can imagine it.

Heaps of love to you. Hettie

CHAPTER FIFTEEN
GOOSE GIRL

"Kapalawai"

Jan. 3, 1913.

My dearest Mother –

The Von Holt girls are visiting us now – Mrs. Von Holt is a cousin of Mrs. R's – a daughter of Mrs. Valdemar Knudsen. They are lovely girls – and it is such a pleasure to have them here. Mary is about my age – and Hilda is seventeen.

Wednesday, New Year's day – we had a *grand* time. Soon after breakfast we all went in the auto away around the island, to Kapaa, where the Spauldings' were holding a "gymekana" – a day of equestrian sports, you know. Men & women both, entered – many of whom we knew – and the races of all kinds were *most* fascinating. They had potato, obstacle, tilting, range, hurdle, pony post, nosegay, lasooing, and fancy dress & relay races – all on horseback – and you cannot imagine how exciting & fascinating it all was. Sinclair and Selwyn entered – and Sinclair won *three* blue ribbons – was first in the hurdles, lasooing & fancy dress races – and Selwyn had two blue ribbons & one red – we were *so* proud of them. We had luncheon on tables, altogether – and a delicious one it was – we all put our eatables together. Towards the end of the performance – they insisted on the young ladies who had not ridden in the races, to enter the "driving geese" contest. Of course I entered – but my stupid goose *wouldn't* go – tho' I whipped him until I was ashamed of myself.

---

* Colonel Zephaniah Swift Spalding lived with his wife Wilhelmina in Keālia in the amazing, expansive Valley House. Their name has two different spellings in historical records: Spalding and Spaulding.

Yes, I'm the original "Goose Girl". It was a *jolly* day! And the ride going and coming was *perfect*.

New Year's eve – we had a grand celebration here – twenty four to our dinner party – and a hilarious time we had – while alternately a native men's band played, & women's band sang. After dinner we had fire works – such brilliant ones – and so *many* in the front yard. Our guests departed at about eleven – then we stayed up until midnight, and fondly embraced each other (at least Mrs. R. and I did) and wished each other all good wishes. New Year's morn very early, the native bands played in distance and then right by the house – and it was even more lovely than last year. Dear loves, from your *Hettie*

The Garden Island, Tuesday, Vol. 9 NO. 1, January 7, 1913

> The Spaldings were responsible for a unique entertainment on New Year's Day at the Kapa'a race track. They gave what is known as a 'gymkana,' being a program including most every mode of athletics and then some. The program began in the forenoon and ended about 5 P.M., during which time, everybody 'gymkanad' to their hearts content. The day's celebration was befittingly closed in a most enjoyable dance at Mr. and Mrs. Spalding's beautiful valley house during the evening.

This event was probably at the racetrack in Waipouli in the Kapa'a area.[63] It is entirely possible that the track was built by the Spaldings.

One's imagination can go wild wondering what a "nosegay" race was, and did they use a mallet to hit the potato along the ground like a polo ball? Polo was a popular sport in the islands at this time. Then to think of girls rushing along after geese in their long skirts, trying to maintain their dignity and still move their geese to the finish line!

"Kapalawai"

Jan. 7, 1913.

Mother, my dearest –

This afternoon Selwyn starts back for California and college – and Mr. R. is going with him – he will remain in California between two weeks and a month, visiting Mrs. Welcker in Berkeley & other relatives in southern California. We shall miss him terribly – he is so dear and jolly.

Selwyn will not return to "Kapalawai" until late in May, after the close of the college term – realizing this, he is a rather miserably looking boy today. But he has had an awfully good time while here – a cattle drive or goat hunt nearly every day. He's an awfully dear boy – I'm fond of him.

Yesterday afternoon we tried to have tennis here – invited many people – but it grew so stormy & threatening during the afternoon, that few of our guests arrived – just the Sandows & Knudsens. We amused them by billiards and music on the graphonola and served our tea, sandwiches, ice & cake on the lanai. However, late in the afternoon it cleared up enough for us to have three good speedy sets. Lots of fun.

Of course the Von Holt girls are still here – so we have a merry household at present. But – sad as it is to relate – as I fear is often the case – there is a family feud of long standing between the Knudsens & Von Holts – (Eric Knudsen & Mrs. Von Holt are brother & sister) – so we have to be very careful in planning affairs not to bring these two factions too closely together. I think that family quarrels are disgraceful and shameful – don't you? And these are such delightful people, too. I can't quite fathom such "goingson."

You must not expect a long letter today – for I have some booking and checking to finish up for Mr. Robinson before he goes. I wish that you could all see him – and he see you – but that is probably impossible this time – but I hope that when they pass thro' California next August on their way to Boston – that we can all see them all!

And now, here is as tremendous amount of love for you, Mother dearest – and each dear Matthew.

From your "Cynthia"
(Someone nice calls me that.)

"Kapalawai"

Jan. 13, 1913

Mother dearest –

I was so happy to hear all about your wonderful Christmas in detail – I was sure that you would have a glorious time – and am surely glad if my little thoughts and love helped to make it as happy as it was. But I did very little, I am sure.

Robinson Family Governess: Letters from Kauaʻi and Niʻihau, 1911-1913

Mr. Robinson and Selwyn left on Tuesday last for Honolulu – and there were tears in poor Selwyn's eyes. They left Honolulu on Saturday – we had a wireless from them – so they are even now on the briny deep. Wish that I was with them!

On Wednesday Mrs. Lindsay and Mrs. Ewart came to luncheon – and we had a most delightful time – Mrs. Lindsay is more than charming – and tho' I have seen her but two or three times – I feel quite well acquainted with her – and she was sweet enough to say that she felt that she had made a dear new friend and made me promise that when I came to Honolulu to meet my sister from Japan that I would let her know – and that we were to have luncheon with her. Won't that be lovely?

Friday was the great day! We had a big expedition up that marvelous Koula Valley – we all went – the Spauldings, Knudsens, Charlie Rices, Philip Rices [Charles' brother and new wife], and several others going with us as our guests – among them a jolly and very famous little portrait artist – a Swede, Mr. Kronstrand by name – great artist by fame. He was imported to our country to paint the official portraits of President & Mrs. Taft. He wishes to paint your illustrious daughter's portrait – and perhaps – but I am digressing – about our trip. Unfortunately we had a rainy day – and the river was high – which means a good deal, considering that you have to cross it twenty five times going up and twenty five times going down. But as we were all soaking wet five minutes after we started out, we didn't mind our bedraggled condition during the remainder of the day – simply ignored it – and had a glorious time. The Valley was even lovelier than before – for every leaf glistened in the rain – and the mist and rain effects were glorious! As the artist said, "Am I dreaming – or is this beauty all true?" Because of the heavy rain – there was more water than usual in the fall – and it was so very beautiful. Oh! how I love it! Everyone declared that in spite of the rain, it had been a very perfect day.

On Saturday we were invited over to Lihue to Mrs. Rice's to luncheon – and then we had a swim in the ocean right in front of her home. The waves come almost up to the front lawn. And the swimming is glorious there. Maud and I nearly swam out to the steamer, which was lying at anchor in the harbor.

Saturday night, Maud and I went out to Mr. & Mrs. Eric Knudsen to the first meeting of the Waimea Literary Club. Everyone in the "district" was present – and we adopted a constitution, elected officers & had an address from pastor Lidgate [Lydgate] of Lihue – then served light refreshments (soft drinks) & had some music – I played & also accompanied Mrs. Sandow when she sang.

Sunday was a quiet day, as usual – but today we have been "going it" again. The Spauldings gave a *lovely* party – and we all went over. Went in autos and met them at a certain bridge, away around at the other side of the island. There were about thirty in the party – we all got into a great big Japanese sand-pan [sampan] – the band boys sat in one end, playing – and we were rowed up the river, by Japanese men, about four miles – there we landed, for that was to be our lunching place. While the servants prepared lunch, we walked about and gathered ferns – then watched them dig up the roasted pigs which had been buried in the ground with hot stones, and cooked thusly – then all sat down to a feast of every conceivable delicious dish – the band playing as we ate. Then we visited a very crude rice mill & poi factory – and all too soon took to our sand-pan and started down the river again. The scenery is perfectly glorious – the river's banks are so beautifully wooded – and you cannot imagine how delightful – how *heavenly* it is to just float downstream to the strains of this charming Hawaiian music. The wee artist was there today, and was very attentive – made me a charming little sketch, (ahem) really he is *most* interesting, and even fascinating – if he were *only* taller – and *not* bald headed!! Alas, Alack! But I don't want a man that I can put in my suit-case at will. It was a *charming* day!

Altho' I "go" a good deal – I am really *not* "fly away," Mother dear – and I love you just heaps & *heaps*! Your own Hettie.

Kalapaki Rice home (courtesy of the Kauaʻi Historical Society)

Going up the Wailua River on a sampan for the Spaldings' outing to the rice mill and poi factory. Second from the right is one of the Robinson brothers. (photo by Hettie Belle)

In Hettie Belle's day, trips of even a short distance could take several hours. Even today, a short trip can seem far, as Hettie said, "away around at the other side of the island!" Author Fleeson calls it the "island effect."[65] The destination with the Spaldings that day was almost certainly the Wailua River. Rice mills were common on Kaua'i at that time, and there was one near the fork where the north and south branches of the Wailua River come together.[66]

Rice growing began in Kaua'i after 1852 when Chinese contract laborers began arriving on the island. The Robinsons did not employ Chinese workers, but other plantations did. Many Chinese immigrants were energetic businessmen themselves, acquiring or leasing land for rice production and for shop keeping. The Chulan and Company rice-growing operation leased a large plantation at Hanalei. The growing Chinese population on Kaua'i consumed some of the rice, but much of it was exported to California.

To keep the Chinese plantation workers in Hawai'i and to add to the labor force, the businessmen arranged for "gunny sack wives," orphan girls brought from China. They had sacks over their heads to keep the men from seeing their faces when they were choosing a bride.[67]

Judith Marion Burtner

"Kapalawai"

Jan. 20, 1913.

My dearest Mother –

First, I must beg your forgiverness – for I missed the last mail – and failed to write to you – but I know that you will generously forgive me this time – even tho' I confess that I was merely busy having a good time – but even so it really was impossible to write. Those Von Holt girls are *most* charming – I count it really a rare privilege that I had the opportunity of being with them – and learning to love them. And they seemed to love me a wee bit in return, too. We parted awfully good friends.

Today, Mrs. McBride [McBryde]*– an old friend of these people – and her two charming old bachelor sons called – and we had tea together and lots of fun. One son, Walter (whom these people have always teased me about) was awfully jolly today – and we had stacks of fun. We planned our costumes for next Saturday night – and I generously offered to make his. He was covered with confusion but thanked me profusely. I simply did it to embarrass him.

You see, Dr. & Mrs. Sandow have been remodeling their home and it is now completed. They are to have a housewarming next Saturday evening – which will take the form of a children's Costume Dance – that is – grown-ups are to go in children's costumes – and be silly & ridiculous for once. Really, I think that it will be *stacks* of fun – don't you? I have planned a little pink dress for myself – made like that blue one that Sally made for Babe last summer – shall wear half sox & slippers – and my hair down in curls – with my big ribbon or velvet (pink) around my head. Won't I be fetching? Must have a snap taken – and send you one. Mrs. R. & Aylmer are too dignified to dress up, or to *go*, even – but Sinclair and I are going – and are planning to be silly enough to make up for the whole family. Of this marvelous party, you shall hear later.

Yesterday was Sunday – we were either early for church, or the parson & organist were late. Mrs. R. said that I would need to play the organ. Mr. Aaser (Oh! Sir) was standing near – and I declared that I would be more than willing to play the organ if Mr. Aaser would preach the sermon. That poor uncomfortable man shifted from one foot to the other – turned a pinker hue – then gently said –"I would be glad to pump the organ." (*So* sweet of him?) But the parson finally came as did the organist – so we were released from our promises & therefore relieved.

---

* The widow Elizabeth Moxley McBryde had two bachelor sons, Walter and Alexander.

Mary E. Von Holt (circa 1907) was about the same age as Hettie Belle when she spent time with the Robinsons on Kaua'i. (courtesy of the Bishop Museum)

Mrs. Spaulding's house party guests left on the steamer – Mr. Kronstrand the artist among them of course. I was jealous that the [Von Holt] girls should go up on the same steamer with him – but then he was nice – and said at parting that it would be hard to forget me – and that he wouldn't try to.

We had tennis here on Friday afternoon. Among the guests was our dear aforementioned Mr. Aaser – he did not play but drank 3 cups of tea & ate 17 sandwiches. When he was "plum" full – I offered him another sandwich – in fact carried it clear across the lawn & insisted that he take it – he refused – & we had quite an argument over it – finally I declared that I would never speak to him again if he didn't take it – but he still refused – that was the first time that I have *ever* admired him – when he had backbone enough to refuse me – such is the nature of perverse woman!

I went out to tennis at Knudsen's at "Hoea"– they dedicated their new court. Mrs. Eric K. has the most charming little teahouse that you can imagine – made of braided cocoanut palm leaves – *lovely*!!

The lights have gone out & I am writing by candle light – but really feel that this is all that you can stand at one sitting so Gute Nacht – and *heaps* of love to you all.

Your own Hettie.

Chapter Sixteen
Pineapple Dreams

"Kapalawai" –

Jan. 23, 1913.

Mother, dearest –

Now what do you 'spose this daughter of yours has been up to today? Well, she taught school this morning – and this afternoon made her gown for the ball Saturday night. I told you about being invited to Dr. & Mrs. Sandow's Children's Costume Dance didn't I?

The other day I went down into the metropolis of Waimea, selected my materials, & it took me just 5 ½ hours to make my gown – not much time wasted, eh? I cut it out and worked a bit on it yesterday afternoon then finished it this afternoon – then to celebrate, I played two sets of tennis – I won, too.

Dr. Derby is with us this week – came down Wednesday morning. We all like him at meal times & after 5 o'clock in the afternoon but hate him between times. Tomorrow comes my turn, that's why I am writing you tonight – this may be my last will and testament. Every one from the grandmothers down has visited the torture chamber, and it is frightful to be one of the last after having heard all the others groan. I'm afraid that I have quite a bit of work as I haven't had my teeth touched for more than a year – & recently I have lost one or two fillings to my knowledge. But we'll pray for the best. Dr. Derby is a "crack" at billiards and last evening he and I beat Mrs. R. and Aylmer horribly.

On Tuesday morning Mrs. R. Aylmer *&* I went over to inspect Mr. McBride's [McBryde] pineapple factory. It is situated about half way to Lihue – the morning was glorious – and my! How I enjoyed that ride. The canning process is *most* fascinating and interesting – we saw the whole thing – the pineapples peeled, cored, sliced, canned, sealed, cooked, cooled and packed – *and* we tasted them in the third stage mentioned – and they were *delicious!* One of these days you will be buying some cans, and if they are *extra* good you'll be sure that they came from McBrides Cannery – and that I inspected the canning of them. So! Gee! But there's a *mint of money* in it! When I'm no longer Governess, I think I'll start a pineapple patch or get a job in a pineapple factory – really the work there is fascinating! And you would be pleased to know how very sanitary everything is – each and every workman wears spotless white rubber gloves – and everything is very clean.

We've been hearing wonderful things of late of the cold in California – the papers have been full of it – and the Vallejo paper which Father so kindly sent me said that you had snow there. And I hear that the snow has been pretty general, has fallen in Berkeley *&* San Francisco and many other places – what fun! Wish that I could be there to help snowball. And yet there has been a serious side hasn't there? Such a tremendous loss to the orange *&* lemon growers – is it true that they have lost many millions? Too bad.

Your own Hettie

Hettie Belle half jokes that she would one day go into the pineapple business. By the late nineteenth century, Hawaiʻi was the pineapple hub of the world. The cayenne variety of pineapple, *Ananas comosus*, was raised there and distributed worldwide. Yet today the old McBryde pineapple cannery at Lāwaʻi is no longer operative and most pineapple is raised in other parts of the world where labor is less expensive. However, for a time the pineapple symbolized Hawaiʻi: lush, delicious, mass-produced in the tropics, and available in cans to the ordinary housewife, no longer a luxury item for the rich. It was a symbol of hospitality, of "*aloha.*"

---

* Walter Duncan McBryde, a community-minded businessman, not only founded the pineapple processing company, but also owned a sugar company, served in the government, and developed the Kōloa tree tunnel and the Kukuiolono Park.

Author Okiro states that this "rather mocked the Hawaiian dispossession by American capitalists."[68]

Pineapple canneries were patterned after the sugar plantations, becoming the second largest agricultural business in Hawai'i. Employees helped invent machinery to streamline the production. The ginaca machine was invented in 1913 by worker Henry Gabriel Ginaca. It removed the skin, cored, sized, and sliced the fruit. Hettie Belle did not realize the drudgery involved in this work, but Ida Kanekoa Milles, a trimmer at Dole's Hawaiian Pine in 1946 said,

> To tell you the truth, I sat on that table and looking at the pineapple coming through the Ginaca to me look like 100 pineapples a minute. Before I finish one pine, there's another one coming down. I put this pine down, I pick up another. I didn't finish, another pine coming down. Before I realize, there was a pile of fruit in front of me.[69]

"Kapalawai"

Jan. 27, 1913.

My own dearest Mother –

You must know that Saturday nights Children's Costume Dance at Dr. & Mrs. Sandow's was an unusual and most unique affair! We had such a good time. All day Saturday I wore my hair up of "rags" for I wanted curls for the party – and lo! And behold, at five o'clock when I took down my hair it was still wet and hadn't curled! I flew to Mrs. R. in my dire distress. She got out her electric hair drying machine, proceeded to dry my hair and then curl it on irons – as you may know it was some task to curl my hair! The regular curling tongs were so short, that we despaired of ever finishing my hair with them, but Mrs. R. had a brilliant idea – sent to the kitchen for two long steels, that you use when sharpening carving knives. Even so it was a job, and took some two hours – we didn't even stop for dinner. Yes, Mother dear, I did feel awfully guilty about letting her do it, but she would do it – and was so dear and interested in it – she really deserved a leather medal, too, for when she had finished I was really a "thing of beauty and a joy forever." And that curl is apparently in to stay – hasn't commenced to come out yet! But as I was saying – when my hair was curled, and I was ready, I was quite presentable – and quite like a little *overgrown* girlie! My pink dress really looked quite pretty & quaint, and I wore pink stockings and black slippers, a band & huge pink bow around my head, and my curls all hangin' a down oh! Then I carried a huge fuzzy brown Teddy bear – and pitched my voice in a high childlike key – and was just as naughty as a 'model' child dares to be. These people all seemed pleased and quite approved of me – of my costume at least – the grandmothers were quite delighted. Mrs. R. and Sinclair and I went, and while we were going, were still on this side of the River, we could see the Sandow place all lit up – a perfect fairy-land of light and beauty.

Of course everyone in the "district" was there, and almost everyone was in costume, and the costumes were *splendid*. Dr. Sandow was not in costume, simply in evening dress, but Mrs. S. was a *darling*, in dainty white French dress – with pink sash and hair ribbon. She is small & dark, with pretty fluffy curly hair, and you cannot imagine how *very* sweet she was & how child-like. And such a cunning & charming hostess she made! Mrs. Eric Knudsen & Maud L'Orange were *lovely* big French dolls (twins) – Mr. Eric was Tom, the piper's son. There were several babies in long dresses still, who danced remarkably well, considering. There were sailor boys & sailor girls – and you *should* have seen the great big six-footer men in Russian blouse suits …. and some in rompers! Really ridiculous! I laughed myself sick. But they were made so swell that they really were splendid. Mr. Aaser was a *dear*!! I really quite fell in love with him, and *told* him so – for children are ever sincere and frank, you know. I said, "I have quite fallen in love with you" – but as he started to beam, I continued – "Don't take that too seriously, for I really believe that it is your costume that I am in love with"! You know he has light curly hair, great big brown eyes – rosy cheeks – and such an innocent child-like expression – and he was dressed in dear pink & white rompers, & had on *such* a cunning wee round straw hat – and looked so kissable and spankable – really I did *quite* fall in love with him! And he with me! He tried to hold my hand, even!

There were old-fashioned children with tight trousers & pantalettes, as the case might be (boys or girls), and modern children of every sort. But really you have no idea how these costumes changed people – and how *really* pretty most of them looked, when they danced especially! We watched them from the balcony – it was a gay scene. They had supper out in the yard – great tables everywhere – so beautifully decorated, and charmingly lit up with hundreds of Chinese & Japanese lanterns. We sat overlooking the cliff, and the moonlight on the river was something to dream over. We had a delicious supper, after which we went in and had a musical program before the dancing was resumed. I played – & then accompanied Mrs. Sandow and others who sang. Then they begged me to play again – and then I made *the* hit of the evening – so they all declared – I sat down and played a couple of those wee pieces that beginners always play, and when I had finished you should have heard them applaud and laugh! It really took *awfully* well. Yes, it was an awfully enjoyable evening – and it was *nearly* Sunday morning before I arrived at home. Those Sandows certainly know how to entertain.

I believe that I told you in my last letter that our dear Dr. Denby had been with us for a few days – well Friday *my turn came* – before lunch for an hour, and after lunch for two hours and a half, I was in the torture chamber with the result that my teeth are shining and bright. I am in five new fillings & out $10.00. He does remarkably good work and is *so quick!* I certainly prefer one long session, to week after week and appointment after appointment as it is in Berkeley – one certainly does waste time & patience – don't you think? But of course we cannot all afford to have a dentist in the house for a week at a time – *hardly!*

Who calls me "Cynthia"? That's another story – not now – only *love*
Hettie.

"Kapalawai" –

Jan. 31, 1913.

Dearest "Mothery" –

Isn't that a pretty new pet name? Or do you not approve, and fail to appreciate it? You must at least admit that it is far superior to "Ma" or "Bedelia"– and besides, because I am at a distance, I should be allowed to call you most anything within reason, that helps me to express myself – and is within limits.

The last day of January! My! How the months do fly! In three more months Margie will be here – and in four or five months more I will be leaving these golden shores and marvelous isles, forever? So often the thought comes to me "*Why* did I come"? –"why did this chance come into my life – and un-sought!" Was it simply that I would have two wonderful years to look back upon? Or was there some other reason that I cannot now see or know? I cannot answer these questions – and *who* can? Perhaps it is best after all that we cannot see ahead – and yet how interesting it would be to know certain things, wouldn't it?

Mrs. R. says that I must tell you that you mustn't feel worried if you fail to hear from me for a few weeks or month, even. It seems that a serious strike is pending among the Captains of all the Inter-Island steamers – and it may be that we will have no steamers either from or to Honolulu after this one for several weeks. The management anticipate a very serious time. So don't worry if you don't hear from me – for you must know that I am very well and happy and quite safe. But just sympathize with me – knowing how I'll be longing for my letters and news from you all. I trust that the trouble will be over quite soon, however.

Mrs. R. has had a very heavy cold this week – I gave her a lomi lomi [massage] last night for a couple of hours – used eucalyptus ointment. I am so much stronger than the little Japanese maids that she says I really give a much more satisfactory rub. She was so thankful to me – and I was so glad to do it for her – and so glad that she was really better today.

While the Von Holt girls were here, Eleanor missed her practice – there were so many interruptions. After they had left, she told me that she had kept count, and had missed 27 hours practice, and that she intended to make it all up. True to her word, she has been practicing three hours a day instead of her regular hour & a half and has almost made up her deficit. Isn't she a *most* conscientious little girlie? Few children are like her in that respect, I think – and that is what makes her so satisfactory to teach.

Are you still cold over there? Even we have had three real cold nights of late – so cold that I have longed to "cuddle" with my beloved little "Mutt." *So much* love to you all. Your own Hettie.

"Kapalawai"

Feb. 3, 1913.

My dearest Mothery –

My! But we are having cold weather! I actually had to wear a sweater all morning – the first time that I have ever needed a coat or wrap in the daytime since coming to these Islands. And usually I don't feel the need of a wrap in the evening even – simply wear one for respectability's sake & convention when going out in the auto. We were so cold Saturday morning after breakfast that Eleanor and I decided that a couple of good sets of tennis would warm us up – and they *surely* did. We felt fine after them. I then came in and "booked" all the letters & receipted bills etc. that have accumulated during the past two months – wanted the books in good condition before Mr. R's return. We have not yet heard when he is to come – but it will be this month probably – and perhaps within two weeks. I'm wondering whether or not he has seen any of my beloved family – am hoping so – but fear that perhaps he has not. I spent a couple of hours Saturday afternoon correcting papers – a teacher's job once in a while, at least – I'm certainly fortunate in this respect – have so few papers and can almost always correct them within school hours. Sometimes they mount up, tho'.

Saturday evening the Waimea Literary Club met at Mr. Gay's home, and an intensely interesting and lively meeting we had. Our subject was the "Balkan Situation" – with three interesting papers on the historical and present aspects – also some keen character sketches of King Ferdinand and others. After the papers we had an interesting open discussion. Usually, I think such discussions are dead, but we are fortunate in having many people in our "district" who love to talk, and fortunately some of these know what they are talking about. It was interesting and altogether a most profitable evening. I really know something of the situation as it now stands. After the "literary" part, we had refreshments & gossip and some music.

Then tomorrow afternoon we go to the big Spaulding reception – Wednesday is mail day (if it comes) – Thursday is tennis day at the Knudsen's – and Friday we will probably go up Olokele canyon, taking a party of about twenty. And so the weeks fly past – and soon I'll be flying home to you, my precious Mother. Love to you all.

Your Betty.

The European/American people on the island of Kaua'i were hungry for news of those mainland worlds from which they came. When Mr. Aubrey Robinson and his cousin Francis Gay were boys, they attended Doles' school in Kōloa. The parents of students there had a magazine club. They shared subscriptions and passed them around. Each family checked off their names on the back cover after having a turn at reading the publication.[70]

The Waimea Literary Club was formed to raise discussion on important topics.[71] There was already such a club in Līhu'e, so Mrs. Brandt went to Līhu'e to confer with Mrs. Lydgate* about forming a club at Waimea. Hettie Belle attended their first meeting.

---

* Helen Elwell (Mrs. Lydgate) was a leading matron and organizer of Kaua'i society.

Judith Marion Burtner

"Kapalawai"

Feb. 6, 1913.

Mothery, dearest –

Would *you* go eighty miles to attend a reception to a fair bride and groom? Well, your daughter would – and did – in fact we all, Mrs. R., Aylmer, Sinclair and I all went around the island to the Spauldings' reception, forty miles each way. We left here at two P.M. and arrived home at 8 P.M. and had a *grand* time in between. The Spauldings gave the reception to Mrs. Spaulding's brother & his California bride, and everyone was there dressed in "Sunday best" to greet them. It was a delightful occasion. The bride is a charming & striking blonde, her groom dark & handsome, so they are a charming pair. They are to live here – two more nice people! People stood about and gossiped, as usual at such affairs, and drank either chocolate, tea, coffee or punch, as best suited their taste – and nibbled sandwiches cakes & candy – enough to spoil their appetites for dinner. During the afternoon Mrs. S. decided that she wanted some music, so I had to play and accompany Mrs. Sandow, who was there. The Spauldings' home is a typical country mansion – magnificent furnishings – and wonderful grounds about the place. It is quite romantic – and looks to have a history – and *has* – for the Spauldings were interesting people – always *did* things. Going over, we stopped in Lihue for Mr. & Mrs. Charles Rice. Mr. Rice delights in teasing me, so that my face was the color of the flaming bougainvillea all the way from Lihue and back to it. But the reception was a *great* success. You know, they said that when they went down to the wharf to meet the bridal couple, they set a phonograph going playing the wedding march – imagine! Old shoes & rice were not enough, but they must needs have a canned wedding march besides – wasn't that funny?

I'm all "broken up" tonight for I have had Father's letter telling of poor dear Sally. Oh! Mother has something happened again? Does his letter mean that she has lost this dear wee baby? If so – it is really *too* cruel – it doesn't seem right. But do tell me quickly – am I wrong? Or *did* she lose this wee baby? If it *has* happened *again* – why did it happen? Something must be *vitally* wrong – is something out of place with dear Sally, or something else wrong? Isn't this about the same length of time as elapsed in the other case (seven months)? I thought that she was *unusually* well – and being very careful. I know you will do everything that can be done for her. And wee Billikin will be *such* a comfort – the *dear* that he is.

Remember that I am waiting impatiently for further news. Love to all.

Your Hettie Belle

Miscarriages were not uncommon in the early 1900s. Poorly trained or untrained medical practitioners often provided obstetric care. It could have been such a case with Sally. Hettie Belle grieved over these losses and her older sister's sorrow.

"Kapalawai"

Feb. 7, 1913.

Father, dearest –

It was certainly very good of you to write, and I want you to know that I appreciate and thank you for your letter of January 27th telling of Sarah's [Sally's] trouble. You must know, of course however, that your news greatly saddened me, and the first reading of your letter was quite a shock.

I wonder if you dream about your wonderful ranch as much as I do! I have decided to make a lot of money – pay off your mortgage, get things comfortably settled in the ranch – and come to live with you & Mother – for you must have a maidenly daughter to take care of you – & it surely looks as if I were to be that happy maidenly daughter! I can't bear to think of settling down in a city! So, me for your winding paths & huge oak trees – I want two splendid ponies, a grand piano, a bathing pool, a tennis court – and you & Mother – and I shall be more than happy all the days of my life! And I'm sure I could feed pigs, pick eggs – even if I couldn't milk cows!!! ! !

No more nonsense – but heaps of love. Here we are off for tennis – so farewell.

Your loving Hettie

"Kapalawai"

Feb. 10, 1913.

My own dearest Mother –

This evening as we sat at dinner – suddenly great flashes of lightning came – and then crack, smash, bang! Came the terrifying peals of thunder! And then the rain. It has been looking dark and threatening for many days, now, and we are counting on a real storm very soon – perhaps this is the beginning. As you have heard me say before – I'm crazy for a real Kona storm – and hope to see it this winter.

Spalding Valley House. Hettie wrote, "The Spauldings' home is a typical country mansion – magnificent furnishings – and wonderful grounds about the place. It is quite romantic." (courtesy of the Kauaʻi Historical Society)

And what do you suppose I did on Saturday? Ten of the young people from Makaweli plantation – five of them school teachers – and the other five, plantation men – gave a little play called, "Engaged" in Lihue Hall Saturday evening. None of these people were going, so Mrs. Sandow invited me to go with her – she had also asked Mr. Milliken (the minister) – so the four of us went, Dr. & Mrs. Sandow – and Mr. Milliken & your fair (?) daughter. She had invited us to dinner, also – and this we had at five o'clock – and tho' it was all a grand dinner, I must tell you of something that we had that I had never tasted before, and it was so good, that I impolitely asked for a second helping – and wanted a third! Yorkshire Pudding! Have you ever tasted it? And isn't it delicious? Ummmm!

After dinner, away we went. The ride is especially lovely at night – when you are cuddled down in a very "comfy" car, with interesting people, and the car spinning along at 20 or 25 an hour. The Hall was packed – for you must know that this was quite a society event – everyone was there, and in evening dress, too. And the play was unusually good! A very, very cleverly written play, and produced splendidly – the girls were so pretty, costumes lovely and stage settings remarkable good. It was one of the funniest plays that you could imagine – and we simply howled all the time – it was surely appreciated by all, and pronounced a huge success!

Friday afternoon last, the Knudsen's had tennis at "Hoea," and I won my set. Mr. Milliken and I against Sinclair and Maud L'Orange – beat them 6-2 – Wasn't that great? And I must tell you what *especially* delighted me – Sinclair didn't return a single one of my serves! How's that? The side-lines clapped – so I guess that was "going-some" (to use an elegant expression). But perhaps "going-some" may be correct now – I must look in my new 1913 Dictionary – for if you please –"hot-dog" is given as a *real* word with definition as follows –"a name given in the U.S. to a Frankfurter sausage when served hot." How's that? And what are we coming to? Slang will soon be considered beautifully pure English. "Spud" is always a correct word to use now – meaning "a potato," of course. So don't think it vulgar – and teach the children to ask for mashed or fried "spuds"! Really a euphonious word! But I am digressing – to return to tennis, it was "going some" to send balls that Sinclair couldn't return – and I am quite proud of myself. So there!

I have had no further word from any of you as to dear Sally's condition, and can only hope and pray that all is well – for surely you would have cabled had complications set in. And while we are mentioning it – I want you to solemnly *promise* me right now that should *anything serious* happen to *any one* of you – that you will cable or send a wireless to me *immediately!* I don't care if you have to pawn the piano or mortgage the house to do it – I want you to *promise* to do it, and I will make it right afterwards. I will never forgive you, if you don't, but am sure that now that you understand my feelings on the matter, that you will comply with my wishes.

A great deal of love. Hettie.

Advertising page of the Līhuʻe play program, "Engaged."

"Kapalawai."

Feb. 14, 1913.

My own dearest Mother –

You have no idea, Mother, what a tremendous relief I experienced upon receiving you letter on Wednesday – you explained the whole situation *so* thoroughly – I couldn't have asked for more information. Poor Sally has indeed had a very sad, trying experience – and here to think that it is all because of the neglect and ignorance of those two physicians – they have been the cause of her physical pain and mental agony. You say that you are indignant – I am *furious!* Mother, what has become of this dear wee son and daughter that *should* have been hers – are they in Heaven – were they old enough to have souls? Is there a *soul* from the very start? And what becomes of these dear wee things that haven't had a chance to live? I wish that I knew.

So you met Mr. Robinson on the car and thought him splendid, to look at, at least. But I have later news than that – for Mr. Robinson arrived here at daylight this morning – and has brought me even later news from you. He has cheered me up so – for I must confess that I have been decidedly depressed during the past week – something most unusual for me – I am usually quite optimistic, you know – but have been so worried about poor, dear Sally that Mrs. R. said she was about to send me home. Mr. R. has told of the car introduction, and of their call upon you all later. That dear Sally was at *home* – and that Mrs. Welcker saw her and that she was getting along *splendidly!* You should hear his praise of my beautiful Mother – of dear sturdy Beckwith, of beautiful Helen Marion and Daisy. My! I am quite bursting with pride tonight. Am *so* glad that he knows what a beautiful family I have. You cannot imagine how wonderful it seems to receive *direct* word from home folks – it means *so much.*

Three tennis days this week! My tennis muscle is increasing.

Last night, Mrs. R. Sinclair Aylmer and I went to the Baldwins' to a gorgeous reception which they gave to the directors of the Hawaiian Sugar Co. The Makaweli young people gave their play "Engaged"– again – and it took *awfully* well.

Did you hear that Mr. Preston's wee two year old son died from small pox? You remember Mr. P. of course – sang tenor in our choir. Isn't this sad? Three children that I have known have died.

Now I must seek my virgin couch – sending dear love to you one and all. Mr. R. wishes to send his *very* kind regards to Mrs. Matthew please.

Your loving Betty

Mr. Aubrey Robinson met some of Hettie Belle's family during his time in California. He was already acquainted with Hettie's oldest brother Allan through his sister-in-law Mrs. Welcker when he hired Hettie Belle. Daisy was Allan's wife and their little daughter, Helen Marion, would reappear on Kaua'i years later due to Hettie Belle's connection with the Robinson family when as a young woman, Helen Marion would meet Lester. (The name Marion/Marian was prominent in the Matthew family, alternating generations between the "o" and "a" spelling. Hettie Belle's sister spelled it with an "a"; and her mother and daughter, with an "o.")

Three small children Hettie knew died of smallpox. This disease had ravaged populations for centuries. In the early 1800s, Edward Jenner discovered that cowpox could be used to inoculate people. He called it "vaccinia." Still after many outbreaks, Americans often refused the vaccinations. In 1905, the Supreme Court upheld the constitutionality of mandatory vaccination programs, and in 1922, it was decided in court that schools could insist on student vaccinations before entrance.[72] Meanwhile, many people suffered and died.

Baby Morton Matthew and Helen Marion Matthew, circa 1913
(Marion Wright files)

"Kapalawai"

Feb. 17, 1913.

Mother dearest —

There is something new and startling that I can tell you — we are all going up to the Floral Parade which is on Washington's birthday — next Saturday. You remember what a *glorious* time we had when we went up last year — this means another gay time. I, of course protested — but they declared that it didn't matter if school was broken into for a few days — that we must go. So Mrs. R., Sinclair, Eleanor, Lester (*perhaps*) and I, are going. They say that the parades will be more gorgeous than ever this year. And I hope that there will be a Japanese lantern parade at night, too.

Did I tell you of my marvelous feat the other day going out to tennis? Mr. Gay was driving his car — I was sitting in front with him — Sinclair and Aylmer were sitting behind. As we started out of the gate, Mr. Gay told me to steer the car – so I leaned over and steered it – after we passed thro' Waimea, he insisted that I take his seat (the driver's seat) – so I was "game" and did – and drove all the way out to Knudsen's, and even in at their narrow gate – the first time that I had ever had my hands on a wheel or tried to run a car. I managed the steering, honking, brakes and exhilerater, and he changed the spark and gasoline whenever necessary. I went as fast as 23 miles an hour a couple of times, but in the main, I tried no fancy tricks, but was very careful indeed. The boys in the back seat were very quiet, but declared afterwards that they were not frightened, only watching and admiring my skill. Both Mr. Gay and the boys gave me many compliments upon my coolness and steady driving I tell you – I'm a wonder! Mr. Gay said that I would know it all in one or two more lessons. A year ago he wanted to teach me – do you remember? But these people rather frowned upon the idea – however they now seem quite delighted about it, and quite proud of me.

And now dear love to you all – and many, many goodnight kisses all round – and please Mother dearest, come out on the vine-covered porch in the morning, and waken me with a kiss, as you did last summer. Oh! How I wish you could! Sometimes I long too hard for you – and all the rest.

Your own loving Hettie

Chapter Seventeen
Singing from the Heart

Alexander Young Hotel

Honolulu –
Feb. 23, 1913.

My dearest Mother –

You see we *are* really here – and tho' this is only our second day, it seems that we have already been here a month, for we have done *so* much. We left Kauai Friday afternoon at five – Mr. Robinson and Lester went over to Lihue and saw us safely off – and as we planned, Mrs. R., Sinclair, Eleanor and I came. We had a *crowded* steamer, the Knudsens and many other Kauai people coming at the same time. And such a delightfully smooth trip we had – *unusually* smooth – so unusual that I celebrated by going to bed at about 6:30 and being a *trifle* sick – just a trifle, nothing serious – and after it was over I went to sleep and slept soundly until 4:30 in the morning, when we arrived in Honolulu. And now I must tell you something funny. You must know that at this Floral Parade season, Honolulu is overflowing with people, and the hotels are *terribly* crowded. We didn't realize that we were coming to Honolulu until late, so only wired for rooms last week. Upon arriving at the Hotel, imagine our surprise to find that they had reserved for us the only remaining available space – the *immense* parlor of the hotel, beds in every corner, some single some double – and they told us that they were planning to put *screens* between! Needless to say, we did not remain, but went on up to Wailele, Mr. Gay's beautiful home up the valley – about 15 minutes ride in the auto from town. The home is *most complete in every respect* – eight guest rooms beautifully furnished, baths, etc. He has servants there who are accustomed to bringing your breakfast to you in bed – and waiting on you hand and foot. We arrived there between five and six, Saturday morning – had coffee and toast – then had baths and went to bed – arising later for a nine o'clock breakfast. We then dressed and went down town for the day – and we certainly made a day of it. In the morning we first witnessed a splendid military parade – then we drove about a bit – seeing many friends all about town – then came here to the hotel for luncheon. After luncheon came the gorgeous Floral Parade – and it *was* pretty! We saw it twice – once as it passed along the streets, and again in the Poonahs Grounds as it passed the judges stand. While it was there, I took at least 20 pictures of the different floats and all and am hoping that they will be so good that you can get some small idea as to what I witnessed. But you can never even imagine the brilliant and vivid coloring, such *masses* of pink, lavender or green – such unique exquisitely beautiful floats.

Then I had heard that the "Mongolia" was in and as I wanted to see Dr. Dukes – and as the Robinsons had some friends who were leaving for Japan, we went down to see the "Mongolia" off. How Dr. Dukes *beamed* when he saw me.

We leave for Kauai late Tuesday P.M. and the next couple of days will be crammed full of *shopping & going*, dinner & luncheon engagements. Of all this you shall hear later.

Heaps of love to you <u>all</u>.

   Your own Hettie.

Haven't time to read this over – so please forgive all mistakes.

One evening while in Honolulu, Mrs. Sandow, Mr. Gay, Sinclair, and Hettie Belle went into town to see a "Roaring Camp" area that represented a western mining town street. She wrote about this later in her 1973 memoir.

> We went into *everything*, altho' we had to come out of some more suddenly than we went in. Many things were *very* good — but some were common and even coarse. After this we needed something to strengthen us, of course, so down to the Rathskella we went and had some delicious fried oysters. Then home again to refreshing Wailele.

Flower parade floats (Hettie Belle 1913)

Flower parade floats. Hettie Belle said, "You can never even imagine the brilliant and vivid coloring, such *masses* of pink, lavender or green – such unique exquisitely beautiful floats." (Hettie Belle 1913)

"Kapalawai" –

Feb. 28, 1913.

Mother, *dearest* –

I believe that I wrote you last from Honolulu – but what I told you I cannot remember – that entire trip is rather confused – as you may well imagine. I found a dozen wonderful American Beauty roses awaiting me at the hotel – and later a very charming gentleman called, and called me "Cynthia"! Wasn't that nice?

Eleanor & I went home with the Von Holts, remaining over night with them. They are the most *charming*, interesting family – I'm quite madly in love with them all – from the jolly, huge fat Father to the little skinny Ronald, who reminds me of "Johnnie Boy," four years ago. And those dear people have invited me and Margie to stay at their beautiful home when we are in Honolulu. Are they not lovely?

We were at the dock to take the "Kinau" at 5 P.M. We had a very very rough trip – but I wasn't a bit ill and slept beautifully all the way. Someone who calls me "Cynthia" was on board and gave me his room, 'cause it was nicer than mine – and yesterday that same someone called on Mrs. R. and me and is now again in Honolulu. [This gentleman was never identified, but we later learn that he was married. So, what were his intentions?] Mr. R. met us at Eleele [named Port Allen in 1909] Wednesday morning, and we were glad to be on shore again – home looked most inviting.

I was so happy to find your beautiful letter awaiting me upon my return from Honolulu. Indeed I rejoice with you, Mother dearest – and all the world is looking bright again. How *perfectly lovely* for you all, and for our dear blessed Sally, that she can be with you to recuperate! Of *course* she will get well and strong quickly – she couldn't help it.

Yes, I too, was delighted that Mr. R. could call on you – and you certainly all made a *most* favorable impression. You should have heard his praise of you, one and all. Do you wonder that I love him to death – a safe expression, for no one understands its meaning.

We had a lovely walk to the sea beach – and witnessed a most gorgeous sunset. Such *brilliant* coloring, the water *so* blue – lovely Niihau *so* purple – and a brilliant golden, red sky behind. This world is really a *marvelously* beautiful place. Don't you think so?

Heaps of love to you all.

Your own loving Hettie

"Kapalawai" –

March 7, 1913.

My own darling Mother –

Last evening Mr. R. and Aylmer left for Niihau where they will remain for one week. It seems quiet without them – we always miss them so. I am *so* glad that they gave up their contemplated three months trip to the Orient and the Colonies. Mr. R. had planned a pleasure and business trip to Japan, China, Philippines, India, New Zealand, etc. leaving next month – they were going especially to find new stock.

(He was planning to take Aylmer.) But they have given up their trip because of the "red tape" and many restrictions in shipping livestock. Now they will be here the rest of my stay, and I am glad. We all went down to the wharf last evening at about eight o'clock to see them off. It was stacks of fun! We wished them "Bon voyage," and tucked in all sorts of "seasick" wishes. You should have seen the many, many old bent men and women sitting along the wharf, fishing – some for fish, some for crab. We found an old woman who had been most successful – had about 2 dozen crabs. These we persuaded her to sell to us – and how we enjoyed them this noon!

We have had two delicious sea baths this week – so refreshing – for the weather has been sultry. And Monday after luncheon we all (that is Mr. & Mrs. R. Sinclair, Lester & I) had a horseback ride to "Makaweli House." It was a *most* wonderful day in the mountains – so fresh – and no rain! My! How *green* everything was and how *blue* were the distant mountains. I just drank it all in so thankfully – and nearly burst with joy and happiness. Such a day just gets hold of me and fills me to overflowing with joy and peace and love! Then I long to be good, and true and beautiful. Sermons are not confined to churches, are they?

Mr. R. wanted to give the man up there directions about planting some trees and shrubs – this accomplished, we found and ate beautiful ripe mulberries and fresh lilikois! And watched and fed the new silver & golden pheasant that Mr. R. recently imported. Then we came home – facing the glorious sunset sky or afterglow all the way down. Before we had reached the lowlands it was quite dark – the myriad stars were out – and in the distance blazed a tremendous cane fire. But I must not get sentimental – to tell the truth, I couldn't "get" for I fear that I am already "got." But *is* it sentimental to really enjoy such beauties? Or should we just silently enjoy them and never exclaim over them? I can hardly help speaking of them – for when I am enjoying them to the fullest, my continual wish is that you, and you *all* could see them, and as long as you cannot, I feel that I must mention them to you – tho' I describe them *so* inadequately.

Your letters are *so* satisfying, Mothery, I love them *so*! Indeed, I should *love* to see dear Sally now – if she is as well as you picture her. I am *so* glad and thankful. Yes, indeed, I take the Gazette – and so learn all the news and gossip – but you are very good to send along the bits that you hear – these engagements & weddings are all *very* interesting – and who can say that I have not brought my "boys" up well? Are they not sensible in marrying young, and [are] they not all doing well and becoming famous? I told you so. And soon they will all be disposed of, and I can fold my hands, put on a cap – invest in a cat – and settle down. But I shall never, *never* enjoy *tea!*

You know that I have about decided, *if* I marry at all – to marry a *real grown man!* Say twice my age, or *nearly* twice. What think you? Always the boys that I have gone with – and they have been from two to five years, or even more my senior – (the usual difference, I believe) – have seemed very immature to me, almost *infants*. I am not just saying this – I have always felt it – that is why I have never been satisfied, but could always laugh at them, tell them that they loved me in a "sisterly" way and hand them out sisterly or almost motherly advice. Older men have *always* interested me and fascinated me the most – I enjoy them more – this is the absolute truth, if I ever told it – and I really am reaching an age when I should be able to judge – I am near twenty five, and have certainly met *heaps* of men and good and interesting specimens, too. Would it break your heart if I married a white haired man? And would you disinherit me? Answer me – but do not worry, I am not, as yet, planning to marry such a man – but am planning to return to you in a couple of months, "heart free." It has *not* worried me that I have not lost my heart during my stay here, I did not come expecting to – but I must whisper to you that the fact that I did not has sorely disappointed certain people. You understand.

"Who calls you Cynthia"? Why "Reuben" calls me Cynthia. "And who *was* Cynthia?" Why *I* was Cynthia – and *am* Cynthia – and always *will be* Cynthia, to Reuben. And that's about all that I know to tell – and surely that isn't very exciting – and surely you won't stay awake nights thinking of it. If anything more develops, I shall tell you of course. In the meantime this is all a good joke. Believe me.

Guess I'll go to bed now. Love and kisses all round – *heaps* and *heaps!*
Your own Hettie

"Kapalawai"
March 10, 1913.

Dearest Mother o' Mine –

Mrs. R. and I have been out calling today – Lester accompanied us gallantly. We went in the carriage, for our auto is disabled, its wheels being in Honolulu, for you must know that we are henceforth to have demountable tires – a very splendid thing, so they all say – for in case of blow-out or puncture you merely have to unscrew a few bolts, pull off the tire, put on a new already inflated one, screw up the bolts, and off

223

you go – a matter of a moment or two. The old way takes from 15 minutes to a half hour, even when one is clever and quick. So no more pilikia – pilikia pau now.

We called on Mrs. Brandt this afternoon, and she showed us her bedrooms which have been newly papered. Some awfully attractive papers she has – and the nice thing about them is that she found cretonnes to match them – thus making her rooms most complete. The wallpapers of today are certainly fascinating and charming – no excuse longer for gaudy or horrid wallpapers. Do you remember your red room at 2009 that writhed at night – and that you had to have repapered. That was funny!

Lester was quite delighted because Mrs. Brandt promised him some Japanese gold fish, today – he wanted to clinch the bargain, childlike – and promptly said, "when"? Then she quite immediately became definite, and he came home thoroughly happy – is at present hunting a glass bowl, I expect, tho' he should be practicing.

I intended to stop at the girls' sewing circle on the way home, but it was so late that I was afraid it would look as if I were merely dropping in for the "eats"– so I came on home. We did stop at the store, however, and almost bought it out. We had to lay in a stock of things to try on the chafing dish. Mrs. R. has a beauty, new one, and we are quite fascinated by it. I christened it last evening at dinnertime, made chocolate and it was good. Mrs. R. made scrambled eggs this morning. We are thinking of discharging the cook!

If you don't ever hear from me again, just know that I am reading and have forgotten everything – really I have such a mania for it that I am apt to be neglectful, I fear. But I have had such charming books lately, too fascinating to put down. I realize that I may not have such an opportunity again for reading, and time to read, as I am having this year, so am making the most of it.

I just finished a wonderfully sad, human book, "The Green Vase" by Dean Castle of Harvard – William Castle Jr. Was especially interested in it as I know his family in Honolulu, brother (a tennis champion), sister, and other members of the family. A brilliant family they are, too! Are we not to have an author from our illustrious family? I should love to write – if only I had the talent – I have plenty to say, numerous futile ideas – but how to put them down, cleverly – that's the question.

Yesterday we went to the kirk and heard a sermon on "ghosts" and learned that we are ruled by tyrannical ghosts, ghosts of convention, etc. All of which is true to a large extent. Convention and Dame Grundy certainly do keep us from being absolutely free – and from being our natural selves. We have to respect them, or *we* are not respected. Is this not true? But I am digressing – the sermon only *suggested* this line of thought.

Here – we are in disorder, have taken up the matting in Library, living & dining rooms – and are having the floors polished – We now eat on the lanai, and it is *jolly!*

The dinner bell has rung – so I must run.

Heaps of love – for *all!*

Your own Betty.

I must add one word of condolence before I can sleep peacefully – you said that you received *four* letters from me at one time! *Horrors!* You poor dear things! From the bottom of my heart I pity you! And believe me when I say that I'll try *never* to let it happen again. Never! How could I, when I love you as I do – so afflict you?

No answer – only Echo answers.

Mrs. Grundy worried everyone. Although a fictional English character, she was a symbol of rigid respectability and purity. She first appeared offstage in Thomas Morton's play in 1798, never seen, but her voice is heard judging the onstage characters. The other characters were continually worrying about Dame Grundy's criticism. The term Mrs. Grundy then became part of everyday speech when referring to convention and community censorship. On Kaua'i, Hettie Belle was guided in local conventions by Mrs. Robinson and by the grandmothers' presence in the household. However, as the family grew to know and love her, Hettie was allowed more leeway as was demonstrated by her chance to drive the car.

Hettie Belle finished reading *The Green Vase* by William Castle, Jr.* *The Green Vase* has the flavor of an O'Henry story. It is a tale of passion, misplaced love, tragedy, class struggle, and finally a happy resolution. Although written in 1912, the book is still a page-turner today.

---

* William Castle, Jr. was the Dean of Harvard, author of *The Green Vase* and a guidebook of Hawai'i.

Judith Marion Burtner

"Kapalawai"
March 14, 1913.

Mother dearest —

"All's right with the world" — at least, all is right in *our* little world, for Mr. R. and Aylmer have returned from Niihau safely, and we are again a united and happy family. It is so much more complete when they are here. To celebrate their home-coming, we are going to have a big swimming party this afternoon — about twenty people are coming. Won't that be fun? It is just the kind of a day for swimming, too — just warm enough. Perhaps we'll have a couple of sets of tennis before we go in, just to warm up a trifle more.

You can imagine what a *wonderful* swimmer I am becoming when I presume to teach others! On Wednesday I taught Ethel Bannum to swim! She had never swimmed? swum? a stroke in her life — and before she left the water that afternoon she swam *fifteen* strokes without stopping. How's that? And here Mr. Gay has tried four times to teach her and failed utterly — she was so terrified — wouldn't let herself go. I merely said, "Come on"–"Lay out flat"–"Wiggle your toes and fingers"– "Breath naturally"– and she somehow succeeded. She is the proudest thing that you can imagine, and thinks that I am a *wonder!* She comes this afternoon and shall receive another lesson. I hope that we can take out the canoe this afternoon. It is *such* fun — paddling over the blue — and you glide *so* swiftly!

Last night Mr. Hime called, a very pleasant, eligible bachelor or *widower*, he is — but cold as a fish — I cannot wonder that his wife left him. Deliver me from a cold unresponsive man! I would kill him! Put poison in his coffee, or some such. A woman has a right to expect to be *loved* if she marrys a man, not be treated coldly. "Them's my sentiments"! Mr. Hime soon leaves for a six month vacation — Canada and California being his two destinations. Possibly you shall meet him in California — who knows — he asked to call upon me there.

Our dear friend Mr. Aaser called, and we amused him with billiards and small talk, with a deal of joshing thrown in. He is quite crazy about Maud L'Orange, you know, and as she is now in Honolulu, we found cause to condole with him, etc. Poor little fellow — poor little unprotected man — it is really a shame to tease him — but it is good fun — he takes it so seriously and gets *so* embarrassed.

No Coast mail this week — and I'm so hungry to hear what is happening in your world, and what you are all doing. You really *do* seem in a different world — not as far away — for you usually *seem very* close to me — but the environment is so absolutely different that it seems that I must surely be on another planet. However, I like your world well enough to want to return to it and to you — and I'm coming soon, too. Each time that I write, I am nearer home, do you realize that? Soon I can touch you — so beware, prepare yourself!

So much dear love to you each and every one.

Your own Hettie.

"Kapalawai"

March 17, 1913.

Mother, dearest —

St. Patrick's Day! And *more* important than that, Mrs. Robinson's birthday. You should see the elegant jewelry that she received — a *wonderful* platinum & diamond brooch from her beloved husband, a pearl & sapphire pin from her Mother, a lovely jeweled hat pin from her mother in law, and lovely pictures, etc from her children. The Governess made her a fancy lavendar silk bag — and she seems to really love it — tho' it is but a trifle. You should see how her oldest sons decorated her and her chair, and themselves! Wore *green* neckties all day and did other ridiculous stunts, reminding me of Win's antics in the good old days when the Matthews celebrated birthdays. Do you remember how he used to tie rags about his knees & elbows, etc? What a *great* boy he was! And *is*!

Something *extraordinary* happened today! I had my first lesson on the Ukulele, if you please. I believe that I told you that Waipa and his men have been polishing the floors in the front of the house. You must know that Waipa is *quite* a musician — has a *very* good orchestra which plays on all festive occasions such as dances, dinners, etc. and Xmas mornings. It was *his* music which first thrilled me two Christmas mornings ago. Well, I have been wanting to learn to play the Ukulele, of course, and thought that as long as he was here working he might as well help me & teach me. Mr. R. asked him if he would — and you should have seen him *grin*! He brought his instrument today, and when work was pau, we went out to the schoolroom, and he proceeded to give me my first lessons. He taught me how to tune up — also the "stroke"— and chords of "C" and "G." By the time he had been ten minutes with me — his men (four of them) were on the school house veranda watching intently, then remained there until the lesson was pau — then came in — I played the piano — Waipa his ukulele, and we *all* sang — and I tell you it was *some music*! I wish that you might have heard them sing Aloha Oe – and some others. Mrs. R. said that the only complaint she had to find with the music was that it stopped all work on the place while it lasted. She said that she went into the kitchen only to find all the household servants leaning from the windows listening. Then Sinclair said that all work in the garden and near the stables ceased – that they all pressed as near as they dared & sat with mouths agape. He said that one man was so enraptured that he failed to realize that he was sitting on a picket fence! But it *was* lovely! And I can play some chords – and he has left his ukulele for me to practice upon until my new one arrives. I have written for one. So you see we'll have some music next summer of a new kind.

You should have seen us at the table tonight – tho' you probably *heard* us away over there. We got to laughing about something funny – then one after the other said something funny, and finally we all got hysterical – we laughed and we cried – and we laughed some more. Laugh & grow fat – you know – that is our policy!

How are you all – and *when* shall I hear from you? Tell about ten of your children that they owe me letters.

Your most loving –
Hettie Belle.

Hettie Belle finally mentions a Hawaiian by name when she writes about Waipa. The male owners of the plantations had more opportunities to know and work with Hawaiian men. However, at that time the European/American plantation women had very little contact with other ethnicities, except as servants. In Hettie Belle's letters, the servants were rarely thought of as having similar wants, dreams, problems, and celebrations. In this rare instance, we see Hettie looking up to and admiring someone outside the Robinsons' circle.

The guitar and the ʻukulele are important instruments in the music of Hawaiʻi. The guitar, possibly brought over by the vaqueros, was first used by the paniolo of Hawaiʻi. The six strings were open-tuned based on a chord, creating the slack-key guitar or *ki hoalu*. It was an instrument that became popular in the cowboy corrals and moved to the court.

The ʻukulele was first introduced in urban Hawaii, "a contribution by Portuguese immigrants during the Monarchy period,"[73] It was modeled after the Portuguese *braguinha*, a plucked instrument. The 'ukulele is the instrument identified exclusively with Hawai'i.

Hettie Belle loved to hear the native bands play, wishing the family good things for the New Year. She was eager to learn, and she had her 'ukulele for many years after her time on Kaua'i. She learned the way the paniolo did: by talk and watching and listening.

A yodeling technique developed in Hawai'i during the nineteenth century, before country-western singers in the U.S. used yodeling.[74] The paniolo music touches the heart, especially when *leo ki'eki'e*, the falsetto voice, is used. One of the many gifts that has influenced the American mainland has been the gift of heartfelt music. The tenderness of leo ki'eki'e can bring tears to the listener. On special nights, even today, Na Kama'aina group, musicians with Ni'ihau and Kaua'i roots, can still thrill hearts of those that hear it.

"Kapalawai"
March 21, 1913.

Mother, dearest –

This is "Good Friday"– and we have a holiday, and are keeping it by taking a ride to the mountains today. Mr. Gay's party are to be our guests – we shall lunch at "Makaweli House"– and expect to have a *grand* day of it. We shall start very soon, now – so if I stop suddenly, you will understand *why*. I did up all our bathing suits in a bag – for we shall probably have time for a dip in the pool near "Makaweli House" this afternoon. They will go up in the cart, along with the lunch, etc. Tonight Dr. & Mrs. Sandow are going to call, as they are leaving for Honolulu tomorrow – the Dr. to go on to the coast for a rest.

Mr. R. and Sinclair have gone around to "Haena" with the Rices for a couple of days – left yesterday morning and shall return this evening. Mr. R. shall probably pick out a lot over there – they expect to build later. As I have already told you, it is a *most* charming spot – a *wonderful* spot.

We must go, now – so goodbye for this time.

Loads of love to each one of you.

Your own Hettie Belle.

Judith Marion Burtner

My dear, *dear* Mother –

Did you know that yesterday was Easter Sunday and that I really didn't realize it until we reached the church and found it decorated with Easter lilies and crosses. I had had one or two reminders – Easter cards, etc. – but it is hard to realize that Easter is really here, there being no change of seasons, as in California, no peeling off of dark winter clothes, and appearing in light spring things and Easter bonnets. We've been wearing our "Easter" bonnets since Christmas – and even before – we celebrate all the year round.

During our Easter garden walk, Mr. Robinson plucked a ripe pomegranate for me – and also a pomegranate blossom – and they were responsible for the dreams that I had *before* retiring last night. As I sat holding the blossom, I went way back into my yesterdays and dreamed of the Sunday afternoons, when returning from a walk or drive – with the very dearest and kindest of Fathers – we would pass by a pomegranate tree, and that Father would pluck some fruit. Then passing on to the steps he would dust off my wee boots, then prepare the fruit for me. And I can remember how tempting the red seeds looked – and how delicious they were as I munched them.

You should see the rooms that have been polished – they are *elegant!* We have moved back into them, and they are such a pleasure. The color is lovely! and goes beautifully with their Koa panels. I take a little credit to myself – as I was the

The pool at Makaweli. (Hettie Belle.1913)

one who suggested polished floors – said that they would be so much more elegant than the matting. Do you think me *"nervy"*? Well, you shouldn't have made me so opinionated – and so truthful and out-spoken. I told the truth, and they are glad that I did, I guess – for the change is for the best and is *most* satisfactory.

After our ride to "Makaweli," Mr. Gay said that they were going to have "farewell" tennis for the girls at "Kekupua" at four o'clock, and as it was impossible to think of riding down on horseback, changing and *then* going over, they persuaded me to go down in the auto with them and let the Gay's chauffeur ride my dear "Telephone" down. So I came down with them, changed, and went over for tennis. We had some splendid tennis – and I have never served as well in my life – they were all talking about it. Sinclair came for me a little later – he and Mr. R. had returned from Haena. And after he had a set we came home.

Heaps of love–Your Betty.

The living area of Kapalawai in all its Victorian splendor
(courtesy of the Kaua'i Museum, circa early 1900s)

Kapalawai wooden floor uncovered. After encouraging the polishing of the
floors, Hettie Belle asked her mother, "Do you think me 'nervy?' "
(2013 by J. Burtner)

Kekupua, Mr. Francis Gay's home, late 1890s
(courtesy of the Kaua'i Museum)

Robinson Family Governess: Letters from Kaua'i and Ni'ihau, 1911-1913

"Kapalawai"
March 28, 1913.

You poor darling Mother! –

Are you really quite worried about me, and the American Beauty Roses, and the Honolulu man and all? If so – pray calm your fears *immediately* – for there is *nothing* to worry about, more is the pity!! For he is a *married* man with grey hair! Now are you *quite* relieved? I'm not – I'm quite indignant to realize that *all* the delightful men in this world are already married. Why should it be so??? But really – I'm not quite as skeptical and pessimistic as I try to make out, for I *really* believe that somewhere in this world there is *one* perfect man left, and that he is waiting and hunting for *me*! Poor dear! Think what he is missing all these days! But I shall strive to make it up to him after we are married. But you shouldn't be alarmed just because I *hope* to have a *home* and *husband* and *library* of my own, some day. Shouldn't any normal *young* spinster have such hopes? Perhaps something serious *is* the matter with me – but anyhow I am really coming home soon – and you can immediately take me in charge, put me on a diet, and even give me castor oil, if you think advisable. Perhaps a tonic would not be without its effect.

Indeed, Mother, it *will* be very, very hard for me to leave this wonderful home, fascinating life, and this family that I have come so to love. I cannot bear to think of it – and the other day when we were speaking of my plans, "booking" etc.– I began to "blubber"– I couldn't help it – the tears just came to my eyes all themselves. As you well know, I have been *wonderfully* happy in this beautiful home – and because they have treated me so beautifully, and so like a daughter – it is almost heart-rending to think of leaving – but let me tell you that there is just one *great big* compensation – I am going *home*! And if you knew how much that means to me, you could realize that I am not altogether miserable at the thought. The parting will bring tremendous pain – but *greater* pleasure – I shall leave this home, but shall go to my *real* home. And then I shall see these dear people quite often, as they will be going to Boston in August, and returning thro' California to the Islands at Christmas time, and each summer, of course. So I expect to see them quite often. But I shall not dwell on the "parting"– I'm going to think merely of the "homecoming." Indeed I shall always love these people very dearly – and trust that they shall never forget me.

So Hurd is in S. Wellington again – I must write him. But he hasn't answered my last letter yet. He must be very busy – so I forgive him.

You do write the *grandest* letters, Mother dearest – I just devour them, enjoying them *hugely*! I wish that *I* had inherited your letter-writing talent. But woe is me – I seem to write heaps, and say nothing! But then I may do better when I have twelve children – which is another way of saying that I am a hopeless case, and will never improve – for how can I ever hope to have twelve children, when I haven't the prospect of even having *one*! Woe is me!!

Our men folks have just returned from a "horse drive," and we have been all refreshing ourselves with fresh cocoanuts on the back veranda. Umm! they *are* good.

Here is *so much* love for you all – *you* especially.

Your Betty

"Kapalawai" –

March 31. 1913.

You dearest Mother –

What kind of a letter do you suppose I have just written? A letter to the private girl's schools of Boston, telling of Eleanor's standing, studies completed during the past two years, etc. These people are now in touch with several such schools, trying to decide in which to place Eleanor – and of course each school that they correspond with, wants to know of Eleanor's scholarship and standing. She has accomplished a great deal during the past two years, and I am quite proud to write about her accomplishments – she will stand *very* well, I have no doubt. It is a great comfort to be able to be *proud* and not ashamed of a pupil, isn't it?

Lester will enter Voltman's – a boys' school – and I have no doubt will do quite as well as Eleanor, altho' he is not as quick as she is. But I feel that the competition of a boys' school will be *just* the thing, just the incentive that he needs to do his best work. Alone in his class as he is – he is inclined to be lazy and dreamy. I feel sure that they will do splendid work in the east, and I shall never have course to be ashamed of them – nor will their parents. It is *most* gratifying to me to realize how perfectly satisfied Mr. & Mrs. R. are with their schooling, and the progress that they have made.

Mr. & Mrs. R, Sinclair, & Aylmer and several natives went to Koholuamanu today, on horseback. Mrs. R. & Sinclair have just returned – but Mr. R. and Aylmer will spend the night at the Mountain home there. They went up especially to see that the roads were in good order, as we are planning an expedition very soon – before I leave, for my benefit – as it is the one place where I have not been. I'm certainly looking forward to it – I love the mountain trips, so!

Saturday night we had a *picnic*. Mr. Gay, Dr. Lyman,* Mr. Milliken, and Mrs. Sandow took me to see a wonderful Hypnotist out at Kekaha. It was Mr. Gay's party, I believe, and we had a great time. The Hypnotist, a woman, was truly remarkable, better than any that I have ever seen or heard of before. And the things that she did were amazing! She worked with any volunteers from the audience, some twenty boys and men – Japanese, Natives and Philippinos and whites. They were all Kekaha men that our party knew, so it was no *"fake."* It took only a moment or two for her to put them under the hypnotic spell, and then she made them do all manner of strange, impossible and ridiculous things – chase flys that were tickling their noses, sing to imaginary babies that they were holding in their arms, fish in an imaginary stream, have toothache, dress for a ball, preach sermons, make love, and many other ridiculous things – things that no men would do unless under a spell. Then she put a hat-pin thro' one man's arm – and broke with a sledge hammer a heavy slab of granite weighing at least 300 pounds on another man's chest, who was suspended between two chairs. It was very interesting and remarkable.

I have many letters pressing – so no more tonight – but *heaps* of love to you all – Your Hettie

Hynotism was a popular entertainment around the turn of the century. A Scottish surgeon, James Braid, developed his technique of hypnotism after witnessing a stage performance by a Swiss Mesmerist called Charles Lafontaine in 1841.
Braid wrote:

> Persons in a perfectly wakeful state, of well-known character and standing in society, who come forward voluntarily from among the audience, will be experimented upon. They will be deprived of the power of speech, hearing, sight. Their voluntary

---

* Dr. Francis Anderson Lyman replaced Dr. Sandow as Waimea physician.

motions will be completely controlled, so that, they can neither rise up nor sit down, except at the will of the operator; their memory will be taken away, so that they will forget their own name and that of their most intimate friends; they will be made to stammer, and to feel pain in any part of their body at the option of the operator – a walking stick will be made to appear a snake, the taste of water will be changed to vinegar, honey, coffee, milk, brandy, wormwood, lemonade, etc., etc., etc. These extraordinary experiments are really and truly performed without the aid of trick, collusion, or deception, in the slightest possible degree.[75]

"Kapalawai" –

April 4, 1913

You dearest Mother –

This morning the "lace" woman and man came – do you remember that they came last year, and these people bought hundreds of dollars worth of things from them – among them, a lovely Irish lace collar for me? Mrs. R. did not buy so many things this time – but she bought me the *most exquisite* lace collar – a lovely "Pointe le Venice" one this time – which I am quite *mad* about. I have already planned the gown which it shall adorn. Isn't she just *too* lovely to me? You will *love* my collar, too, when you see it – it is *such* a dream! But I shan't tell you what it cost. Real lace *does* cost!!

Yesterday we went away out to Mana to call upon Mrs. Danford and Mrs. Heapy (?) who is living with her – a *charming* middle-aged woman. Mrs. Heapy knows our Margie! Met her some three years ago in Tokyo. She was there about seven months – and simply raves about Margie and her *dear* home – *so* artistic, she says!

Last mail I had a *dear* letter from Hurd from S. Wellington. He sounds well & happy – he is certainly a dear, interesting chap.

My eyes are so tired with riding many hours in the strong wind today – that I must stop.

Heaps of love to all.

Your Hettie

Robinson Family Governess: Letters from Kaua'i and Ni'ihau, 1911-1913

"Kapalawai" –
April 7, 1913.

Mother, my dearest –

Yesterday, Sunday afternoon Mr. & Mrs. Wilcox⋆ called – bringing their tiny son, Sam, whom I am quite crazy about. We took them for our walk in the garden – Sam accompanying me – and hugely delighted with all that I showed him, from flowers & strawberries to turkeys and pigs. After they left, we went over to the fishpond for a walk – watched the myriad fish jumping at sunset. A pretty sight that!

Saturday evening we all (that is Mrs. R., Sinclair, Eleanor & I) went in to Waimea to the Hall to hear the school children in concert. They had been trained by a Portugese girl, and they really sang remarkably well. The selections were not all that they might have been, being "popular" music or "rag time," but the voices of the girls (all Hawaiian) were so sweet – and they sing in such a naturally artistic way – that we were quite charmed. Some things were most killing – and we laughed ourselves almost sick. It wasn't late when we started home, so we went for a wee joy ride. That was all right, considering, wasn't it?

What a beautiful Easter week you did have. Wish that I, too might have enjoyed it with you. No – we did not observe Lent – ours is a "Union" Church, more Congregational than anything else, I think. Our minister, I fear, is too lazy to prepare or inspire anything more than the one weekly service.

About the $200.00 – of course I can give it to Father, and shall be only too glad to help you out at this time. I am so sorry that you are having such a struggle, but you did perfectly right, and the only right thing in telling me of the situation, and asking my help. My money is not in the Berkeley bank, but as soon as transfer and deposit there can be made, I shall send Father a check. You needn't tell anyone about it – just we three shall know the secret. Your asking me made me feel most happy – made me feel that you loved me & trusted me enough, as much as I want to be loved & trusted. Am so glad that I am able to assist at this time.

Heaps & heaps of love. *Your Hettie*

---

* Charles Henry and Marion Butters Waterhouse Wilcox were part of the large and community-minded Wilcox family of Kaua'i. Little Sam later became president of Grove Farm.

CHAPTER EIGHTEEN
ON THE *PŪNE'E*

"Kapalawai"

April 13, 1913 –

My dearest Mother –

If you tried *very* hard, even you could not imagine the wonderful experiences that I have had since I wrote to you last. I have *never* enjoyed anything as much as our wonderful trip to the mountains – to "Koholuamanu"– it was beyond even *my* wildest dreams – but first I must tell you of our day in Lihue with the Rices. We went over there to tennis last Wednesday afternoon – had many splendid sets – then all piled into our autos and went down to "Kalipaki" [Kalapaki] (the Chas. Rice's place) and had a *splendid* swim there. That is the beach that I have spoken of to you before – a *splendid* place for swimming – and they took out the Hawaiian canoe, also, and we paddled away out. It was *heaps* of fun.

After our swim we had our "shower" and dressed and went back to the W.H. Rice's [William Hyde Rice's home Halenani in central Lihu'e] where a *beautifully* decorated round table, was set for thirty of us. Such a *jolly* meal as we did have! And such good things to eat! Everything – pork, chicken, salmon & salt fish – all cooked in native style (which is the same as saying, "cooked *perfectly*") – and salads, desserts etc. A perfect *feast*! People always enjoy eating, don't they? We surely enjoyed this. And later, the ride home in the moonlight.

We did not leave for "Koholuamanu" on Thursday as we expected as Mrs. R. did not care to be away from the grandmothers two nights, so we left very early Friday morn. Had an early breakfast and started right off. I took my camera – so that you people could enjoy to a tiny degree at least, my wonderful trip. We went up Waimea

Canyon, following the glorious winding river and fording it several times. Then suddenly we began to climb, starting up a *very* rocky, steep mountainside – the trail seems almost a pair of stairs, cut out of the rock – and you rise almost a hundred – no, they said, almost a *thousand* feet in less distance than a mile. After this hard steep climb, you come out into open country, covered with cactus.

About the middle of the morning we reached one of their small mountain cottages – the "half-way" house, they call it. Here we refreshed ourselves with bananas, and drank from the clear, cool river, which runs by the house. Then on we went – but I haven't yet told you who "we" are. Mr. *&* Mrs. R. Sinclair, Aylmer, Eleanor, Lester *&* I – seven of us – and seven natives – two pack mules – and a Japanese cook – quite a "caravan"– only we *weren't* passing thro' a desert. After leaving the half-way house, the mountains grew larger and larger, and grander and grander and ever more thickly wooded. And oh! The *coloring!* If I only could make you see that – but it is so impossible to describe the vivid blues, lavenders, reds and greens. *Brilliant,* is the only word that comes near describing the coloring – and it was even more brilliant than that. One huge range towering above the other, each grander than the last, and the canyons <u>so</u> deep and rugged. At times a mist would subdue everything – and the greys *&* lavenders would be lovely – then the sun would burst out *&* all would be more gorgeous than ever – with a huge, brilliant rainbow spanning the heavens.

We reached the house at about noon. A very comfortable house it is, too – eight small bedrooms, a *large* dining room – (large enough to dance in) kitchen *&* pantries – and three large verandas – then of course there are servants' quarters. About the house is a perfect *tangle* of white Cherokee roses and pink roses, that look *&* smell just like our dear wee pink California wild rose, grown up. Then there are masses of Shasta daisies. We had a delicious luncheon – unpacked our things *&* soon were on our horses again, preparing for a ride of investigation in a neighboring valley and "hunting" on the side. This later, however, you must *never* mention when starting out if you want to get anything. The trail that we took was very wonderful leading thro' a really tropical forest or jungle – imagine if you can a perfect *tangle* of ferns *&* all kinds of wild vines in a forest, and you will know what we passed thro'. The flower that grows in the greatest profusion is the Begonia – both pink and white – great masses of it everywhere, especially along the riverbanks. It looks so wonderfully delicate in the forest. Suddenly we were all startled by the dogs barking and a huge wild pig tore across our path – just in front of my horse. The boys and dogs all gave chase – with the result that Sinclair killed it – so that we had plenty of fresh pork during our stay – and I am the proud possessor of a magnificent pair of *tusks* which you shall all see. Also I have learned how to cook & extricate the tusks from an animal – smart?

Mr. R. got some splendid wild duck – you should have seen him slipping along (reminded me of Father), and you would be surprised if you knew how very quiet fourteen horses and people can be when game is sighted. The ride was beautiful *and* exciting – as you can imagine – and we returned to the house at about five. Then with clean clothes and towels under our arms, Mrs. R., Eleanor and I walked swiftly in the other direction (than that of our ride) about a mile & a half to a glorious mountain pool. The *most* beautiful spot – a wee waterfall at the head – and ferns and begonias covering the steep sides & reflected into the pool. It was really an *unusual* sight, *especially after* we went in. For you must know that we did not have bathing suits, but went in as nature intended that we should. You really cannot imagine how delightful it is – and I now sympathize with small boys & hardly wonder that they play "hooky" from school or defy the law to go in thusly. We didn't want to *come* out – almost longed to turn into mermaids, and we found a delightful cave where we might have spent the night. There was a huge log covered with slippery moss, leaning down into the pool – and we thought it great fun to slide down this and splash into the water. But when the sun began to set, we decided that we must leave our pool – tho' we were loath to do so. When we reached home, we found that the men folks had thoughtfully made all the beds – and Mr. R. was more than delighted with himself, because he had found my "nightie" and tucked it under my pillow. My bed was made well, too.

We had a splendid appetite for dinner, after which we all piled on to the huge punei [pɒneʻe] in the warm dining room – and as the wind howled without, listened to wild cattle hunting stories & Hawaiian legends & ate salted almonds. Later we all got hysterical and silly – and decided that it was best to disperse for the night. The next morning, after a good breakfast, we were off on horseback again for a long ride thro' the woods to a beautiful waterfall, "Hihi Nui". There was a fine mist most of the morning, making the trail rather slippery, but the trees & leaves were all the more beautiful. The waterfall was very, *very* beautiful and some of the views that we had were *grand* – imagine the views from such high mountains (3,000 ft.) to the sea! And other islands in the distance. *Perfectly marvelous!* We returned to the house for luncheon, then packed up for going home. Before we left, however, we went into the woods and gathered fragrant maili leis, so that we could return home properly decorated. We hated to come home, but the ride down was very lovely – especially at sunset and afterwards when the stars and moon came out.

Riding the Mokihana Ridge, Lester at the right (Hettie Belle 1913)

Mr. Gay was here when we arrived, he had stayed here with the grandmothers. We had dinner and prayers – and then it felt pretty good to have a hot bath and get into bed. I was *awfully* sleepy, but not the *least* bit stiff or tired. This morning, I felt as fresh as ever, upon awaking. Went to church this morning – and since the children's Bible study this afternoon, I have been writing. So you see, I am none the worse for wear. And didn't I have a *wonderful* time!? Yes, more wonderful than this has given you any idea of – so wonderful that I trust its memory will always be with me – and I trust that the many pictures will always be fresh in my memory. I only wish that *you all could have enjoyed it*. It seems *so* selfish that I should enjoy so many very beautiful and wonderful things, doesn't it? Why should such privileges have all come

River crossing on horseback. "We followed the glorious, winding river fording it several times," wrote Hettie. (Hettie Belle 1913)

to me? I cannot understand it – for I don't deserve it all. But I *do* appreciate all that I see, I think.

Time for our Sunday walk – pineapples, lettuce etc. so goodbye.

Loads of love to you all – *especially my mother!*

Your loving Hettie

Rugged terrain on ride to Koholuamanu. Hettie wrote, "the trail seems almost a pair of stairs, cut out of the rock." (Hettie Belle 1913)

Sitting on the soft, movable couch at Koholuamanu Cottage, Hettie Belle enjoyed the laughter and stories. She may have heard the following story shared by William Hyde Rice in his manuscript *Hawaiian Legends*.

Hettie Belle beside Koholuamanu cottage (Hettie Belle's photos 1913)

Mr. Aubrey Robinson on horseback (Hettie Belle 1913)

Hunting party at Koholuamanu, but Hettie said they never mentioned hunting, just that they were going on a "ride of investigation." (Hettie Belle 1913)

Holua-Manu: A Legend of Kauai

Manu, Bird, lived with his parents in the mountains above Waimea valley. His greatest delight was to slide down the steep *pali* sides on his sled.

This sport caused his parents a great deal of worry, for they feared that he would meet with some accident. So they placed two immense rocks on the path he used most. But Manu could not be stopped by this. He jumped over the rocks, and struck the path below. However, he did not enjoy the jar, so he climbed back, and rolled one of the rocks down to the river, where it stands today, as large as a house.

Manu's parents prevented his crossing the river by sending a freshet to stop him. The freshet would start at the same moment that Manu started to slide and it would always reach the river first.

At last, discouraged, Manu took his sled, and went to the highest *pali* of the Waimea valley, where he enjoyed his sport, without interruption. This spot is still called Ka-holua-manu, or the Slide-of-Manu.[76]

Registered Mail, No. 636

"Kapalawai"
April 17, 1913 –

Father, dearest –

Thank you *so* much for your Easter postal, bearing your love and loving Easter thoughts – it was appreciated more than I can tell you – a little thing, means a *great* deal, sometimes. Thank you.

All plans for dear Margie's coming and going, seem to be quite definitely made now – and I trust that everything will work out as well as we have planned it. Just think – she leaves Yokohama the day after tomorrow, April 19th and arrives in Honolulu April 29th. I shall be there to meet her, of course and this is our plan – I leave Kauai for Honolulu, Saturday April 26th, arriving early the following morning. Margie will arrive on Tuesday the 29th – and we will start the following day, Wednesday the 30th for Hawaii and the *marvelous* volcano. We arrive at the volcano early Thursday morning and have until late the following day, Friday, before leaving again for Honolulu – reach Honolulu Saturday evening. Then we will have until the following Tuesday afternoon in Honolulu, when we leave for Kauai, reaching these dear people early Wednesday – then Margie will have four days here in my wonderful home, from Wednesday morning until Saturday afternoon, before she leaves for Honolulu – and then on to *you* dear people. She reaches Honolulu early Sunday morning – and has until Tuesday May 13th her sailing day, there. Are you *quite* dizzy? And do you think that *she* will be? Well, I thought that you folks would want to know all our plans.

I can scarcely wait for Margie to arrive – I'm simply *crazy* to see her and "show her off" to these dear people! Won't they *love* her? And won't she love *them*? We shall *tell* you all about *everything* that we do while she is here – everything.

You, no doubt, found my check for $200.00 upon opening this letter – a "little bird" told me that you had need of it – so I am forwarding it – trusting that it arrives in time to help you a bit. I'm so glad that I am able to help you at this time – only wish that I could do more.

With *heaps* of love – *dear* love to you all – *you*, very especially.

Your loving daughter

Hettie Belle

Makaweli, Kauai, T.H.

April 18, 1913 –

Mother, my dearest –

In a letter to Father which I mailed today, I enclosed that check – I trust that it reaches him safely, and that it comes in time to help a bit. I was very glad to be able to send it to him.

I had lots of lovely mail on Wednesday – tho' none from home proper. I heard all the latest gossip, news and scandal. The last *most interesting* engagement news to arrive from Berkeley – is that of your beloved daughter Hettie Belle to Mr. Robinson !!!! Isn't that *exciting?* It was to me. Florence thinks me "horrid"– not to have told her before it is "out." Don't be alarmed – and *don't* you believe it.

You'll forgive a short letter this time, please? More next time. *Heaps of dear* love to all. Your Betty.

"Kapalawai"

April 21, 1913 –

Dearest Mother o'mine –

Do you realize that our Margie has been two days on the ocean blue, already – and is every moment coming nearer and nearer to us? And that by the time this letter reaches you, she will no doubt be with *me?* It really seems too good to be real – and yet it is true. I shall pack my trunk today and lock it – for we shall go to "Makaweli House" any day, now, and not come down until Saturday when I leave for Honolulu. The trunk has to leave here very early in the morning, before we come down.

The work at "Makaweli House" starts today – re-shingling, etc.– and Mr. & Mrs. R. have gone up – left at about 6:30 this morning – Mr. R. will stay up there – Mrs. R. will be down again by lunch time today.

After I had closed your letter last Friday evening (about 9:30) we had some excitement here. Mrs. R. and I were talking, and Aylmer came and told us that we were wanted by Mr. R. to come immediately up on top of the tank. It is about three stories high – and from its top you have a remarkable view – (it was from there that we watched the cane fires that I told you of before). From its top Friday night we watched a *tremendous* forest fire – which burned off acres and hundreds of acres – before they could backfire it, and so put it out. Fortunately it did not reach the cane fields nor get into the high forests, but acres & acres of the land between were well burned over. The main loss was to the grazing country & algarroba trees. We staid up there watching it, perfectly fascinated and horrified as we watched it spread – until way after midnight. It wasn't until after four in the morning that they finally got it out. The boys went to it, of course, and also all the native men about the place and many from the plantation.

It started thro' the carelessness of a man, up the valley, who in burning off his kuliana [kuleana] up there, preparing it for cane planting – failed to put out his fire entirely, and it smoldered on finally setting fire to the whole place. Poor man! He came tearing down in the middle of the night to tell of the fire – but to assure Mr. R. that it wasn't his fault – as he had put his fire out that afternoon! Poor man!

Heaps of love to all. Hettie.

"Kapalawai"
April 26, 1913 –

Mother, *dearest* –

This is Saturday morning – my trunk has gone – and about two o'clock we shall be leaving for Lihue – and from there I shall leave for Honolulu. Mr. Gay (Mrs. R's brother) is going up, and will take care of me on the steamer. In Honolulu the charming Von Holts will meet me – for I am to be their guest while in Honolulu, you know. After Margie's arrival, she will also be there, of course. They are the loveliest people, and have a *most* wonderful home – and it will be *so* much nicer to be with them than at the Hotel. You cannot imagine how excited and happy I am at the very thought of Margie's coming. I fear that I shall squeeze every breath out of her body when I meet her on Tuesday. Of all our good times, you shall hear later, of course.

We did not go up to "Makaweli House" this week as we expected – as the Grandmothers didn't seem to feel strong enough. Mr. R. has been up there all week, superintending the work, and Mrs. R. has made almost daily trips up and down. The boys have taken turns staying up there at night.

Monday afternoon Mrs. R. and I had stacks of fun – with the help of half a dozen of the native boys we planted a huge "rockery" in the front garden – planted it with numerous ferns, begonias, etc. The natives always make work into play, and are awfully funny.

Ladies and sister Marjorie next to William Hyde Rice (Hettie Belle, 1913)

Hanalei area - Emily Rice Sexton (?), sister Marjorie, and Hettie
(from Hettie Belle's photos)

247

Wednesday night we all went for a quiet "Joy" ride – Sinclair driving – Mrs. R and I, sang nearly all the time. Thursday night our beloved Mr. Aaser called, and we had music and billiards and fresh strawberries & cake. He is *such* a dear little pedantic man! He declares that he will *miss* me! And thinks of coming to California in the fall! Don't worry – I *haven't* encouraged him – and won't *"fall,"* even if he *does come!*

Really, I must stop and get ready. Pray that I won't be seasick tonight, won't you? Remember how *dearly* I love you all. *Heaps* of love and kisses.

Your own Hettie Belle

Hettie Belle with her camera. Sister Margie is to the right.
Gentlemen unknown. (Hettie Belle's photos)

"Kapalawai"

May 12, 1913 –

You dearest Margie –

I guess you were right, dear – altho' I wouldn't admit it before – he *must* be a "Mutt"– or else he would not have presented you with such a volume as he did, on such very short acquaintance, too. Altho' I have never read that book the author is known to fame because of her "free love" ideas, etc.– and tho' she is considered a *most remarkable* woman by the world today – I don't think that we all have to agree with her in the least. By this time you know that "Eugenics" is a much discussed subject – perhaps he feared that coming from a "heathen" land you needed enlightenment. As for me, dear, have no fear – I shall never see him again – I don't care to.

You are with the family tonight – and I can just see all your shining faces! It is wonderful to think of you together again. Now, I must send a note to Mrs. Von Holt – and there are other letters. Heaps of my dear love to you – you darling.
Betty

These people think that you are a most wonderful person! (Strange) And when I reach home, if I find that the family haven't made a frightful egotist of you – and spoiled you to death – I shall tell you a few of the many beautiful things that they have said about you.
Your "Betty Helle".

The details of Marjorie and Hettie Belle's travels are missing, but her letter implies that the two sisters met a man whom they do not wish to see again, a man who gave Marjorie a book on free love, or eugenics, or both. Her older sister must have warned Hettie Belle in a letter about this person.

Based upon supposedly scientific principles, proponents of eugenics wanted to control which people reproduced so that the characteristics considered "desirable" would "win out" over characteristics labeled "undesirable." The outcome of this theory allowed those with racial prejudice to justify it with the false "science." Within twenty years, this "science" would be taken to its genocidal extreme in Nazi Germany.

Margie had been working in Japan, so her experiences with another ethnicity may have triggered the discussion on Eugenics. The theory gained some ground in the U.S., and on Kaua'i a Eugenics Club was formed, organized by Mrs. Lydgate and Mrs. Dean.

The Garden Island newspaper featured an amusing letter on page one. In part, it read: "…what is or are Eugenics anyway. Is or are they some kind of breakfast food or some kind of contagious disease or some kind of wild animal?" The letter continues to say that if the ladies need something to *do*, there are pants to mend and socks to darn. It is signed, "Ignoramus."[77]

Judith Marion Burtner

Dearest Family –

I realize that I owe *each* one of you – Father, Mother, Marian, John, Theo & Gertrude a letter – but I have decided to answer them each and all in *person!* Really there is no time for letters these days – besides school, luncheons, dinners and *all sorts* of pleasures are filling the days *more* than full. Besides you really

wouldn't care to receive a letter from me at present – as I am not very happy these days – my tears seem too near the surface, and I have been ashamed to realize that I cannot control myself. It began last Saturday evening when we were eating and drinking just before retiring, and I suddenly realized that it was my *last* Saturday night – I began to weep. I didn't mean to. Then all day Sunday I disgraced myself – one thing after another seemed to almost break my heart – the hymns, the prayers at home – the goodbyes at church – everything seemed to *hurt* – I could scarcely stand it. I have tried to be more sensible today, but fear that it will not last very long. You must not misunderstand me – it isn't that I am unhappy about returning to you all – it is only that this has come to be such a "home" to me that it needs must hurt to leave. But *home* and my blessed family & friends I know will prove compensation enough. I leave here on either "Siberia" May

Desk at Kapalawai - This may have been the "wee desk" where Hettie Belle sat to write. (Photo taken by J. Burtner at Kapalawai, 2013.)

250

27th or "Sierra", May 31st – arriving in S.F. June 2nd or 6th. This is the *last mail* that will reach you before I do – expect me June 2nd – as I am *almost certain* that I shall get passage on the "Siberia." You see I cannot know for sure until she reaches Honolulu from the Orient. However, I leave here, next Saturday, May 24th. Will any of you be in B. [Berkeley] upon my arrival? Do you think that I had better stay a day or so in B. before leaving for Vallejo? Then I could kind of "settle down" when I did reach Vallejo. Please write plans for me and send them to Sally's care. You will know best what you want me to do.

Remember that the last time that I sat at my wee desk at "Kapalawai" writing – it was to *you all* – it is a wonderful moonlit night, too. I love *you all, dearly*. Hettie.

EPILOGUE

Hettie Belle returned to California and her family, but she was forever changed by her two years with the Robinson family on Kaua'i and Ni'ihau. The rest of her life was deeply influenced by these experiences she had as a young woman. She retained many of the values she had acquired with the Robinsons: she married well, treasured beautiful possessions, never talked of money, and enjoyed live musical entertainments. She indulged in travel to exotic places including India and China. Like Mrs. Robinson, she cared for her garden and always did mending: hemming and sewing buttons on her grandchildren's clothing. She became a wonderful storyteller in the manner of Mr. Robinson. She treated guests extravagantly, taking them on excursions to Muir Woods, the ice follies, fancy dinners, theater, and musical performances. And, she *did* marry an older man, nine years her senior.

Not long after her return to California, Hettie Belle stepped down from a train to attend a friend's wedding ceremony. In the crowd on the platform was Henry Charles Marcus, sent with his mother, Virginia Frank Marcus, to meet this young woman and guide her to the festivities. It is rumored that he took one look at her and said to his mother, "This is the woman I'm going to marry."

Their wedding took place at the Palace Hotel in San Francisco on August 8, 1916, three years after Hettie Belle left Kaua'i. It was a double wedding with Henry's brother Frank and his bride. The couple traveled by ship to Alaska and the Yukon on their honeymoon. After a few years, they moved to a house at 1040 Lombard Street in San Francisco, then a steep hill with goats grazing on its grassy side within sight of the Italian fishermen's homes by the Bay. Today that block of Lombard Street is the famous twisty hill in San Francisco. Hettie Belle and Henry had three daughters: Virginia, Marion (my mother), and Patricia. She adored her husband and was devastated when he died in 1938. This home on the crooked street was beloved by three generations. I lived there when I was born.

Hettie Belle continued to play her grand piano until she had to move out of her home into the San Francisco Athletic Club. I remember how she would sit down and play Mendelssohn's *Lieder Ohne Worte, Op. 19: No. 1* with great feeling. After her husband's death, she took up wood carving, and it is interesting to note that some of her furniture patterns mimicked the furniture in the Robinsons' Kapalawai bedroom.

Hettie Belle Matthew Marcus 1917, and Henry Charles Marcus
(photos from Marion Wright's collection)

Hettie Belle returned often to her beloved Hawaiʻi. Her life continued to be much more connected to the Robinsons than she could have predicted when she left Kauaʻi. The darling toddler Helen

Marion Matthew, whom Mr. Aubrey Robinson saw on a visit to Allan Matthew's home in California, grew to be an accomplished musician and horsewoman. Hettie Belle wrote to the Robinson family to tell them that her little niece Helen Marion was coming to Hawai'i, and could they show her around Kaua'i?

Double-wedding. Hettie Belle is the third from the left with Henry Charles Marcus next to her. The other couple were Frank Marcus and his wife. (Marion Wright's collection)

Hettie Belle in Whitehorse, Yukon, Canada on her honeymoon trip (photo from Marion Wright's collection)

Marcus family: Hettie Belle holding Patricia, Marion Pomeroy,
Henry, Virginia (Marion Wright's collection)

Furniture carving in Robinson's Kapalawai bedroom (2013, J. Burtner)

Furniture Hettie Belle later carved (2011, J. Burtner)

As Keith describes in the Foreword, the Robinson's were preparing to leave for a summer visit to Niʻihau. Eleanor insisted that Lester, who had loved his teacher Miss Matthew, should be the unfortunate one to stay behind and entertain her niece on Kauaʻi. Lester felt totally disgusted. But when the family returned they noticed a strong attraction between the two young people, sparks flying. Eleanor was somewhat fit to be tied at the developments. Lester and Helen were married in 1937, and so, Hettie's niece, Helen Marion, became Mrs. Lester Robinson. She was a superb rider, a beautiful woman, and is remembered as an inspiring organist at the Waimea United Church of Christ, formerly the Foreign Church.

Lester and Helen had two sons, Keith Pomeroy and Bruce Beauclerk. The "axident" did not slow Lester down too much. At Harvard he was a champion shooter in the prone position, going a whole year without missing a shot. His son Keith recounts that Lester ran the 100-yard dash at a speed that was only one-tenth of a second slower that the then existing Olympic Games record. On Kaua'i he outran a raging freshet on a mule. Helen Marion still went out on cattle drives late in life. At the age of sixty-five, she was in the saddle for eleven hours on a Ni'ihau drive. She is remembered for climbing a mango tree in her later years to show her grandchildren how to get the fruits.

The Gay and Robinson Corporation continues to manage the family's assets. Bruce is involved in this business and actively working the land along with his children. With no more sugar production on the island, the family has gone back to ranching and formed the Makaweli Meat Company, LLC with a slaughterhouse at the location of the old sugar mill.[78]

Lester's two sons own the island of Ni'ihau. Hunting Safaris are now allowed by appointment on this private island. Hybrid sheep and wild boar that have become destructive to the landscape are targeted. As when Aubrey Robinson lived, these grandsons have also imported some animals; in this case, large antelopes for hunting. Helicopter tours are also offered on Ni'ihau.

Lester and Helen Marion's family. Lester, Helen Marion, Bruce Beauclerk, and Keith Pomeroy Robinson at Lois Robinson Somers's wedding reception. The lady greeting them is Lois's mother, Ethel "Ethelyn" Nowell Robinson. July 1948 on the front porch of Kekupua House. (photo courtesy of Lois Somers)

Keith uses his knowledge to continue the work with native plants that Isabella Sinclair so lovingly documented, trying to preserve the fragile endemic species as Manager of Kauai Wildlife Reserve. His passion is to save the beautiful ecosystem that Hettie Belle found so fascinating. He has worked tirelessly and been able to grow endangered plants and trees, but these native plants had evolved in benign isolation, so lost their competitive survival mechanisms, and they are unable to compete with more efficient, aggressive introduced species.[79]

Eleanor Robinson mid-1900s (courtesy of Lois Somers)

Matthew second cousins – Keith Robinson, Judy Burtner, and Bill Matthew 2013 (Les Burtner)

Lack of water is still an issue on Niʻihau, but as with their ancestors, the Robinsons do what is necessary to protect the island. The waters around Ni'ihau sparkle, large shivers of sharks gather, and monk seals bask safely on the shores. Soon another generation with ties to Ni'ihau will come into the management of this special island.

Sinclair married Ethel Glade shortly after Hettie Belle's marriage. Alymer never married but tended to Ni'ihau. His room at Kapalawai still holds his books and pictures. The family speaks of him with great respect. Selwyn married Ethel Pickering Nowell, and their daughter Lois Somers lives at Kekupua, Francis Gay's house during Hettie's stay. Eleanor never married and stayed at the family home of Kapalawai until her death in 1988.

The Kapalawai house is today being renovated; plans are to restore it as the centerpiece of a resort there. I did not get to see the Makaweli House and grounds that Hettie Belle loved so dearly.

My research took me to Kaua'i many times and to Ni'ihau twice. Trying to visit the places Hettie Belle saw, I visited the Fern Grotto, Hanalei, the Wainiha Valley, Koke'e State Park, the "metropolis" of Waimea, and the McBryde gardens. I tried to slide on the Barking Sands, but before I could disturb the "dogs," I was turned away as a missile from Barking Sands Pacific Missile Range Facility was fired out over the ocean. I rode down an irrigation ditch in an inner tube and explored Kekaha on bicycle. I was warmly welcomed at the church Hettie Belle attended. Kaua'i is now a bustling island with many conveniences and visitors, but the spell it casts calls me to return as it did my grandmother.

Years ago in 1885, Francis Sinclair wrote a nostalgic poetic verse that illustrates the family's close ties to their place, specifically Ni'ihau.

A Sketch in the Pacific
There would they pause, each happy, laughing face,
Waiting the highest wave that landward swept;
Then with a merry shout began the race,
As huge rolling billow onward leapt;
Each swimmer flying with the lightning's pace,
Poised on the buoyant wave, and deftly kept

> Fair on the sparkling crest, and light and free,
> As sea-gulls sweeping o'er a summer sea.[80]

Hettie Belle wished she could write a book, but felt dismayed, thinking she did not have the talent, even though she had plenty to say! She didn't realize how highly vivid her letters were. Hettie Belle had no idea that her letters would someday entertain readers far in the future and provide a glimpse into a world long past.

ENDNOTES

Notes

Introduction

1. Igler, *The Great Ocean*, 34.
2. Joesting, *Kauai: The Separate Kingdom*, 158.
3. Igler, *The Great Ocean*, 34.
4. Wichman, *Kauai: Ancient Place-Names and Their Stories*, 22.

Chapter One

5. *The Garden Island*, 09/12/1911, Vol. 8, #36.
6. Kinghorn, Jonathan. *The Atlantic Transport Line, 1881-1931*.
7. Kapalawai literally means "the ripe fresh waters."

Chapter Two

8. Joesting. *Kauai: The Separate Kingdom*, 243.
9. Tabrah, *Ni'ihau: The Last Hawaiian Island*, 122.
10. Ibid., 155.
11. Baybrook and Hofgaard, C.B., "Waimea Foreign Church."

Chapter Three

12. Von Holt, *Stories of Long Ago: Niihau, Kauai, Oahu*, 10.
13. Tabra, *Ni'ihau: The Last Hawaiian Island*, 94.
14. Von Holt, *Stories of Long Ago: Niihau, Kauai, Oahu*, 14.

15. Mengies, "Charles Barrington Robinson 1812-1899" Unpublished partial history of Banks Peninsula, Kaua'i Museum files.
16. Tabrah, *Ni'ihau: The Last Hawaiian Island*, 96.
17. Ibid., 96.

Chapter Four
18. Joesting. *Kauai: The Separate Kingdom*, 201.
19. Keith Robinson conversations; Lincoln, *Amy Greenwell Garden Ethnobotanical Guide to Native Hawaiian Plants.*
20. Von Holt, *Stories of Long Ago*, 18.
21. Tava & Keale. *Niihau: The Traditions of an Hawaiian Island*, 71. The Robinsons question Tava & Keale's veracity. However, Keith Robinson remembers one breadfruit tree on the south of the island had red sap and was said by the people to be human. He does not believe that there are any breadfruit trees left on Ni'ihau today. The Robinsons knew a professor of botany who went to Tahiti and asked if there were different varieties of breadfruit trees. His search seemed futile until finally an old timer spoke up saying that once upon a time there had been that variety of breadfruit that had red sap like blood.
22. Knudsen, E., *The Kaua'i Papers*, "Early Days at Waiwa," 100.
23. Mr. Cropp was probably the son of the manager of Kōloa Sugar on Kaua'i. Conversation with Andy Bushnell, 2012.
24. Opening date was 1904, but it was constructed from 1889-1891, designed by Henry P. Baldwin. ("Sugar Water: 6-West Kauai," excerpted by Carol Wilcox, http://muse.jhu.edu/chapter/258020, date 01/14/17.)
25. William R. Castle, Jr., *Hawaii Past and Present*, 150-151.
26. Blay & Siemers, *Kauai's Geologic History: A Simplified Guide*, 82.

Chapter Five
27. Joesting. *Kauai: The Separate Kingdom*, 199.
28. Martin, *Na Paniolo o Hawaii*, 15.
29. Knudsen, *Teller of Hawaiian Tales*, 157-162.
30. Tabrah, *Ni'ihau: The Last Hawaiian Island*, 105.

Chapter Six

31. Moriarty, *Niʻihau Shell Leis*, 24.
32. Daws, *Shoal of Time: A History of the Hawaiian Islands*, 182-183.
33. Joesting. *Kauai: The Separate Kingdom*, 144.
34. Hemphill, "Gay and Robinson Tours."

Chapter Seven

35. Beltz, Unpublished paper, 2012.
36. Hackfeld and Company, 1913 booklet, Hawaiian State Archives.

Chapter Eight

37. Titcomb, *Native Use of Fish in Hawaii.*
38. According to Keith Robinson, after World War II, even with improved communication between Kauaʻi and Niʻihau, the pigeons continued to carry messages.
39. Eric Knudsen, *Teller of Hawaiian Tales*. These are stories that Eric told on the radio to entertainment-hungry citizens during World War II.

Chapter Nine

40. Wichman, *Kauaʻi: Ancient Place-Names and Their Stories.*
41. Arthur C. Pillsbury, "Paradise Unknown." His trip to Hawaiʻi was chronicled in a Sunset Magzine article in 1912.

Chapter Ten

42. Joesting, *Kauai: The Separate Kingdom*, 35.
43. Isabella Bird, *Six Months in the Sandwich Islands*, 207.
44. Casciani, "The History of the Suffragettes, 10/2016.
45. Whyte, *The Life of W. T. Stead.*
46. Keith Robinson remembers a story about the phonograph and a family cat named "Widey." The cat would catch lizards and pull off their tails, getting very frisky and racing around the house. On the back porch was a stack of fragile records, and the excited cat jumped on the record pile. They fell with a crash and shattered. Later the family reminisced and called that story "the night Widey broke all the records."

Chapter Eleven

47. There are some differences in the measurement of Niʻihau: 72 square miles (http://www.niihau.us/island.htm 01/13/17), 69.5 square miles (https://en.wikipedia.org/wiki/Niihau 01/13/17.)
48. Tava & Keale, *Niihau: The Traditions of an Hawaiian Island*, 11-15.
49. W.H Rice, "Bernice P. Bishop Museum – Bulletin 3," 68.
50. Jones International and Jones Digital Century, "History of the Phonograph," intekom.com/restore/History_Of_The_Phonograph.html, 04/06/18.

Chapter Twelve

51. Department of the Navy, Naval History and Heritage, "Mongolia: Passenger-Cargo Steamship," 1904.

Chapter Thirteen

52. "October 14,1912, President Roosevelt Shot in Milwaukee," This Day in History, 05/20/16.
53. Bird, *Six Months in the Sandwich Islands*, 289.
54. Wikipedia, "Flinch (card game)," 04/19/2018.
55. Aylmer was not really a woman-hater but was a very serious person who was focused on his work and did not enjoy the glib society of the day. He is much admired by his nephew, Keith Robinson, who wrote, "From Hettie's writing, it is clearly evident that even in those early years, Aylmer was already developing the careful, sober, intensely workaholic habits that would characterize him for the rest of his life."
56. Okihiro, *Pineapple Culture*, quoting Davida Malo, 97.
57. Von Holt, *Stories of Long Ago*, 18-19.
58. Blay and Siemers, *Kauai's Geologic History: A Simplified Guide*, 56.

Chapter Fourteen

59. Wikipedia, "Hazel Hotchkiss Wightman," 10/31/2017.
60. Fayé, *Touring Waimea*, 5.
61. Ibid., 5-8.
62. *The Garden Island*, Vol. 8 #35, 09/05/1911, 4.

Chapter Fifteen

63. Location of gymkana: conversation with Andy Bushnell, 2012.

65. Fleeson, *Waking Up in Eden*, 55.

66. Conversation with Andy Bushnell, 2012.

67. Joesting, *Kauai: The Separate Kingdom*, 207.

Chapter Sixteen

68. Okihiro, *Pineapple Culture*, 176.

69. Ibid., Ida Kanekoa Milles quote, 140.

70. Joesting. *Kauai: The Separate Kingdom*, 157.

71. *The Garden Island*, Vol. 9, 1913.

72. College of Physicians of Philidelphia, "The History of Vaccines: Smallpox," 04/05/18.

Chapter Seventeen

73. Martin, *Na Paniolo o Hawai'i*, 95.

74. Ibid., 95.

75. Wikipedia "Stage Hypnosis," 04/2016.

Chapter Eighteen

76. W.H. Rice, "Bernice P. Bishop Museum – Bulletin 3," 90.

77. *The Garden Island*, Dec. 3, 1912, p. 1.

Epilogue

78. "Agicultural Land Assessment for Robinson Family Partners: Proposed Important Agricultural Land, Makaweli, Island of Kaua'i," June, 2016.

79. Robinson, Keith, "Letter to Gay & Robinson Environmental Manager," 02/29/16.

80. Sinclair, Francis, "A Sketch in the Pacific, Verse VII, 20.

APPENDIX A
ROBINSON/GAY FAMILY WITH NICKNAMES

Francis Sinclair 1797-1846
m. Elizabeth McHutcheson "Eliza" 1800-1892

Six children with <u>descendants mentioned in book.</u>

1. George Sinclair 1824-1846 (died at sea)
2. Jane Sinclair "Jean" 1829-1916
      James Gay (son of Thomas)
   m. Thomas Gay 1814-1865
         2.1. George Sinclair 1850-1933   m. Marion Rowell
                  2.1.1. Ethel Gay
         2.2. Annie (died) 1859-1861
         2.3. Francis 1852-1928 m. Lily Hart
         2.4. Elizabeth "Eliza" "Lila" 1859-1947   m. Welcker
         2.5. Charles 1862-1937
         2.6. Alice 1865-1960
               m. Aubrey Robinson 1853-1936

3. James McHutcheson Sinclair "Hamie" 1826-1873
4. Helen McHutcheson Sinclair 1831-1913
   m. Charles Barrington Robinson
         4.1. Aubrey Robinson
               m. Alice Gay
               4.1.1. M. Sinclair 1886-1964

4.1.2. Aylmer Francis 1888-1967

4.1.3. Selwyn Aubrey 1892-1984

    m. Ethel Nowell

      4.1.3.1. Lois Ethlyn 1925-

          m. Lawrence H. Somers

      4.1.3.1.2. David L.

          m. Susie Summers

4.1.4. Eleanor 1898-1988

4.1.5. Lester Beauclerk 1901-1970

    m. Helen Marion Matthew 1910-2002

    4.1.5.1. Keith Pomeroy 1941-

    4.1.5.2. Bruce Beauclerk 1943-

CODE KEY

4.1.1. = Fourth child of the 6.
      First child of the fourth.
      First child of the first.

Underlined name = if second name is commonly used

---

5. Francis Sinclair "Frank" 1834-1916

   m. Isabella McHutcheson

6. Anne McHutcheson Sinclair "Annie" (1839-1922)

   m. Valdemar Knudsen "Kanuka" (1820-1892)

      6.1. Ida Elizabeth Knudsen "Eliza"

         m. Valdemar Knudsen "Kanuka" (1820-1892)

      6.1.1. Mary Elizabeth 1892-

      6.1.2. Hilda Karen 1897-

      6.3. Eric Knudsen

         m. Cecilia L'Orange

      6.3.1. Alexandra Lilikoi "Sandy"

      6.3.2. Valdemar L'Orange

APPENDIX B
MATTHEW FAMILY WITH BIRTHDATES AND NICKNAMES

Dr. Winfield <u>Scott</u> Matthew 1848
m. Marion Lillian Pomeroy 1857

Twelve children with <u>descendants mentioned in book</u>

1. Margaret Lillian 1879 "Margie"
2. Allan Pomeroy 1881
   m. Daisy Lincoln 1883
   - 2.1. Helen Marion 1910
     m. Lester Beauclerk Robinson
     - 2.1.1. Keith Pomeroy 1941
     - 2.1.2. Bruce Beauclerk 1943
   - 2.2. Morton Pomeroy 1912

3. Melville Richard 1883 "Mel"
   m. Ida Rhoton 1884
   - 3.1 Melville Richard, Jr.
     m. Irma Heoch
   - 3.2. Raymond Pomeroy 1913 "Ray"
     - 3.2.1. William Melville 1942 "Bill"
       m. Vicki Faught

4. Sarah Wheat 1885 "Sally"
   m. Phil <u>Beckwith</u> Hackley
     4.1 "Billiken"
5. Winfield Scott, Jr. 1886 "Win or Winnie"
6. Hettie Belle 1888 "Betty"
   m. Henry Charles Marcus 1879
     6.2 Marion Pomeroy Marcus 1920
       m. Hollis <u>Garrett</u> Wright 1916
         6.2.2. Judith Marion Wright 1945 "Judy"
           m. Homer <u>Leslie</u> Burtner, Jr. 1945 "Les"
7. Samuel <u>Hurd</u> 1890
8. Raymond 1892 "Boy Dear"
9. Marian Hilliard 1894 "Mutt"
10. John Britton 1896 "Fats" "Johnny Boy"
11. Theodore 1898 "Dordie" "Ted"
12. Gertrude Willard 1900 "Babe" "Gert"

CODE KEY

3.2.1. = Third child of the 12.
         Second child of the third.
         First child of second.

Underlined name = if second name is commonly used

APPENDIX C
HISTORICAL FIGURES

Fredrik Hiorth Aaser was born in Christiania, Norway, in 1884. He came to Hawai'i in 1906 and joined the staff of Kekaha Sugar Co., Ltd., where he became a bookkeeper and cashier. As cashier, Mr. Aaser would take their pay to the workers in the fields at Mānā via the plantation's narrow-gauge railroad. On one such occasion, the locomotive slowed at a curve, and a man with a revolver called out "Stop and dismount." Mr. Aaser was carrying about $11,000 in payroll money, and all was taken in the holdup. The police soon captured the culprit. Almost all the loot was recovered, found in a tin hidden in a swamp.

In 1919, after unsuccessfully courting women for several years, Mr. Aaser married Hazel Moody at Waimea. (Siddell, Men of Hawaii, Vol. 2; Gage, *The Garden Island*, March 7 and 13, 2014)

Louise Theresa Voss Baldwin married Benjamin Douglas Baldwin. He was born at Kohala, Hawai'i in 1868. His grandfather was the Reverend Dwight Baldwin, who arrived in Hawaii in 1831 with the fourth company of missionaries. After working on Maui, Mr. Baldwin became the manager of the Hawaiian Sugar Co. at Makaweli and then became the plantation manager at Makaweli in 1903. (Siddell, *Men of Hawaii, Vol. 2*)

Claire Edesse Borron Brandt was the daughter of Edward Barnes and Marie-Edesse Février of Canada. She married her husband, Thorvald Brandt, in 1905 in Honolulu. They lived in a large mansion and were active members of the

270

Norwegian community in Waimea. (Hawaii Kauai Bios, Genealogy Trails.com; conversation with Christine Fayé.)

Thorvald Brandt was born in 1861and educated in Christiania, Norway. While Hettie Belle was on Kaua'i, he managed the Bishop and Company Bank in Waimea, which opened July 1, 1911. He married Claire Borron in Honolulu. Mr. Brandt was active in many community organizations on Kaua'i, including serving as treasurer of Hofgaard and Co.; president of Waimea Stable Ltd.; trustee of both the Waimea Foreign Church and Waimea Hospital; and president of the Kaua'i YMCA. Thorvald was also named Commissioner of Education and was the president of the Kaua'i Chamber of Commerce. He served on the Kaua'i Board of Supervisors for two terms in the early 1900s. In Hettie Belle's time, there was a small, influential Norwegian community in the Waimea-Kekaha part of Kaua'i, which included the Brandt, Fayé, Knudsen, and Hoffgaard families, a group of Norwegians apparently following in the footsteps of Valdemar Knudsen. Mr. Brandt died in 1925. (Geneaology Trails.com; Leonard, *A Who's Who in Finance and Banking, 1920-22*; "Thorvald Brandt;" conversation with Christine Fayé.)

Alexander H. Brodie was Superintendent of Kaua'i Schools during Hettie Belle's time on Kaua'i. He had previously been a teacher and was also a small-scale farmer in the Waimea district. His son Lex later became famous in Honolulu for his tire business, with commercials that always ended with "Thank You, Very Much!" (Andy Bushnell conversation)

William Richards Castle, Jr. (born 1849) served King David Kalakaua as attorney general, one of several missionary descendents active in government during the movement to annex Hawai'i to the United States. He was later Dean of Harvard and an author. His grandfather, Samuel Northrup Castle, founded the prosperous agricultural company Castle & Cooke. (Wikipedia, "William Richards Castle, Jr.,"; Siddell, *Men of Hawaii, Vol. 1*)

William Danford was born in 1878 in Dublin, Ireland, the son of William and Anna "Annie" Sharpe Danford. His mother later remarried, becoming Lady Herron. William attended high school in Ireland then immigrated to Hawai'i by ship around Cape Horn in 1894 with his mother and stepfather, retired Scottish businessman and Magistrate for the County of Dublin, Sir Robert Herron. Mr. Danford was sugar boiler on Oʻahu and then employed by Hawaiian Sugar Co. at Makaweli for eleven years. He married Jean Harwood, a San Franciscan, at Kekupua in 1903. After that he advanced to supervisor, and in 1907, he was hired by H.P Fayé as head overseer, Mānā section, at Kekaha Sugar Co. Many laborers followed this popular supervisor to Mānā, and by 1908 he became assistant manager. In 1928, at the death of H.P. Fayé, he became manager of Kekaha Sugar Company. (Siddell, *Men of Hawaii, Vol. II*; Blain, "Anglican History")

Jean Harwood Danford was the wife of William Danford, assistant manager of Kekaha Sugar Company. She was from San Francisco and was married at Kekupua in 1903.

Dr. Harrison Columbus Dukes was born in Indiana in 1848. By 1895, he was proprietor of Dukes Sanitarium in Oakland, CA. He married Isabella Jane Shaw, and they had several children. Later, this physician and surgeon worked for the Pacific Mail Company, where he was apparently honored and loved.

An article in the *San Francisco Call* illustrates Dr. Duke's character and why Hettie Belle may have considered him a suitable chaperone.

"Popular Physician Transferred --- Dr. Dukes, the physician aboard the steamer Korea of the Pacific Mail Company, has been ordered to the steamer Mongolia of the same company. Doctor Dukes will remain over one trip and go out on the Mongolia on the next run. He removed his belongings from the steamer Korea yesterday, but before he took his departure a large number of the Chinese crew, who were great admirers of the doctor, assembled in front of his stateroom. One of the number, who was delegated as spokesman, informed the physician in broken English how sorry they were to have him leave. A box containing choice eatables was presented to the doctor as a token of their regard." (Ancestry.com; *The San Francisco Call*, Vol. III, No. 81, February, 1912)

Elizabeth Lindsay Ewart was born in 1880 and lived until 1947. She married George Robert Ewart, and they had three children. Her sister was Margaret Lindsay Fayé, and their brother, Alexander, was Attorney General of Hawaiʻi during Hettie Belle's stay. ("Elizabeth Lindsay," Records Ancestry.com)

George Robert Ewart was born in Sacramento, CA in 1875 and was educated at Punahou School, Honolulu and McGill University in Montreal. He married Elizabeth in 1904. His first job in the sugar business was at the Kilauea Sugar Plantation. Later he worked as a civil engineer for the Territory and became head *luna* (foreman) at the Hawaiian Sugar Co. From 1906 through 1912, George was manager for Gay & Robinson, Inc.'s Makaweli Sugar Plantation. Following this, his engineering expertise helped with work at Kekaha Sugar Company and in improving the water ditching system. (Siddell, *Men of Hawaii, Vol. 1*)

George Hendrick Fairchild, born in 1869, was the manager of the Makee Sugar Company at Keālia on Kaua'i and was a Territorial Senator in 1911. He left Hawai'i in 1912 and established a sugar plantation in the Philippines. ("George Fairchild," Geni.com; Andy Bushnell conversation.)

Margaret Lindsay Fayé of Kaua'i married Hans Peter Fayé in 1893. They had eight children. One of her sisters was Elizabeth Lindsay Ewart. Her husband Hans was born in 1859 in Drammen, Norway. His mother Ida's maiden name was Knudsen. On his father's side, he descended from a French family that had settled in Norway in the late seventeenth century, thus the French name. Hans Peter came to Hawai'i in 1880 to learn the sugar business, and he eventually became a cane planter and the plantation manager of the Kekaha Sugar Company, as well as the president of the Waimea Sugar Mill Company. (Siddell, *Men of Hawaii, Vol. 1*)

Ethel Eliza Gay was a cousin of the Robinson children. She was born in Hawai'i on November 17, 1882 and died in San Diego, CA on May 11, 1965. Her family lived on Coronado Island, San Diego, CA. Not long after her stay with the Robinsons, she married Chester Allen Sumner in July 1914 and continued to live on Coronado Island.

Ethel's parents were George Sinclair Gay and Marion E. Rowell. Marion was known as a brilliant student at Mills Seminary. She left California to return to her island home and taught in the family of Jane (Mrs. Thomas) Gay on Ni'ihau, and Alice (Mrs. Aubrey Robinson) was one of her students. After a short time there, she married her pupils' oldest brothers, George. While her daughter Ethel was on Kaua'i staying with the Robinsons, Marion died, April 11, 1912

The Rowell ancestors, Ethel's maternal grandparents, were George Berkeley Rowell and Malvina Jerusha Chapin. They were early missionaries to Kaua'i and Ni'ihau, part of the tenth company of the Hawaiian Board of Missions. Reverend George Rowell helped build the Waimea Church, but later he was censured and withdrew from the Hawaiian Board of Missions. He continued work with the Hawaiian Church in Waimea. (Tabrah, *Ni'ihau: The Last Hawaiian Island*, pp.86-89; "Waimea Church Early History"; U.S. Find-a-Grave)

Francis Gay was born in 1852 in New Zealand. He was a businessman, and in 1880 he founded Gay & Robinson, Inc., a family corporation, with his cousin Aubrey Robinson and his grandmother Eliza Sinclair. His home in Makaweli was called Kekupua. Today it is the home of Lois Somers, Selwyn Robinson's daughter. Mr. Gay figured large in the life of the Robinson family when Hettie Belle was governess. He died in 1928.

Jane "Jean" Sinclair Gay (1929-1916) was the daughter of Francis and Eliza Sinclair. She and her husband, Thomas Gay, had six children, and Alice (Hettie Belle's Mrs. Robinson) was their sixth. Jean was the oldest of the three Sinclair sisters, and along with her next sister, Helen, was one of the two grandmothers who lived in the Robinson household.

Lily Hart Gay was raised in Honolulu by her father, Judge Hart of British heritage, and her Hawaiian mother. A noted beauty, she and her sister were well educated, and she graduated from Mills College in California. She married Francis Gay but preferred the Wailele home in Honolulu to life on Kaua'i. Hettie remembered Lily dancing the real hula on a moonlight night. Lily and Francis had one son, Ernest. Toward the end of Hettie Belle's stay with the Robinsons, the Francis Gays left for Boston and Paris. Francis Gay soon reappeared back on Kaua'i without Lily. There was no explanation of this unexpected occurrence in Hettie Belle's letters. Lily later married artist George Burroughs Torrey and became known for her own decorative paintings of flowers. (Hettie Belle's 1973 memoir; "Lillie Hart Gay Torrey," Ask Art.com/Artist Bio).

Captain Thomas Gay, born in Scotland, was a British Merchant Service captain who engaged in whaling in the Pacific Ocean. He first met the Sinclair family at Pigeon Bay, New Zealand when he was skipper of the whaler *Offley*. Later he captained the *Corsair* and continued whaling until it was no longer profitable. His ocean travels as merchant and whaler took him as far as Scotland and Alaska with frequent trips to New Zealand and Australia. Already father of one son, Captain Gay married a second time in New Zealand to the eldest Sinclair daughter, Jane, who later became Mrs. Aubrey Robinson's mother. In Canterbury, New Zealand Gay was considered a daunting whaler, known for his courage and enterprise. Soon after steering the Sinclair family safely to the island of Ni'ihau in 1863, he set sail again to take a shipment of cargo back to Auckland, New Zealand. On this journey, he was involved in an altercation with an unscrupulous member of his crew, and Captain Thomas was sentenced to five months in prison. Before he could return to his family on Ni'ihau, he died at Newcastle, New South Wales, Australia. He and Jane had six children, and the last child, Alice Gay (Mrs. Robinson), never saw her father. (Ogilvie, "Dauntless Captain Gay, the Forgotten Whaler" *The Press*.)

Gustav Henry W. and Helen Emlie Whittington Hansen. Mr. Hansen was born in Hamburg, Germany in 1873. He arrived in Honolulu in 1894 or 1895. In 1901, Gustav married Helen Emlie Whittington on Kaua'i. The census listed their residence in Waimea in 1900 and in Kekaha in 1910. His occupation was a timekeeper in 1900. (Ancestry.com)

Arthur Gilmour Hime was born in Canada in 1865. His father was Irish by birth, and his mother was from Canada. He was divorced by 1910 and had moved to O'ahu and then Kekaha, Kaua'i. At the time Hettie Belle met him, he lived with Brodie and Aaser. In the 1910 census, Mr. Brodie was listed as his partner and employee and Mr. Aaser as a boarder. Mr. Hime became a bookkeeper at the Kekaha Sugar Company. He later married a woman named Agnes (maiden name unknown). By 1921, the couple lived in Seattle. He died in 1950. (Ancestry.com; United States Federal Census)

Christopher Blom Hofgaard was born in Norway (1859) and educated there. He worked in Christiania before moving to Hawai'i in 1882. After arrival on Kaua'i in 1885, he married Marie at Waimea. Mr. Hofgaard founded C. B. Hofgaard & Co., which was the main store in Waimea at that time. He became postmaster for Waimea as well as District Magistrate, a position he held while Hettie was on the island. He was involved in various community organizations and businesses: President of the Waimea Foreign Church; treasurer of Waimea Stables; owner of the lumberyard; treasurer of the Hawaiian Church including its Sunday School and Christian Endeavor; member of the Masons, Knights of Pythians, and Eastern Star; and active in the Waimea Chamber of Commerce. Gertrude who came to play tennis with Hettie was the daughter of Christopher and Marie Hofgaard. (Siddall, *Men of Hawaii, Vol. 1*, p. 141; "Hawaii Kauai Bios," Genealogy Trails.com; conversation with Christine Fayé)

Marie Mahlum Hofgaard was the wife of Christopher Blom Hofgaard. They were a prominent couple in Waimea business and society. They married in Waimea in 1889. Hettie Belle played tennis with their daughter Gertrude.

Victoria Kamāmalu was born in 1838, the sister of King Kamehameha IV and King Kamehameha V. She was appointed Kuhina Nui by King Kamehameha IV when she was only seventeen. This was her destiny, as she was the highest-ranking female chief and expected to serve in this prominent leadership position as head of the king's council. King Kamehameha IV's young son had died, and he did not name an heir to the throne before his own unexpected death in 1855. Because of her pivotal position, Victoria then had influence in proclaiming her brother, Lot, to be Kamehameha V.

In 1824 an attempted revolution against the Kamehameha dynasty, led by Kaua'i chiefs, was crushed in a bloody battle. The rich lands of Kaua'i were then divided among the descendents of Kamehameha I. As his granddaughter, Victoria Kamamalu was awarded 51,000 acres on the island. Her ownership of these lands was recorded in the Mahele book in 1848. In 1865, she sold the Makaweli ahupua'a (over 21,000 acres) to Eliza Sinclair. ("Victoria Kamamalu," Hawaii.gov; Joesting, *Kauai: The Separate Kingdom,* pp. 112-113, 193)

King Kamehameha I, renowned as Kamehameha the Great, united and ruled the Hawaiian Islands. He lived from the mid 18th century until 1819. A great warrior, he made use of Western technology as well as his own impressive leadership skills to create a single Hawaiian Kingdom, ruling the entire archipelago by 1810. (NPS.gov "Kamehameha the Great")

King Kamehameha III, Kauikeaouli, lived from 1813 until 1854 and was the longest reigning monarch of the Hawaiian Kingdom. He formalized the Hawaiian government and set up the system of land ownership under the Great Māhele of 1848, trying to balance modernization with Hawaiian traditions. After his two children died in infancy, he adopted his nephew Alexander Liholiho at birth and named him as his successor.

In a speech celebrating the return of sovereignty to the Hawaiian Kingdom (after a brief British takeover in 1843), Kamehameha III used the phrase *Ua mau ke ea o ka `aina i ka pono,* the life of the land is perpetuated in righteousness. This is still the state's motto. (HawaiiHistory.org; Wikipedia.)

King Kamehameha IV, Alexander Liholiho (1834-1863), ruled the kingdom of Hawai'i from 1855 until his death. He was the grandson of Kamehameha the Great and adopted son and heir of his uncle, King Kamehameha III. His wife, Queen Emma Rooke and young son Albert visited Kaua'i in 1860. Sadly, after their return to Honolulu, Prince Albert became ill and died suddenly in 1862, devastating his father.

King Kamehameha IV favored the British over the encroaching Americans. He and Queen Emma promoted public hospitals to care for their people. ("Kamehameha IV," Aloha Hawaii.com; Joesting, *Kauai: The Separate Kingdom,* p. 182.)

King Kamehameha V, Lot Kapuāiwa (1830-1872), ruled the Kingdom of Hawai'i from 1863 until 1872. He was the older brother of King Kamehameha IV, serving under him as Minister of Interior and Minister of Finance. He traveled to Europe, Canada, and the United States. After refusing to take an oath to the 1852 constitution, he eventually was able to draft another one giving more power to the king. This constitution lasted twenty-three years. He promoted the cattle industry on the islands. A lifelong bachelor, he named his sister Victoria Kamāmalu as heir, but she died before him. King Kamehameha V died before he named another selected successor, so the constitution required an election after his death. He was the last direct descendant of Kamehameha the Great to rule as king. ("King Kamehameha V," Aloha Hawaii; Hawaii History.com.)

Anne "Annie" McHutcheson Sinclair Knudsen (1839-1922), the youngest of the three Sinclair sisters, was the last child born to Francis and Eliza Sinclair. She emigrated with her family from Scotland to New Zealand and on to Hawai'i. She married Valdemar "Kanuka" Knudsen of Kaua'i who was the first family friend of European descent to visit the widow Eliza and her family on Ni'ihau.

Annie was the first Sinclair to leave the family home and move to Kaua'i, causing concern for some in her tight-knit family. She was the sister of both grandmothers living in the Robinson household. Hettie Belle also met her two children, Ida and Eric. (Veech, interviewer, The Watumull Foundation Oral History Project, "Ruth Knudsen Hanner.")

Cecilia Alexandra L'Orange Knudsen was Eric's wife during Hettie Belle's time on Kaua'i. Hettie Belle remembered her as a fascinating woman, "full of life and humor – at the dances she had an admiring audience when she and a German partner danced the waltz." The children were Alexandra "Sandie" Lilikoi Knudsen and Valdemar L'Orange Knudsen. Cecilia was from a Norwegian family.

Eric Alfred Knudsen was born at Waiawa, Kaua'i in 1872, the son of Valdemar Knudsen and Annie McHutcheson Sinclair. He was educated in New Zealand, Europe, and at Harvard. In 1905, he married Cecilie Alexandra L'Orange in Christiania, Norway. Hettie Belle met two of their three children, Alexandra "Sandie" Lilikoi and Valdemar L'Orange. Eric was the manager of the Knudsen Brothers ranch in the Kekaha area. Over several years, he served in the Hawai'i territorial government in the legislature and Senate. For the 1911 to 1913 sessions, Eric was president of the Senate. According to Hettie Belle's letters, he was lively and entertaining. (Siddell, *Men of Hawaii, Vol. 1.*)

Ruth S. Knudsen was born January 6, 1901 in Oakland, CA. She was the only surviving child of Augustus Francis Knudsen and Margaret Russell. Her paternal grandmother, Anne Sinclair (Mrs. Valdemar Knudsen), was the sister of the two grandmothers (Helen and Jane) in the Robinson household. Ruth's father, Augustus, was interested in how the religious beliefs of the *kahunas* might be connected to other religions. He was a kind of mystic and stated that he once saw a *menehune* sitting across from him at a campfire. Thus, he got involved in Theosophy and Hinduism and spent some time in India.

Augustus returned to Kaua'i and worked for a time on the family ranch after the death of his father, Valdemar. Augustus' wife, Margaret, became physically and emotionally incapacitated after the death of their baby, and they divorced. Augustus left Kaua'i and moved to California, where he remarried and settled in Hollywood. Ruth was left in the care of her grandmother and her Japanese nurse, Hirokichi Ito.

As an adult, Ruth traveled widely, including trips to Norway and Germany. In 1947, Ruth married Eric K. Hanner in Maine, but soon she returned to Hawai'i. In her later years, she helped form the visitor center at Kōke'e, along with Isabel Faýe. She established the Annie Sinclair Knudsen Fund to benefit the people and environment of Kaua'i and to honor her grandmother's deep love for the island. (Ancestry.com; Veech, interviewer, The Watumull Foundation Oral History Project, "Ruth Knudsen Hanner,")

Valdemar Knudsen, "Kanuka" was the first European/American visitor to the Sinclairs on Ni'ihau. He helped them as they were learning the language and customs of the islands. His respect for native customs and religion made him a natural go-between for the Island's native and *haole* populations. Valdemar was living at Waiawa, Kaua'i, the seat for *konohiki* (overseers of crown land). He became the caretaker of the royal herd, and sold hides, tallow, and sweet potatoes to ships at the Waimea port. He was an American citizen from 1852 on, as he had earlier been in a transport business in the gold fields of California. (Veech, interviewer, The Watumull Foundation Oral History Project, "Ruth Knudsen Hanner.")

Deborah Kapule of Kaua'i was the favorite wife of Kaumuali'i, the last King of Kaua'i. After his kidnapping by Liholiho and later death, Deborah stayed on Kaua'i. She was an active participant in the history of Kaua'i during the first half of the nineteenth century. (Joesting, *Kauai: The Separate Kingdom*, pp. 94-96, 113-114)

Lili'uokalani, Hawai'i's Queen (1838-1917), born Lydia Kamakaeha, was the last sovereign of Hawai'i. Raised in Honolulu, she became fluent in English and toured the Western world. She married John Owen Dominis, son of an American sea captain. When her brother King Kalākaua died, she became queen, but her power was limited by a previous constitution. In 1893 pro-American forces in Hawai'i overthrew her government and named Sanford B. Dole as president of a Provisional Government and then of the Republic of Hawai'i. Although President Cleveland thought the overthrow was illegal, his successor McKinley did not. Dole, backed by powerful forces, refused to step down. In order to avoid bloodshed among her people, the queen chose not to resist, but others staged a rebellion, and she was arrested and ultimately forced to abdicate. Queen Lili'uokalani was a skilled musician, writing many songs and chants. While detained at Iolani Palace, she wrote the beautiful song "Aloha Oe" (Farewell to Thee). ("Hawaii's Last Monarch, Queen Liliuokalani," Aloha Hawaii. com; *Liliuokalani, Hawaii's Story by Hawaii's Queen*; "Liliuokalani," History.com.)

Fannie Louise Young Lindsay married Alexander Lindsay, Jr. in Michigan in 1906. Alexander was born in Fifeshire, Scotland in 1871, and he was educated in the public schools of Hawai'i and at the University of Michigan. Fannie and Alexander had two children. He practiced law in Honolulu, moving up through the ranks to become Attorney General, Territory of Hawai'i, 1910 to 1913. Fannie was sister-in-law to Mrs. Fayé and Mrs. Ewart. (Siddell, *Men of Hawaii, Vol. 1*)

Hans L'Orange, one of the young men Hettie met (and perhaps the mystery man she admired), was from Norway. In later years, he became the manager of Oahu Sugar Company. He persuaded his bosses in 1924 to donate several acres of low-yielding sugarcane land for a recreation area for the workers. This became the Hans L'Orange Baseball Park. He was beloved for his high regard of Hawaiian people. After the December 7 attack on Pearl Harbor, he reportedly said, "You don't have to worry about the people of Hawaii; they're all loyal." (Ohira, *Star Bulletin*, October 11, 1999)

Helen Elwell Lydgate was a social matron of Kaua'i. As a young teacher, she worked at Malumalu School for Hawaiian boys and girls. She married John Mortimer Lydgate (1854-1922) in 1898. He was a renaissance man: surveyor, botanist, plantation manager, journalist, and Congregational minister. He preached in both English and Hawaiian. He made an early decision not to become a landholder on the island, but years later the County of Kaua'i dedicated a large park in his honor. Helen entertained many guests both local and international. She organized groups such as the literary clubs and eugenics association. She started circulating her collection of books that eventually became the Līhu'e Library. ("The Story of Hawaii and It's Builders," *The Honolulu Star Bulletin*; Soboleski, "The Reverend John Mortimer Lydgate: Kaua'i's Renaissance Man," *The Garden Island*, February, 14, 2007; "History of Steelgrass Farm.")

Dr. Francis Anderson Lyman replaced Dr. Sandow as Waimea physician from 1913 to 1917. Born in Honolulu, he was the grandson of two couples who were early missionaries to Hawai'i. (Hank Soboleski, "Plantation Doctor Francis Anderson Lyman," *The Garden Island,* April 20, 2014)

Davida Malo (1793-1853) was a leading early Native Hawaiian historian. Educated after King Kamehameha I's death, he wrote in the 1830s and 1840s. He later became a Christian minister and built a church on Maui. He was a poet, author, and translator as well as a founder of an early Hawaiian historical society. (Wikipedia, "David Malo," 10/2/16)

Alexander Moxley McBryde (born about 1861) loved the beachfront of Lāwa'i. With his brother Walter, he founded McBryde Plantation, and when the family corporation formed in 1899, he procured the lower valley and fishing rights in the bay. He moved Queen Emma's house down the cliffs to the valley floor, enlarged the gardens, and added many exotics to Queen Emma's plantings. After his death, Alexander's property was sold to Mr. Robert Allerton and his companion, John, in 1938. The property ultimately was incorporated into the National Tropical Botanical Garden. The Queen Emma cottage was preserved. Both Alexander and his brother Walter were highly regarded by Hawaiians in the area. In his will, Alexander gifted his collection of Hawaiian artifacts to the Kaua'i Library Association, and these items eventually formed the beginning of the Kaua'i Museum collections in 1960. (Forbes, *Queen Emma and Lawai*; Donohugh, *The Story of Kōloa: A Kaua'i Plantation Town*; "Kauai Historical Blog: Alexander McBryde," Kauai Museum Collections.)

Elizabeth Amelia Moxley McBryde's husband Duncan was a Scotsman. He arrived on Kaua'i in 1856, working as a cattle rancher. In 1876, Queen Emma leased the land of Lāwa'i to him for fifteen years, reserving a house plot and taro patch for herself. He died when his son Walter was fourteen years old. Elizabeth McBryde raised her two sons, Walter Duncan and Alexander. These were the bachelors Hettie Belle teased. In 1886, after Queen Emma's death, Elizabeth McBryde purchased the entire ahupua'a for $50,000. (Nellist, *The Story of Hawaii and Its Builders*, incorporating *Vol. III of Men of Hawaii.*)

Walter Duncan McBryde (1864-1930) was the founder of the McBryde Sugar Company, Ltd. and Kaua'i Fruit and Land Company, Ltd. Born at Wahiawa he was an energetic, community-minded businessman who served on the Kaua'i Board of Supervisors and as a representative to the Territorial Legislature. His "Kaua'i Pine" company, which produced up to 250,000 cases of canned pineapple, allowed him to grant homesteads to his workers and to invest in his garden. In 1907, he purchased the land for Kukuiolono Park in Kalaheo. (The park name means "torch of the god Lono" and is located in a place where a torch was lit in long-ago times to guide fishermen at sea.) He spent years and his own resources designing this beautiful spot "to benefit the public regardless of race, color, or creed." He gave the Nōmilu Fishpond part of his land to the family of Philip Palama, Sr., a dear friend and a partner whom he loved. Hettie Belle's teasing probably made a man of his persuasion more embarrassed.

The beloved Kōloa Tree Tunnel was also a product of Walter's energy. In 1911, Walter McBryde donated and helped plant many eucalyptus trees, a "swamp mahogany" variety that absorbed water and helped dry the roadbed area. About 1/3 of the length of the original Tree Tunnel is left today since the highway rerouted the old road, and many trees on the *mauka* section were cut to clear land for sugarcane planting.

Along with his bachelor brother Alexander, he was highly regarded by Hawaiians in the area. (Forbes, *Queen Emma and Lawai*, p. 9; Donohugh, *The Story of Kōloa: A Kaua'i Plantation Town*)

Charles Dunklee Milliken was born October 12, 1863 in New Hampshire. His education was completed at the Yale Divinity School in 1892. Reverend Milliken lodged with the Hiorth family in Waimea while pastor of the Foreign Church from 1905-1916. Hettie Belle remembered that he rode his bicycle about the District, played the best tennis game, and was "a most delightful dinner guest, much in demand." After his service on Kaua'i, he served at the Union Church in Piedmont, Oakland, CA. He later died in Hawai'i. (*The Pacific*, Vol. 66, p. 14; United State Federal Census.)

Queen Emma (1836-1885) was born a member of high-ranking royal Hawaiian ancestry. Adopted at birth by her childless aunt and Dr. Thomas C. Rooke, she married Alexander Liholiho, King Kamehameha IV. She promoted both a hospital

(Queen's Hospital) and a girls school, traveling to London where she met the British queen and raised funds for her projects. After the deaths of her young son and husband, Queen Emma was defeated in her efforts to succeed her husband. She spent time on Kaua'i sojourning at Lāwa'i, developing a garden and taro patch, enjoying nature, and reading. Her trip into the Alaka'i Swamp is famous on the island. ("Queen Emma," Aloha Hawaii; Forbes, *Queen Emma and Lawai*.)

Charles Atwood Rice of Līhu'e, Kaua'i was a planter and rancher. He was born in 1876, the second son of Wm. Hyde Rice and Mary Waterhouse. Charles was educated on Kaua'i, in O'ahu, and in San Francisco. He was married to Grace King for fifty-two years. Besides his work as a rancher, he managed Kipu Sugar Company and was president of Līhu'e Ice & Electric Power Co. and Kaua'i Honey Co. plus director of Waterhouse Investment Co., and Waterhouse Realty Co. He was a member of the Territorial Legislature during Hettie Belle's time. In 1912, he was a delegate to the Republican National Convention in Chicago and active nationally in that party. Charles was a member of Pacific Club and Chiefs of Hawai'i plus captain of Kaua'i Polo. As Hettie noted, he was an enthusiastic sportsman. Charles and his brother William Henry Rice, the sheriff of Kaua'i, controlled the political machine that ran the island. (Siddell, *Men of Hawaii, Vol. I*, p. 201; Kaua'i Historical Society "Rice Family Papers" MS7; Andy Bushnell, 2014 conversation)

Grace Ethel King Rice was a member of the *kama'aina* (Hawai'i born) King family. Her parents were Thomas J. and Josephine "Phina" Wunderberg King. Thomas was from Nova Scotia, and "Phina" was born on Kaua'i. Their child Grace was born in 1881 and raised on O'ahu. Hettie Belle was fond of Mrs. Rice and enjoyed visiting their Kalapakī Beach home. Mrs. Rice's two daughters who visited the Robinsons during Hettie Belle's time were Edith Josephine Kapiolani (born 1900) and Juliet Atwood (born 1901). In 1946 a tsunami destroyed her house and almost got Mrs. Rice. (Kaua'i Historical Society "Rice Family Papers" MS7, conversation with Andy Bushnell)

Mary Waterhouse Rice (1847-1933) was born at Hobart Town, Tasmania and traveled with her family to Hawai'i when she was four years old. Her father was a merchant in Honolulu, and he brought the first live camel to Hawai'i and gave tickets to his paying customers to see it. As a child, Mary attended Punahou School and spent some time with her family in England. She married William Hyde Rice in Honolulu, 1872, and they established their home, Hale Nani, in Līhu'e. They had eight children. She was known as "Mother Rice," and Hale Nani was a center of cultural life on Kaua'i. Hettie Belle was especially fond of the Rice family. (Goodale, Hobey. *Hobey*; "Mary Waterhouse Rice, Part 2, *The Garden Island*, October 4, 2011; Kauai Historical Society "Rice Family Papers, MS7.")

William Hyde Rice, rancher and sugar planter, was born in 1846 in Honolulu. He had a pet donkey as a child. As a schoolboy he rode horseback or buggy to Kōloa on Monday mornings for school weeks with Father Dole. Later, he attended school in Honolulu and California. Right before his marriage, William Hyde was the youngest member of the House of Representatives under King Kahmemeha V. He served in the Senate and was on the committee that forced Kalakaua to sign the Bayonet Constitution that stripped the king of much of his power. Appointed Governor of Kaua'i by Queen Lili'uokalani, he served until after the revolution of 1893. His favorite recreation was wild cattle hunting. William Hyde said that he always thought in the Hawaiian language. His translations of legends are considered true to the original tales. He became lame when thrown from a buggy—thus the cane in Hettie Belle's photo. (Kauai Historical Society "Rice Family Papers, MS7"; Siddell, *Men of Hawaii, Vol.I*.)

Helen McHutcheson Sinclair Robinson (1831-1913) was the second daughter of Francis and Eliza Sinclair. She voyaged with her family from Scotland to New Zealand, where she married Charles Barrington Robinson. The marriage produced one child, Aubrey, but did not last.

George Berkeley Rowell (1815-1884) was part of the Tenth Missionary Company 1842 sent out from the Boston area to Hawai'i. He was stationed at Waioli and Waimea on Kaua'i. With meager funds and the help of the community, he built the Foreign Church that still stands in Waimea. He later left the Hawaiian Board of Missions and established the Hawaiian Church in Waimea. (Coan Memorial Library "Early Missionary Life In Hawaii: Christian Missionaries to the Kingdom of Hawaii (1820 to 1893)" ; Hofgaard, "Waimea Foreign Church Early History," excerpts from the Kauai Historical Society Manuscript.)

Dr. Bruno F. Sandow was born in 1859 in Baden, Germany. He moved to the United States after being widowed. **Eula Elmira** (Mrs. Sandow, his second wife) was born in 1881 in California and married the doctor about 1900. When Hettie Belle was on Kaua'i, Dr. Sandow was the medical practitioner as well as an active member of Waimea district society. He returned to California and was replaced by Dr. Lyman. Dr. Sandow was later a captain in the U.S. army during World War I. He died in 1935 and was buried in the San Francisco National Cemetery. (Ancestry.com)

William K. Schultz and **Mabel B. Schultz** were a young European-born couple. William had been a sugar boiler and was head *luna* (overseer) for the Hawaiian Sugar Company at that time. He was born in Germany about 1875; Mabel, in England about 1883. An article in *The Garden Island* tells of excitement near the newspaper office: Sugar Boiler Schultz's horse ran away with his sulky and crashed. Apparently the horse was not tied securely, so briefly enjoyed its wild freedom. (Ancestry.com; *The Garden Island*, Vol. 8 #36, 9/12/1911 p. 1)

Eliza McHutcheson Sinclair was the matriarch of the Robinson/Gay family, a strong and determined woman, a pioneer, and businesswoman. She married Francis Sinclair in Scotland, and they traveled by ship to New Zealand with their large family. Later, as a widow, she moved her family to Hawai'i and purchased Ni'ihau.

Francis Sinclair, Jr. (1834-1916), son of Francis and Eliza Sinclair, was the family's manager of the island of Ni'ihau for nearly twenty years. His wife Isabella wintered there with him. In 1883, he turned over management of the island to his nephews, moving to California and then England, where he pursued his interest in literature, publishing several books of poetry. (Soboleski, "Niihau Manager Francis Sinclair," *The Garden Island*, January 24, 1916)

Isabella McHutcheson Sinclair was born in Scotland and immigrated to New Zealand with her family in 1861. She married Francis Sinclair, Jr., a son of her aunt Eliza McHutcheson Sinclair. She and Francis spent many years on Ni'ihau. She explored the flora of Ni'ihau and western Kaua'i, making illustrations that comprised the book *Indigenous Flowers of the Hawaiian Islands*. Some of these paintings can be seen at the Kōke'e Natural History Museum. Sadly, a second book of rare flora was destroyed in a warehouse during the San Francisco fire. (Soboleski, Hank."Author, Illustrator Isabela McHutcheson Sinclair," *The Garden Island*, Sunday, January 19, 2014)

Wilhelmina Harris Makee Spalding was the eldest daughter of James Makee, a sugar plantation owner on Maui. She married Colonel Zephaniah Swift Spalding in 1871, and they eventually settled on Kaua'i. Their home, Valley House in Keālia, was renowned for its expansive porches, gables, and dormers, with sweeping lawns, swimming pools, rock-enclosed lily ponds, pavilions, and many out buildings. (Marley, "A Historical Narrative Of the Valley House Estate on Kauai (part 1); Hite, Kauai Historical Society Spalding family; Cole & Wichman, Early Kauai Hospitality, p. 44.)

Colonel Zephaniah Swift Spalding was born in 1837 in Ohio. He served in the Civil War, was captured and exchanged for another prisoner, and was awarded the rank of Lt. Colonel at age twenty-five, but he always felt the Civil War was a tragedy. He was remembered by his family as a "strong, crusty man" and "indulgent to his children." In 1867, he was sent by Secretary of State Seward, who knew his father in Congress, to Honolulu to investigate the possibility of a reciprocity treaty with the Kingdom of Hawaii. Zephaniah met James Makee, a sugar plantation owner on Maui. He married the eldest Makee girl, Wilhelmina Harris Makee, in 1871. After two of their five children were born, they moved briefly to San Francisco, but returned to the island of Kaua'i. In Keālia, they built the Valley House. The house, which Hettie Belle visited, was impressive and expansive with a dining room that could seat twenty-four comfortably, and there was an enormous crystal chandelier in the drawing room. Colonel Spalding established the Makee Sugar Company. (Marley, "A Historical Narrative Of the Valley House Estate on Kauai (part 1); Hite. "Makee Family Genealogy"; Cole & Wichman, Early Kauai Hospitality, p. 44.)

Heinrich Martens von Holt, Honolulu businessman, was born in 1863. He was educated at Saint Alban's College and Royal School in Honolulu and Bishop Scott Academy in Portland, OR. He married Ida E. Knudsen at Cambridge, MA, and they raised five children. He began work in insurance and real estate, but is remembered mostly for his accomplishments with the ranch department of the O'ahu Railroad and Land Company where he developed irrigation ditches from the mountains. He served on many boards in the community and was chairman of the Central Committee of the Reform Party during the Provisional Government. (Siddell, *Men of Hawaii, Vol.2*)

Ida Elizabeth Knudsen von Holt, (1868 to 1941), was the first child of Valdemar and Annie Knudsen, the older sister of Eric. She was the mother of five children including the two girls, Mary Elizabeth and Hilda Karen, who visited the Robinsons during Hettie's stay. Ida was the author of a book about her ancestry, *Stories of Long Ago*.

Mabel Zelia Palmer Waterhouse (born 1877) was the wife of Alfred Herbert Waterhouse, company doctor for Kōloa and McBryde Plantations. She married him in California in 1907, and they soon moved to Kōloa. Her daughter Florence remembered that her dad, Dr. Waterhouse, was also government doctor. In that capacity, he had to go out to ships to examine the crews. Once he had to attend to a pet monkey that had been burned on board. Mabel was active in the YWCA Girl Reserves, taking groups camping in the hills above Kalāheo and 'Ele'ele. Her children were cared for by three Japanese amahs. She entertained with big full-course dinners. At Thanksgiving, the family invited guests from the bachelor quarters and teachers, those who had no family on the island. Her marriage anniversary was on the fourth of July when her husband Alfred hosted a community-wide train ride and picnic, but she stayed home to answer the phones. Their grandchildren remembered joining in family musical evenings when Dr. Waterhouse played cello and their "Nana" Mabel played the piano and violin. (Smith Family Records, Kauai Historical Society; Nishimoto, "Oral History Interview with Florence Waterhouse Brandt, 1987"; Cook, *100 Years of Healing: The Legacy of a Kauai Missionary Doctor*, p. 160)

William Waterhouse was born in Honolulu in 1852, the son of John Thomas Waterhouse and Eleanor Dickenson. He was educated in private schools in Honolulu and Kōloa where he was a "school chum" of Mr. Aubrey Robinson at Dole's School. He married Melicent Philena "Lena" Smith. Their family moved back and forth between the Mainland and Hawai'i. He was mayor of Pasadena from 1905 to 1907 and is credited with establishing that city's municipal electric lighting system. (Siddell, *Men of Hawaii, vol. I;* Ancestry. com; US Census records)

Elizabeth "Eliza" "Lila" Gay Welcker lived from 1859-1947. She was the fourth child of Jane Sinclair (grandmother Gay in the Robinson household) and Thomas Gay. She married Mendell Welcker of Berkeley, but he became seriously ill on their honeymoon in 1901, passing away in 1910. Mrs. Welcker was a widow when Hettie met her.
(University of California, Berkeley)

Charles Henry Wilcox was born in 1880 to Samuel Whitney Wilcox and Emma Washburn Lyman. The Wilcox family was large and community minded. Among many other philanthropic gifts, his sisters Elsie and Mabel, along with their brother Gaylord, established the Wilcox Memorial Hospital in Līhuʻe.. ("Samuel W. Wilcox," *The Garden Island.*)

Marion Butters Waterhouse Wilcox and her husband Charles had three children. Samuel Whitney Wilcox II (born 1909 or 1910) was the little Sam that Hettie Belle met. He was named for his grandfather. When Sam was president of Grove Farm, the family gifted land for the Kauaʻi Community College. ("Samuel W. Wilcox," *The Garden Island.*)

APPENDIX D
GLOSSARY OF HAWAIIAN WORDS

ahupua'a – land division usually extending from the uplands to the sea. Land division for royal Hawaiian tax purposes.

'ake 'ake – band-rumped storm-petrel (*Oceanodroma castro*)

'akekeke – ruddy turnstone (*Arenaria interpres*)

ali'i – royalty,chief, chiefess, one acting as ruler

akua – supernatural beings

aloha nui – big love

Aloha nui loa – huge love from afar

haole – white person, American, Englishman, Caucasian; formerly any foreigner

heiau – pre-Christian place of worship, shrine

hinana – spawn of the 'o'opu fish

holokū – loose seamed dress with yoke and train, patterned after the missionary ladies' dresses.

kama'āina- native born, "child of the land," one who has lived in Hawai'i a long time, specifically born on the land or in one place, but not necessarily of native Hawaiian ancestry.

kahuna – wonder worker, priest, expert in any profession

kanaka – Hawaiian person

kolohala – a showy ring-necked pheasant (*Phasianus colchicus torquatus*)

kuleana – tract of land given to Hawaiians

kulu'ī – small, endemic trees or shrubs (*Nototrichium* spp.) with small more or less hairy leaves and downy catkin-like flower spikes.

Judith Marion Burtner

lei – garland, wreath of flowers, leaves, feathers
lomilomi – massage, pounding, pressing
lūʻau- feast, named for taro tops
luna – overseer, foreman, leader

mahele – portion, division, section
maile – fragrant shrub, vine leaves used in leis and hula ceremony
makai - toward the ocean
mauka – toward the mountains
make – make dead, or slang for finished, tired
malihini – newcomer
mele - song, anthem, or chant of any kind
menehune – legendary group of small people who worked at night
mokihana – citrus shrub found only on Kauaʻi with fragrant berry-sized fruits
used in lei
moʻo – lizard

nūhou – news, gossip

ʻōhiʻa lehua – shrub/tree of hard wood, grown in wet areas
opihi – cowri shell
ʻoʻopu – goby fish
ʻōpū – belly, stomach, abdomen

paniolo - cowboy
pāpala – light wood used for fireworks
pāʻū – a wrap-around skirt costume worn by women riding in formal parade
attire
pau – over, finished
pilikia – trouble
pipi – cattle (also bipi), came from the English word beef
poi – cooked taro corms, pounded and thinned with water; Hawaiian staple
food.
puneʻe – soft, movable couch
pūpū – shells

ʻulu – breadfruit tree

APPENDIX E
PORTION OF HETTIE BELLE'S
MARCH 7, 1913 LETTER

Explanatory note: Most of the letters were written on folded paper as can be seen by this example.

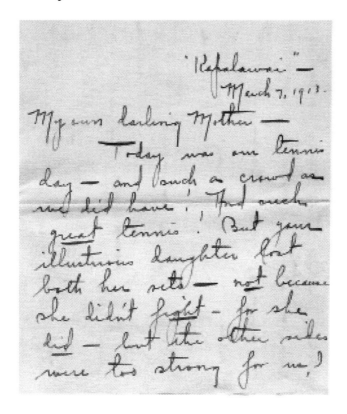

— who had been most successful — had about 2 dozen crab,
then we persuaded her to
sell to us — and how we
enjoyed them this noon!
We have had two delicious
sea baths this week —
so refreshing — for the weather
has been sultry.
    That monday after luncheon
we all (that is Mr. & Mrs R.
Sinclair, Sister & I) had a
horseback ride to "Makaweli
House." It was a most

of my stay — and I am glad.
We all went down to the
wharf last evening, at
about eight o'clock to see
them off. It was stacks
of fun! We wished them
"Bon voyage" and tucked in
all sorts of 'seasick' wishes.
You should have seen the
many, many old kent men
and women, sitting along
the wharf — fishing — some
for fish & some for crab
We found an old woman

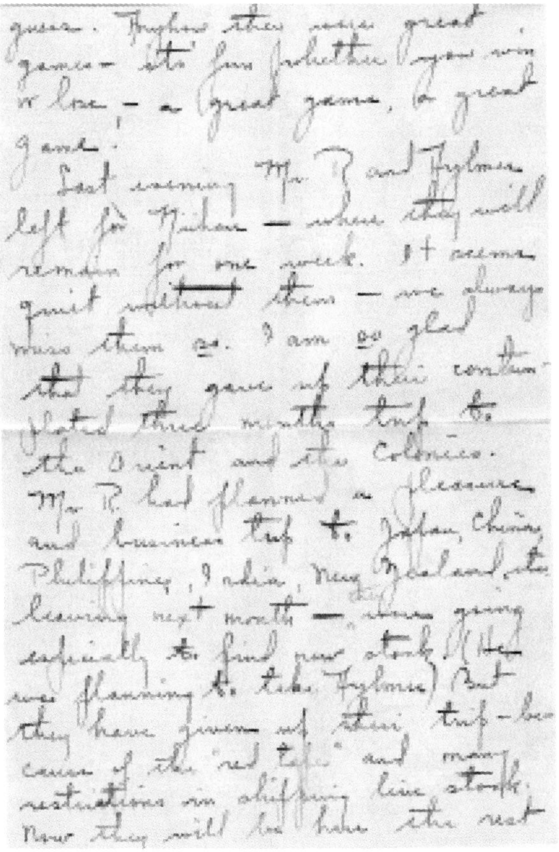

guess. Anyhow they were great games — it's fun whether you win or lose — a great game, a great game!

Last evening Mr R and Fylmer left for Niihau — where they will remain for one week. It seems quiet without them — we always miss them so. I am so glad that they gave up their contemplated three months trip to the Orient and the Colonies. Mr R. had planned a pleasure and business trip to Japan, China, Philippines, India, New Zealand, etc. leaving next month — they were going especially to find new stock. (He was planning to take Fylmer) But they have given up their trip — because of the "red tape" and many restrictions in shipping live stock. Now they will be here the rest

APPENDIX F
SAMPLE PAGE OF HETTIE BELLE'S 1973 MEMOIR

mine was of lovely, fine net - gathered into
a crown at the top of my head board -
decorated with lace and ribbon. A servant
opened your bed at night, and partially
tucked in the net. The trick was to get
into bed and finish the tucking-in process.
Often it was lovely Mrs. Robinson who tucked
me in! At the lowland home - my room was
next to the Grandmothers' lovely ~~suite~~ Mrs.
Robinson, after bidding them goodnight -
would come into my room for a little visit,
and then tucked me into bed. Very soon
I became "Hettie Belle" to both Mr. and Mrs.
Robinson (because they said they liked the
name) otherwise, for all the others, I, of
course, was Miss Matthew, for two years.

APPENDIX G
MRS. ROBINSON'S RECEIPT [SIC] FOR SHORTBREAD OR SCOTCH CAKE

2 lbs. flour
1 lb. butter
1 lb. white sugar

"Heat flour, mix sugar and butter and put in the heated flour gradually – knead 20 minutes. Break into pieces, put the pieces into a juuly [jelly roll] tin, flatten with the knuckles – prick all over with a fork, sprinkle with sugar – bake in a slow oven half an hour until a nice brown."

(Cole & Wichman, Early Kauai Hospitality, p.23, from Dora Isenberg's Central Union Church Cookbook. It is labeled "Mrs. Robinson's receipt.")

Here is another delicious version.

Scotch Shortbread Recipe

Cream together ½ lb. butter with ½ scant cup fine granulated sugar.
Add 3 c. white flour, less 1 T. Replace that T with 1 T cornstarch. Mix this with your hands. It will hold together when squeezed but fall apart easily.
Press evenly into a 9 X 12 pan. Prick all over with a fork.
Bake in preheated oven 325 degrees until light brown around the edges, from 20-30 minutes. Cut right away into 2" rectangles w/ a sharp knife, but allow to cool completely before removing from the pan. Keep in an airtight container.

(http://www.grouprecipes.com/63807/genuine-scottish-shortbread.html#)

Popovers

To make these airy shells you will need 2 eggs, 1 c. milk, 1 c. flour, ¼ t. salt, and 1 T. melted butter.

Beat the eggs until foamy. Add milk and combine this slowly with the flour and salt. Add the melted butter. Pour into oiled and heated popover pans, filling the sections 2/3 full. Place in a hot oven, 450 degrees. At the end of 20 min., reduce heat to 350 degrees for 15 min. The lower temp. at the end is essential as it dries out the hollow centers. Heavy, heated iron pans are best. If the baking is conducted according to rules, the crusts will be crisp. This is a desirable characteristic of popovers.

(from My Better Homes and Gardens Cookbook, copyright 1930)

Molasses Taffy

Place in heavy pot 2 c. sugar, 1 c. molasses, ¼ c. water, 2 t. mild vinegar and bring to a boil. Cook and stir until a small amount of syrup dropped into cold water forms a rigid ball. Remove from heat and add 2 T. butter and ½ t. baking soda.

Pour candy on buttered platter. Let it cool until you can dent it with a finger. Gather it into a lump, and pull with buttered fingertips. Keep folding and pulling the taffy until it is golden brown and too stiff to pull any more. Cut into bite sized pieces and wrap in waxed or buttered paper.

Put into a tightly covered tin.

(Adapted from http://allrecipes.com/recipe/old-fashioned-molasses-taffy/)

Mary Sophia Rice's Yorkshire Pudding

(Her family, the Waterhouses, were originally from Yorkshire)

3 eggs

1 cup flour

1 cup milk

Pinch of salt

Beat eggs slightly, add milk, flour and salt. Pour into hot roasting pan of fat after removing roast of beef. Have pan very hot and bake until brown (about 25 minutes).

(Cole & Wichman, Early Kauai Hospitality, p. 29.)

ACKNOWLEDGEMENTS

I have edited this work over many times, but it was the invaluable assistance of my readers, retired college professors Nancy Worcester, Mariamne Whatley, and Judy Riggin, that set me on track for undertaking this project. I appreciate the careful reading and thoughtful comments of all three. I wish to thank Chris Fayé of Kōke'e Natural History Museum for her generous gift of time as I waded into my research. Many Kaua'i residents were particularly kind and welcoming, encouraging me as I learned more about Hawai'i and its past. Thank you to my second cousin Keith Robinson for taking me into the wonderful folded hills and helping identify old photographs. Dennis Fujimoto, on a chance meeting at a rodeo in the rain, told me how important horses were to growing boys. Aletha Kaohi of the Waimea Visitor Center encouraged me, and Susie Morita at the Grove Farm gave me a glimpse into the plantation past. Lucy Kawaihalau shared her excitement about the project. The people at Waimea United Church of Christ (formerly the Foreign Church where Hettie Belle attended) were welcoming, and I appreciate Lois Somers's interest in my work and the tour of Kapalawai with Susie and David Somers. I was warmed with aloha from Ruth Cassel who showed us her garden and the route into the hills, and I was welcomed by Napua and others at the Kaua'i Museum, and have been assisted by folks at the Kaua'i Historical Society. Visiting various sites with me and reading the original letters, my second cousin Bill Matthew and his wife Vicki have been my cheering section, encouraging me to continue. Thank you both. My Anchorage writing group gave me their blessing as I read portions of the book aloud to them, and Mary Bristol traveled with me for research. Pat Griffin examined and helped identify some of Hettie's photos. Valuable help came from historian Andy Bushnell of Kapaʻa on Kauaʻi, who took time to really analyze my work and make accurate, insightful suggestions. Later, when I was stumped over forgotten names, my sleuth friend, Ginny Moore, pulled them out of the thin air that was the Internet. Louise Freeman, my editor, shared her expertise, and then Kay Koike carefully read the manuscript and gave me valuable suggestions. Thank you, Kay. Finally, my dear traveling companion, husband Les, with me the whole way, supported me in my study and writing. I appreciate you all.

BIBLIOGRAPHY

Aloha Hawaii.com. "Kamehameha IV," "King Kamehameha V", "Queen Emma," and "Liliʻuokalani." http://www.alohahawaii.com, 07/25/2016.

Ancestry.com; "Dr. Harrison Columbus Dukes." *The San Francisco Call*, Vol. III, No. 81, February, 1912, 12/11/2016.

AskArt.com/Artist Bio http://www.askart.com/artist_bio/Lillie_Hart_Gay_Torrey/80478/Lillie_Hart_Gay _Torrey.aspx#, 05/02/2018.

Bannerman, Helen. *The Story of Little Black Quibba.* USA: Frederick A. Stokes, 1903. http://archive.org/stream/storyoflittlebla00bann/storyoflittlebla00bann djvu.txt

Baybrook, George W. & Hofgaard, C.B. (May 3, 1970). "Waimea Foreign Church." http://www.waimeachurch.org/history/earlyhistory.htm.

Beltz, Arnie. "Tea Party." November 14, 2012. Unpublished writing.

Bird, Isabella L. *Six Months in the Sandwich Islands*. New York: G.P Putnam's Sons, 1881.

Blay, Chuck and Robert Siemers. *Kauai's Geologic History: A Simplified Guide*. Kauai, HI: TEOK Investigations, 2004.

Britannica, editors. "Mrs. Grundy." https://www.Britannica.com/topic/Mrs-Grundy, 20/10/17.

Casciani, Dominic. "The History of the Suffragettes." BBC News Online, 10/02/2003. http://news.bbc.co.uk/2/hi/uk/3153388.stm, 4/4/17.

Castle William R., Jr. *Hawaii Past and Present.* NY: Dodd, Mead and Company, 1920. Chapter IX "Kauai."

——. *The Green Vase.* NY: Dodd, Mead and Company, 1912.

Coan, Titus. Memorial Library "Early Missionary Life In Hawaii: Christian Missionaries to the Kingdom of Hawaii (1820 to 1893)."

Cole, Dora Jane Isenberg and Juliet Rice Wichman. *Early Kauai Hospitality: A Family Cookbook of Receipts, 1820-1920.* Lihue, HI: Kauai Museum Association, 1977.

College of Physicians of Philadelphia. "History of Vaccines: Smallpox." https://www.historyofvaccines.org/content/articles/history-smallpox, 02/05/2018.

Conover, Adele. "A Onetime Rancher Wages Lonely War to Save Rare Plants." Smithsonian, November 1996.

Cook, Evelyn E. *100 Years of Healing: The Legacy of a Kauai Missionary Doctor.* Koloa, Kauai, HI: Halewai Publishing, 2003.

Daws, Gavan. *Shoal of Time: A History of the Hawaiian Islands.* Honolulu, HI: University of Hawai'i Press, 1968.

Department of the Navy, Naval History and Heritage. *"Mongolia"* (Passenger-Cargo Steamship, 1904).

Donohugh, Donald. *The Story of Kōloa: A Kaua'i Plantation Town.* Honolulu, HI: Mutual Publishing, 2001.

Faye, Christine. *Touring Waimea.* Lihue, HI: Kauai'i Historical Society Publications Committee, 1997.

Fleeson, Lucinda. *Waking Up in Eden.* Chapel Hill, NC: Algonquin Books, 2009.

Forbes, David. *Queen Emma and Lawai.* Lihue, HI: Kauai Historical Society, 1997.

Gage, Reg. Lihue, HI: *Garden Island*, Feb. 27, Mar. 7, & Mar. 13, 2014.

Garden Island, The, Volumes 8 and 9, September 1911 through May 1913. Editor E.B. Bridgewater. Manager, K.C. Hopper.

GeneaologyTrails.com http://genealogytrails.com/hawaii/kauai/bios_a.htm, 05/02/2018.

Geni.com. "George Fairchild." http://www.geni.com/GeorgeFairchild/6000000011502897577. 12/11/2016.

Goodale, Hobey. *Hobey.* Printed in the United States, 2011.

Hackfeld and Company. "Paradise of the Pacific." Hawaiian State Archives: 1913 booklet, PP63-6.033.

Hatta, Kayo, Mari and Diane Mei Lin Mark. "Picture Bride." Miramax Films, 1995.

Hawaii.gov http://ags.hawaii.gov/archives/centennial-exhibit/victoria-kamamalu/, 04/04/2017.

HawaiiHistory.org. "King Kamehameha III." 16/10/2016.

Hemphill, Allen. "Gay and Robinson Tours: Kauai Sugar Plantation Photo Tour." http://www.allenhemphill.com/Gay%20and%20Robinson%20sugar%20plantation .pdf, 3/10/2016.

History.com, "Liliuokalani," 25/10/16.

"History of Steelgrass Farm." https://steelgrass.org/the-story-of-steelgrass-farm/, 31/10/2016.

Hite, Charles M. "Makee Family Genealogy." Kauai Historical Society Spalding family, subject/file.

Hofgaard, C.B. (1930). "Excerpts from Kauai Historical Society Manuscript." http://www.waimeachurch.org/history/earlyhistory.htm/

Honolulu Star Bulletin, Territory of Hawaiʻi, 1925. "The Story of Hawaii and It's Builders."

Igler, David. *The Great Ocean: Pacific Worlds from Captain Cook to the Gold Rush.* New York, NY: Oxford University Press, 2013.

Joesting, Edward. *Kauai: The Separate Kingdom.* Honolulu, HI: University of Hawaii Press, 1984.

Jones International and Jones Digital Century, "History of the Phonograph," intekom.com/restore/History_Of_The_Phonograph.html, 04/06/18.

Kauaʻi Historical Society. "Rice Family Papers" MS7.

Kauai Museum. "Kauai Historical Blog: Alexander McBryde." http://www. kauaimuseum.org/kauai-museum-collections/kauai-historical-blog/23-kauai-blog/51-alexander-mcbryde-s-collection.

KamaʾAinaʾs. "Sweet Tuberose." Steelgrass Studios recording, 2010.

Kinghorn, Jonathan. *The Atlantic Transport Line,1881-1931: A History with Details on All Ships.* Jefferson, NC: McFarland and Company, Inc., 2012.

Knudsen, Eric. "Early Days at Waiwa.*" The Kauaʻi Papers.* Līhuʻe, HI: Kauai Historical Society, 1991.

——. *Teller of Hawaiian Tales.* Honolulu, HI: Mutual Publishing, 1946 (2004, 4th printing).

Kopesky, Janell. "Kauai North Shore – The Spectacular Fire-Throwing Ceremony." http://www.balihai.com/Blog/kauai-north-shore-the-spectacular-fire-throwing- ceremony/, 11/12/16.

Leonard, John William, editor. *A Who's Who in Finance and Banking, 1920-22.*

Lincoln, Noa Kekuewa. *Amy Greenwell Garden Ethnobotanical Guide to Native Hiwaiian Plants.* Honolulu, HI: Bishop Museum Press, 2009.

Marcus, Hettie Belle Matthew. "Reminicences." Written at Carmel-by-the-Sea, CA: July 7, 1973, unpublished notes.

Marley, Roni. "A Historical Narrative of the Valley House Estate on Kauai, Part 1. www.hawaiilife.com/articles/2012/08/valley-house-estate-part-1, 02/04/2017.

Martin, Lynn J., Ed. and Project Director. *Na Paniolo o Hawaii.* Honolulu, HI: Honolulu Academy of Arts, 1987.

Mengies, Ian. "Charles Barrington Robinson 1812-1899." Unpublished partial history of Banks Peninsula. Kauai Museum, Robinson file.

Moriarty, Linda Park. *Niʾihau Shell Leis.* Honolulu, HI: University of Hawaii Press, 1986.

NationalParkService.gov "Kamehameha the Great." 02/24/2017.

Nellist, George F., editor. *The story of Hawaii and Its Builders, incorporating Vol. III of Men of Hawaii.* Territory of Hawaii: Honolulu Star-Bulletin, Ltd., 1925.

Nishimoto, Warren. "Oral History Interview with Florence Waterhouse Brandt, 1987," *Kōloa: An Oral History of a Kauaʻi Community, Vol. 1*: Center for Oral History Social Science Research Institute, University of Hawaiʻi at Mānoa, 1988.

NOAA. "About Waterspouts." http://www.srh.noaa.gov/mfl/?n=waterspouts, 03/30/2015.

Okihiro, Gary. *Pineapple Culture: A History of the Tropical and Temperate Zones.* Berkeley and Los Angeles, CA: University of California Press, 2009.

——. *Island World: A History of Hawai'i and the United States.* Berkeley and Los Angeles, CA: University of California Press, Ltd., 2008.

Olgilvie, Gordon. "Dauntless Captain Gay, the Forgotten Whaler." *Press,* Saturday, December 15, 1979.

Pacific, Vol. 66. "Charles Dunklee Milliken."

"Passenger List from the Bessie." September 18, 1863. Kauai Museum, Robinson file.

Pillsbury, Arthur. "Paradise Unknown: Hidden Wonders of Hawaii." Sunset Magazine http://www.acpillsburyfoundation.org/1912---Photographing-Hawaii.html, 02/22/2017.

RecordsAncestry.com; "Elizabeth Lindsay." http://records.ancestry.com/elizabeth_lindsay_records.ashx?pid=164786363, 12/10/2016.

Rice, William Hyde. *Hawaiian Legends.* Honolulu, HI: Bernice P. Bishop Museum, 1923. http://hbs.bishopmuseum.org/pubs-online/pdf/bull3.pdf

Riedel, MD, PhD. "Edward Jenner and the History of Smallpox and Vaccination." *Proceedings.* Baylor University Medical Center. Vol. 18, No. 1, 2005. Pp. 21-25. www.ncbi.nlm.nih.gov/pmc/articles/PMC1200696/

Siddell, John William, Editor. *Men of Hawaii, Vol. I & II revised.* Honolulu, HI: Honolulu Star-Bulletin, Limited, Territory of Hawaii, 1917/1921.

Sinclair, Francis [Philip Garth, pseudo]. *Ballads and Poems From the Pacific.* London: Gilbert and Rivington, Limited, 1885. Library of the University of CA, Los Angeles. http://archive.org/stream/balladspoemsfrom00sinc#page/n5/mode/2up

Sinclair, Isabella. *Indigenous Flowers of the Hawaiian Islands.* London: Sampson, Low, Marston, Searle & Rivington, 1885.

Soboleski, Hank. "Author, Illustrator Isabela McHutcheson Sinclair," *The Garden Island,* Sunday, January 19, 2014

——. "Niihau Manager Francis Sinclair," *The Garden Island,* January 24, 1916.

——. "The Reverend John Mortimer Lydgate: Kaua'i's Renaissance Man," *The Garden Island,* February, 14, 2007.

——. "Plantation Doctor Francis Anderson Lyman," *The Garden Island,* April 20, 2014.

Sydney Morning Herald. "1912 Typhoon Caused Devastation in Japan." *Sydney Morning Herald,* Friday, 27 September 1912. http://stevengoddard.wordpress.com/2011/07/30/1912-typhoon-caused- devastation-in-japan/

Tabrah, Ruth. *Ni'ihau: The Last Hawaiian Island.* Kailua, HI: Press Pacifica, 1987.

Tava, Rerioterai, Moses K. Keale, Sr. *Niihau: The Traditions of an Hawaiian Island.* Honolulu, HI: Mutual Publishing, 1989.

This Day in History. "October 14, 1912: President Roosevelt Shot in Milwaukee" http://www.history.com/this-day-in-history/theodore-roosevelt-shot-in-milwaukee, 02/05/2018.

Titcomb, Margaret. "Native Use of Fish in Hawaii." Honolulu, HI: University of Hawaii Press, 1972.

U.S. Find-a-Grave. www.findagrave.com/. 05/02/2018.

University of California, Berkeley, "Mendell Welcker."

Veech, J.A., interviewer. The Watumull Foundation Oral History Project, "Ruth Knudsen Hanner."

Von Holt, Ida Elizabeth Knudsen. *Stories of Long Ago: Niihau, Kauai, Oahu.* Honolulu, HI: Daughters of Hawai'I, 1985.

"Waimea Church Early History" www.waimeachurch.org/history/early history. htm, 10/15/2016.

Whyte, Frederic. *The Life of W.T. Stead.* New York: Houghton Mifflin Co., 1925.

Wichman, Frederick B. *Kaua'i: Ancient Place-Names and Their Stories.* Honolulu, HI: University of Hawai'i Press,1998.

Wikipedia. "Brother Kronstrand." http://translate.google.com/translate?hl=en&sl= sv&u=http://sv.wikipedia.org/wiki /Bror_Kronstrand&prev=/search%3Fq% 3Dbror%2Bkronstrand%26client%3Dsaf ari%26rls%3Den, 02/12/2017.

Wikipedia, "Flinch (card game)" https://en.wikipedia.org/wiki/Flinch_% 28card_game%29, 04/19/2018.

Wikipedia, "William Richards Castle, Jr.," 05/10/2016.

Wikipedia. "Hazel Hotchkiss Wightman." http://en.wikipedia.org/wiki/ Hazel_Hotchkiss_Wightman, 10/31/2017.

Wikipedia. "Phonograph." http://en.wikipedia.org/wiki/Phonograph#History, 05/02/2018.

Wikipedia. "Stage Hypnosis." http://en.wikipedia.org/wiki/Stage_hypnosis, 12/28/2017.

*Wilcox, Carol, editor. "Sugar Water: 61West Kauai." http://muse.jhu.edu/ chapter/258020, 01/14/17.

Winter, Kawika. "Firebrand Ceremony Conducted of North Shore of Kauai." http://www.civilbeat.com/posts/2012/01/09/14472-firebrand-ceremony-, 05/02/2018.